Will of the Father

Atonement Essays

Gospel Insights

*Glen and Jan
To wonderful friends
Best Wishes Always
LaVelle*

2nd Edition

LaVelle Day, All Rights Reserved

© 2009, 2016

i

This book is dedicated to

my wife, Marie and extended Family

Acknowledgements

Judy Day provided the photographs, expertise and time for creating the book covers. She has my deepest gratitude for her creation of the front, back and spine cover.

By providing editing and constructive comments Dorothy Jenkins and Judy Rump have contributed significantly to the final editions. Cynthia Richards gave encouragement following her reading of an earlier version. President Lloyd Campbell, my stake president, has been aware of my continued development and has given me feedback. I am extremely grateful for their encouragement and assistance.

Author's Purpose

This book reflects the views of the author based on many scriptural references and Joseph Smith quotes with a few others to demonstrate the source used for these views. The reader can evaluate them as they may choose.

Provide comments and criticisms about this book, which may be used to upgrade this book at

http://lavellebooks.com/

LaVelle Day grew up in Utah and Eastern Oregon, one of four children. After he became active in the Church of Jesus Christ of Latter-day Saints, He served a mission in the California Mission, married Marie Nielsen and graduated from Brigham Young University with a BS in mathematics and minor in English. He spent one year at Utah State University as a teaching assistant before becoming full time employed.

He started his working career with IBM as a Systems Engineer followed by increasing responsibilities at other companies. During this time, LaVelle obtained his JD degree from Lewis and Clark Law School evening program and passed the Oregon State Bar following graduation. Post law degree, LaVelle managed an information systems consulting firm in Portland, OR, where he earned top performance awards.

LaVelle and his wife Marie have 5 children and 16 grandchildren. His most cherished and anticipated times are bi-annual week-long family reunions.

LaVelle has served in multiple positions within the LDS church including high councilman (multiple times), Bishop Counselor (twice), Bishop and multiple missions including Beaverton Employment Office manager and as the first Portland Transient Services manager, where he organized the office processes and procedures, which were not available from the Church. He and his wife spent 18 months in Pottsville, Pennsylvania as Utah Genealogical Society representatives to collect records from churches, funeral homes, cemeteries and libraries. To obtain filming contracts, a self-developed power point presentation educated interested parties on records preservation, which produced pleasing results.

Table of Contents

v

PREFACE

Many gospel questions and issues are addressed in this book. The writing technique uses scriptural and early Church record quotes to substantiate the discussion points. Research for quotes of Joseph Smith were a priority and used extensively. The reader can evaluate my analysis as he may choose. My purpose is to propose what I see from the scriptures and research that I have conducted.

Members of the Church, who actively read the scriptures and Church scholarly books will recognize many common concepts but may benefit from other contents of this book. Novice readers of the scriptures might have difficulty with the many quotations and concepts.

This book started by my writing personal thoughts regarding the atonement. As time progressed, I added and changed things previously recorded. Eventually I felt that I had something of value so I decided to publish this book. Some book evaluators stated it was well researched and encouraged me to make some modifications and get it published.

The important parts of any quotes used in this book are bolded or <u>underlined</u>. No notifications are included in the body of the book as it is obviously used to emphasize the important parts of the quote. Reference to the Garden of Gethsemane is sometimes shortened to Garden.

An independent essay format was used in early writings. Changing to the current organization retained the essay designation rather than chapters. This purpose reminds the reader that truth in one essay could be significant in understanding another. Cross-references are sometimes used.

--- The WILL of the FATHER ---

Most of us know and understand that our Father in Heaven has provided this earth and the heavens for his children. When we look at the history of this earth we see so much good and evil that has happened upon it. This earth was provided so that his children could live upon it so that we could experience and adopt the good or the evil that exists. This choice between good and evil started in heaven. Moses recorded the Father's purpose in creating this earth. Moses was told,

> *For behold, this is my work and my glory--to bring to pass the immortality and eternal life of man.* [1]

Immortality is the permanent uniting of our spirit with our resurrected body after we die, never to die again. Eternal life is life with our Father in Heaven or in the highest degree in the celestial kingdom. To qualify for this highest degree, we must accept and live in such a way as to qualify for it.

Jesus Christ was the first spirit child born to our Father in Heaven and was chosen from the beginning to be our Savior and judge. For he said

> *And now, verily I say unto you, **I was in the beginning** with the Father, and **am the Firstborn.*** [2]

The Father began teaching Jesus Christ at the very beginning so that he could develop in such a way as to be our Savior and redeemer.

---

[1] Moses 1:39.

[2] D & C 93:21

1

The evil that is upon the earth comes from Satan and his followers who were cast out to the earth from heaven. This was done before there were people upon the earth. Most of us know and understand that Satan made a proposal to the Father, which was denied. That proposal was

> *I will **redeem all mankind**, that one soul shall not be lost, and surely I will do it; <u>wherefore give me thine honor</u>.* [3]

This proposal was for Satan to use force to deprive man of his ability to choose and thereby force every person to keep God's commandments. Satan knew that God had strong feelings of love for his children and wanted them to be with him in eternity. By promising to see that not one person would be lost he thought that God would accept his proposal. He felt that by getting all of Father's children to be with him in the celestial kingdom that he, Satan, should be rewarded and have God's power and honor. Actually Satan desired to control everything including God, the Father.

Satan was very influential among the spirit children of the Father. This is shown in a revelation to Joseph Smith and Sidney Rigdon.

> *And this we saw also, and bear record, that an **angel of God <u>who was in authority</u>** in the presence of God, **who rebelled against the Only Begotten Son** whom the Father loved and who was in the bosom of the Father, was thrust down from the presence of God and the Son,*
>
> *And was called Perdition, **for the heavens wept over him—he was Lucifer, a son of the morning.***

---

[3] Moses 4:1.

And we beheld, and lo, he is fallen! is fallen, even a son of the morning![4]

Not only was he influential in heaven but he had priesthood authority to function therein. This demonstrates that Jesus Christ was chosen prior to Satan's proposal.

While functioning in his priesthood capacity, he developed the desire to control everyone. He proposed to take the Savior's place and be the only begotten Son of the Father. This is further substantiated in the writings of Moses when Moses saw Satan and conversed with him. Moses wrote

And again Moses said: I will not cease to call upon God, I have other things to inquire of him: for his glory has been upon me, wherefore I can judge between him and thee. Depart hence, Satan.

And now, when Moses had said these words, Satan cried with a loud voice, and ranted upon the earth, and commanded, saying: I am the Only Begotten, worship me.[5]

This scripture shows the deep intensity that Satan wanted to control all others. He had that desire when he proposed to make all humankind subservient to him, forcing them to keep God's commandments. This desire to control is what drives Satan to fight against God.

After Satan made his proposal to the Father, the Savior promised the Father

---

[4] D&C 76:25-27.

[5] Moses 1:18-19.

3

Father, thy will be done, and the glory be thine forever.[6]

The Father reconfirmed that Jesus Christ would be his Only Begotten Son and the Savior of the world. Because of Satan's continuing rebellion, he was cast out to the earth. Moses recorded

> *Wherefore, because that Satan rebelled against me, and sought to destroy the agency of man, which I, the Lord God, had given him, and also, that I should give unto him mine own power;* **by the power of mine Only Begotten, I caused that he should be cast down.** [7]

It should be noted that it was by the power of Jesus Christ that Satan was cast down. The book of Revelation shows that Satan was cast down to the earth.[8] When the Savior was on the earth, he never took honor unto himself. He always recognized that it was the will of the Father which he did. He told the Nephites when he appeared to them

> *Behold I have given unto you my gospel, and this is the gospel which I have given unto you--that* **I came into the world to do the will of my Father, because my Father sent me.**[9]

In his intercessory prayer, the Savior was reporting to the Father and said,

---

[6] Moses 4:2.

[7] Moses 4:3.

[8] Revelation 12:9.

[9] 3 Nephi 27:13.

I have glorified thee on the earth: I have finished the work which thou gavest me to do. [10]

Now they have known that all things whatsoever thou hast given me are of thee. [11]

The Savior promised the Father that the glory and honor would be his forever. These two statements from the intercessory prayer show that during his mortal tenure, the Savior had fulfilled this promise to the Father although at the time he uttered these words he had not completed his atonement.

King Benjamin in his address to his people said,

I say, that this is the man who receiveth salvation, through the atonement which was prepared from the foundation of the world for all mankind, which ever were since the fall of Adam, or who are, or who ever shall be, even unto the end of the world. [12]

Here King Benjamin states that the atonement was taught prior to Adam and Eve being placed in the Garden of Eden and that the atonement was for all humankind. That means we knew of the celestial, terrestrial and the telestial kingdoms plus outer darkness before being born to this earth. This plan was the plan of the Father and was his will. The Savior implemented it.

---

[10] John 17:4.

[11] John 17:7.

[12] Mosiah 4:7.

5

----- ATONEMENT PLAN -----

This section begins with a summarized statement by the Savior about his atonement. It is very simple to explain but more complicated to fully understand.

We also discuss the love of the Savior for the Father and all of humankind which is his motivation to accomplish his atonement. "Enduring to the end" is a major key of his atonement and is included in this section.

CHRIST'S GOSPEL

Christ gave a statement to his Nephite disciples near the end of his Nephite ministry in which he explained his "Gospel." This statement of Christ's gospel is the simple essence of and the heart of his atonement. His disciples inquired of him the name of his church. Christ responded that it be called after his name and then he said,

> *And if it so be that the church is built upon **my gospel** then will the Father show forth his own works in it.*[13]

Then the Savior stated what his gospel was.

> *13 Behold I have given unto you my gospel, and this is the gospel which I have given unto you--that I came into the world to do the will of my Father, because my Father sent me.*
>
> *14 And my Father sent me that I might be lifted up upon the cross; and after that I had been lifted up upon the cross, that I might draw all men unto me, that as I have been lifted up by men even so should men be lifted up by the Father, **to stand before me, to be***

---

[13] 3 Nephi 27:10.

6

judged of their works, whether they be good or whether they be evil.

15 And for this cause have I been lifted up; therefore, according to the power of the Father I will draw all men unto me, that they may be judged according to their works.

16 And it shall come to pass, that whoso repenteth and is baptized in my name shall be filled; **and if he endureth to the end, behold, him will I hold guiltless before my Father at that day when I shall stand to judge the world.**

17 And **he that endureth not unto the end, the same is he that is also hewn down and cast into the fire,** *from whence they can no more return, because of the justice of the Father.*

18 And this is the word which he hath given unto the children of men. And for this cause he fulfilleth the words which he hath given, and he lieth not, but fulfilleth all his words.

19 **And no unclean thing can enter into his kingdom; therefore nothing entereth into his rest save it be those who have washed their garments in my blood, because of their faith, and the repentance of all their sins, and their faithfulness unto the end.**

20 Now this is the commandment: Repent, all ye ends of the earth, and come unto me and be baptized in my name, that ye may be sanctified by the reception of the Holy Ghost, that ye may stand spotless before me at the last day.

*21 Verily, verily, I say unto you, **this is my gospel; and ye know the things that ye must do in my church;** for the works which ye have seen me do that shall ye also do; for that which ye have seen me do even that shall ye do...* [14]

This scripture summarizes the plan of the atonement. There are important principles contained in this quotation.

- Because he submitted himself to the judgment of men and was crucified on the cross, then all men must stand before the Savior and be judged by him.

At the end of his ministry immediately prior to his Garden of Gethsemane experience he said,

Now is the judgment of this world: now shall the prince of this world be cast out.

*And I, if I be lifted up from the earth, **will draw all men unto me.**[15]*

Nephi quotes Jacob as saying,

*...for it behooveth the great Creator that he suffereth himself to become subject unto man in the flesh, and die for all men, that **all men might become subject unto him.**[16]*

The expression "*will draw all men unto me*" and "*all men might become subject unto him*" has reference to all men being judged by the Savior at the end of the world.

---

[14] 3 Nephi 27:13-21.

[15] John 12:31-32.

[16] 2 Nephi 9:4-5.

- He will judge all humankind by *"their works, whether they be good or whether they be evil."* It is his judgment that allows us into the Father's presence.

- Those who repent and are baptized would be filled with the Holy Ghost. However, those who endure to the end would earn the greatest spiritual reward. He further promised those who endure to the end that he would hold them "guiltless before my Father."

  In a revelation by the Savior, he stated that all of humankind will be resurrected and that,

  > *The righteous **shall be gathered on my right hand unto eternal life**; and the wicked on my left hand will I be ashamed to own before the Father;* [17]

  Eternal life is life in the highest degree in the celestial Kingdom which means married persons need to be sealed by the temple marriage ordinance. [Read the essay "MARRIAGE COVENANT"]. The wicked in this verse are all that are not qualified to have eternal life by the time the final judgment occurs.

- Those that do not endure to the end will have the *"justice of the Father"* applied and be cast into the "fire". [Read the section "Everlasting Fire" in the essay "JUDGMENTS at MORTAL DEATH" for understanding of this fire]. There is no return from this justice meaning it will be permanent throughout eternity. They will not have eternal life.

- The Savior cautions that his Father's kingdom is a holy place and that "no unclean thing can enter into his

---

[17] D&C 29:27.

9

kingdom." His requirements to enter his kingdom are those

> *who have washed their garments in my* [Savior's] *blood, because of **their faith, and the repentance of all their sins, and their faithfulness unto the end.***

The Father sent the Savior to be crucified on the cross. This was the act, which culminated in his death and was necessary to fulfill his atonement. Because he suffered this, the Father made him judge of the rest of his children. Making the Savior our judge was the goal of the Father from the beginning. All things the Father required of the Savior were required to prepare the Savior to judge the rest of us. This is the key element of understanding the atonement!

At the final judgment, no one will enter the highest degree of the celestial kingdom unless the Savior holds them guiltless before the Father. We start at his right hand when we have faith, are baptized and receive the Savior's forgiveness. At the final judgment, the Savior holds us guiltless before the Father if we continue at this right hand. Without forgiveness, we are at his left hand.

Other scriptures emphasize this same concept. Alma, seeing church members committing sin and not repenting was troubled and went to the Lord in prayer. Alma recorded the Lord's answer as follows,

> *For behold, this is my church; whosoever is baptized shall be baptized unto repentance. And whomsoever ye receive shall believe in my name; and **him will I freely forgive.***

*For it is I that taketh upon me the sins of the world; for it is I that hath created them; and it is I that granteth unto **him that believeth unto the end a place at my right hand.***

*For behold, in my name are they called; **and if they know me they shall come forth, and shall have a place <u>eternally at my right hand.</u>*** [18]

However, there is one additional concept the Savior added to his revelation to Alma. When there is true repentance followed by baptism, the Savior states *"him will I freely forgive"*. When the Savior forgives us is when we begin to qualify to be on the Savior's right hand. To stay on his right hand, we must faithfully *"endure to the end"* by living all of the commandments given.

Therefore, we ask this question "Why did the Father require the Savior to suffer all the things that he suffered?"

The answer to this is that after our resurrection, we will then stand before him to be judged. This is referred to in the scriptures as the final judgment and is referenced in a number of scriptures. King Benjamin taught,

> *And he shall rise the third day from the dead; and behold, he **standeth to judge the world**; and behold, **all these things are done that a <u>righteous judgment</u> might come upon the children of men.***[19]

King Benjamin made this statement prior to the Savior's earthy ministry. He stated that after his resurrection, he *"<u>standeth to judge the world</u>"* and that *"all these things are*

---

[18] Mosiah 26:22-24 See also D&C 29:26-29.

[19] Mosiah 3:10.

done that a *righteous judgment"* would be given to all humanity.

Remember that the Savior stated to the Nephites that he was commanded by the Father to be crucified before men and all would stand before him to be judged. We emphasize that it was the will and purpose of the Father to make the Savior our judge and advocate from the very beginning. The Savior lived in this mortal life and experienced tests so that we who are judged cannot find fault with his judgments. He had to live a life without sin, setting the example, and his experiences had to be of such a nature that we could not say, "You should not judge us because you did not suffer the things that we suffered. You have no understanding of what our suffering was like. How could you judge us?" His judgment will be a righteous judgment because he has suffered greater suffering than what we have suffered.

The Savior's experience on the cross was a prototype. He stood before high magistrates, who pronounced judgments on him, found guilty and suffered their punishment which caused him greater suffering than what we have suffered. The magistrates had the power to find him not guilty of the charges leveled against him. In like fashion the Savior became our judge and will judge us. He will judge us according to our works, whether they are good or evil. The following comparison shows the events pertaining to the judgment and punishment of Christ and the events of his judgment of us.

Christ Suffering Man's Judgment	Christ as Judge
Jewish Leadership & Pilate were judges	Christ is the judge
Christ stood before man to be judged	Humankind will stand before Christ to be judged
Choice between two, Christ or Barabbas to be set free	Humankind separated into two groups, one on Christ's right hand and one on his left hand who will suffer
Barabbas who was guilty of breaking Jewish law was chosen to have freedom	Those on Christ's right hand, the righteous, will be free by inheriting the highest degree in the celestial kingdom
Christ was found guilty of breaking Jewish law and punished	Those on Christ's left hand are guilty of breaking God's law and will suffer accordingly
Christ suffered scourging prior to his final punishment of the crucifixion	Some will be cast into hell to suffer the buffetings of Satan prior to their resurrection
Christ suffered unjustly	Christ's judgments will be just

The whole point of this discussion is the Father gave a commandment to the Savior to suffer maltreatment at the hand of man and upon the cross that by doing this he became our king, judge and our advocate with the Father.

The Savior counseled the early saints and then identified what he would say to the Father when we are on his right hand.

> *And I give unto you, who are the first laborers in this last kingdom, a commandment that you assemble yourselves together, and organize yourselves, and prepare yourselves, and **sanctify yourselves; yea, purify your hearts, and cleanse your hands and your feet before me, <u>that I may make you clean;</u>***
>
> *That I may testify unto your Father, and your God, and my God, that **you are clean from the blood of this wicked generation**; that I may fulfil this promise, **this great and last promise, which I have made unto you**, when I will.* [20]

To be cleansed means to be free or cleansed from the effects and power of this wicked generation so that it has no effect on us to sin. This great and last promise of the Savior is to advocate our cleanliness to the Father so that we are able to dwell in his presence. The Father will accept the Savior's judgment because the Savior qualified himself to be our judge for the Father.

CHRIST AS KING AND JUDGE

This essay will focus on the Savior's completion of his ministry and atonement.

Completing His Ministry

---

[20] D&C 88:74-75.

When the Passover dinner conversation was over, John records the Savior's intercessory prayer. Following that prayer John records that they crossed over the brook Cedron to the Garden. John does not record the Garden prayer recorded by Matthew, Mark and Luke. The content of both prayers is different.

In his intercessory prayer, the Savior said,

> *I have glorified thee on the earth;* **I have finished the work which thou gavest me to do.** [21]

This quote refers to his ministry with his apostles and does not refer to his final atonement sufferings. His atonement sufferings would begin shortly. In his intercessory prayer, he followed with these words

> *I have manifested thy name unto the men which thou gavest me out of the world; thine they were, and thou gavest them me; and they have kept thy word.*
> *Now* **they have known that all things whatsoever thou hast given me are of thee.**
>
> *For I have given unto them the words which thou gavest me; and they have received them, and* **have known surely that I came out from thee, and they have believed that thou didst send me.** [22]

Following the Passover meal and prior to the intercessory prayer, the Savior told his disciples that he would leave them to return to the Father and they would feel sorrow. Then they would see him again and they would rejoice. To this comment the apostles replied,

---

[21] John 17:4.

[22] John 17:6-8.

*Now are we sure that thou knowest all things, and needest not that any man should ask thee: **by this we believe that thou camest forth from God**.* [23]

The Savior fulfilled his promise that the honor and glory would be the Father's. He fully taught that he represented the Father and that all things were done according to the Father's will. This is confirmed by the apostles' statement that " *we believe that thou camest forth from God.*" [24] However, the apostles did not understand the Savior's mission of atonement and resurrection.

Completing His Atonement

The Savior still had to fulfill the commandment of the Father to lay down his life and take it up again to provide the resurrection. [25] It was possible that the Savior might not fulfill this commandment. The Savior had his agency for he said the following in relation to the bitter cup:

> *and would that I might not drink the bitter cup, **and shrink**--.*[26]

Shrink" means to "withdraw." By this statement, he acknowledges that he had the agency to withdraw from suffering the "bitter cup." It was very much on his mind that he had to endure those pains and not shrink or withdraw.

Luke records that in the Garden an angel appeared to him and strengthened him.[27] The heavens were watching this event. If

---

[23] John 16:30.

[24] John 16:30.

[25] John 10:17-18.

[26] D&C 19:18.

16

the Savior withdrew all humankind would be lost forever. The angel would have reminded him of his Father's love and stirred the Savior's love for us. This could have been a very pivotal moment but he prayed that, if possible, he not be required to partake of this bitter cup. [28]

He held true to his commitment to the Father by enduring Gethsemane and the cross resulting in his death and resurrection.

Receiving All Authority

Following the completion of all the Father's commandments Christ received all priesthood power and authority. John's writings shed some light on this concept, including this quotation concerning the Savior's development during his life on the earth. Part of John's record was given by direct revelation as found in the Doctrine and Covenants.

> *And I, John, bear record that he received a fulness of the glory of the Father;*
>
> *And he **received all power, both in heaven and on earth**, and the glory of the Father was with him, for he dwelt in him.*[29]

Abinadi stated,

> *Yea, even so he shall be led, crucified, and slain, the flesh becoming subject even unto death, the will of the Son being swallowed up in the will of the Father.*

---

[27] Luke 22:43.

[28] Matthew 26:42.

[29] D&C 93:16-17.

And thus God [Christ] breaketh the bands of death, having gained the victory over death; [and the Father] **giving the Son power to make intercession for the children of men--.**[30]

When his life was finished he then received a *"fulness of glory"* and then he

> *"received* **all power, both in heaven and on earth"***...* *and* **"power to make intercession for the children of men.."** [31]

The "power to make intercession for the children of men" or to be our advocate to the Father is the power to hold those on his right hand "guiltless" before the Father. He will say to the Father that these on my right hand are worthy to return to thy presence, which is using his judgment powers. For the rest, he will pass judgment to determine their eternal destiny.

The Savior confirmed that he received "all power" following his resurrection when he appeared to his apostles at Galilee. He stated this to his apostles at that time:

> *All power is given unto me in heaven and in earth.*[32]

The expression "is given unto me" represents the present tense and not the distant past. It shows that this power was recently given before he met with his apostles. By this authority, he became our Savior and King.

GETHSEMANE

---

[30] Mosiah 15:7-8.

[31] D&C 29:5; 1 John 2:1; Moroni 7:28; D&C 32:3; D&C 45:3; D&C 62:1; D&C 110:4.

[32] Matthew 28:16, 18.

We need to realize that the Lord has given his revelations in our English language so that we "come to understanding" of his revelations for he said

> *Behold, I am God and have spoken it; these commandments are of me, and were given unto my servants in their weakness, **after the manner of their language, that they might come to understanding**.* [33]

We can examine the language of the Savior's revelations and feel comfortable that the language is precise and true. Trying to understand the atonement, what the Savior suffered in Gethsemane and how he takes upon him our sins is a challenging pursuit for a great many of us. There are many scriptures relating to these topics and putting them together in a comprehensive way is difficult.

But whatever is determined, it must be compatible with what the Savior has said. Trying to understand what he suffered in the Garden has been a major theme relating to his atonement. The Savior said

> *For behold, **I, God, have suffered these things for all**, that they might not suffer if they would repent But if they would not repent they must suffer even as I*
>
> *Which suffering caused myself, even God, the greatest of all, to tremble because of pain, and to <u>bleed at every pore</u>, and to suffer both body and spirit—and would that I might not drink the bitter cup, and shrink.* [34]

Luke identifies that the Savior was in the Garden of Gethsemane when he shed his blood.[35] Here the Savior states

---

[33] D&C 1:24.

[34] D&C 19:16-18.

that he suffered for all humankind so that they would not have to suffer provided they repent.

One of the first things to consider is the expression "for all." This refers to all of humankind. He stated that he suffered "these things for all". All of humankind will hear the gospel and have a chance to repent and receive all the eternal blessings available whether it is in mortality or in the world of spirits. He commands everyone to repent since he suffered for all.

King Benjamin made a statement that suggests that Christ's Garden suffering was only for Christ's people:

> ...for behold, blood cometh from every pore, so great shall be his anguish for the wickedness and the abominations of his people. [36]

There was no suffering for the wicked mentioned in this statement. However, the Savior unequivocally said his suffering was "for all" not just his people who are members of his church. These statements are compatible if understood properly. When a person repents, he is baptized, becomes a member of his church and is forgiven. He becomes a part of "his people." His people are the only ones who repent. So only his people receive the benefits of his suffering in the Garden even though he suffered for all.

To emphasize that the Savior suffered for all he stated in another revelation,

> And it shall come to pass, because of the wickedness of the world, that I will take vengeance upon the wicked,

---

[35] Luke 22:44.

[36] Mosiah 3:7.

for they will not repent; for the cup of mine indignation is full; for behold, my blood shall not cleanse them if they hear me not.[37]

If those of humankind will hear the Savior, his blood will cleanse them. However, the Savior indicates that the blood he shed in the Garden was shed for all but his blood will not cleanse those who do not repent. This quote clearly shows the blood which was shed in the Garden was clearly *"for all"* including the wicked.

The question is "What were *"these things"* he suffer that caused him to bleed at every pore?"

Definition of "These Things
Many have read these words and tried to understand what he actually suffered in the Garden. They have felt they could understand what he meant by this expression by studying all the scriptures. It is a very understandable approach and one at which this author and many others have spent considerable time and effort to research. However, this approach is difficult because the scriptural descriptions vary considerably.

The expression "these things" appears 201 times in the New Testament, 117 times in the Doctrine & Covenants and 366 times in the Book of Mormon. There is not a single definition for the expression "these things" in all of these usages. In actuality each time it is used it refers to different things. In each case, the meaning of the expression depends on the context in which the expression is used. The following are a number of examples showing how the definition of the expression "these things" is determined.

---

[37] D&C 29:17; See also 2 Nephi 9:21; Matthew 11:20.

In writing of his father while preaching to the Jewish population, Nephi stated,

> *And it came to pass that the Jews did mock him because of the things which he testified of them; for he truly testified of their wickedness and their abominations; and he testified that the things which he saw and heard, and also the things which he read in the book, manifested plainly of the coming of a Messiah, and also the redemption of the world.*
>
> *And when **the Jews heard these things they were angry with him;** yea, even as with the prophets of old, whom they had cast out, and stoned, and slain; and they also sought his life, that they might take it away.* [38]

The term "these things" refers to the condemnations, warnings and truths that Lehi preached. These were identified in the first paragraph quoted. The term "these things" is used in place of repeating the things listed in the first paragraph.

Nephi and his brothers returned to their home to get their treasures left behind when Lehi traveled into the desert. These treasures were to be offered to Laban for the brass plates.

> *And it came to pass that we went down to the land of our inheritance, and we did gather together our gold, and our silver, and our precious things.*
>
> *And after we had gathered **these things** together, we went up again unto the house of Laban.* [39]

---

[38] 1 Nephi 1:19-20.

[39] 1 Nephi 3:22-23.

Here the term "these things" refers to the valuables they collected, which were gold, silver and precious things", as stated prior to the usage of the term.

From the Doctrine and Covenants, the Lord told Hyrum,

> *Deny not the spirit of revelation, nor the spirit of prophecy, for wo unto him that denieth **these things**;* [40]

The term *"these things"* is used to refer to things previously stated.

We will now use some examples from the New Testament. In the Sermon on the Mount the Savior said,

> *Therefore take no thought, saying, What shall we eat? or, What shall we drink? or, Wherewithal shall we be clothed?*
>
> *(For after all **these things** do the Gentiles seek:) for your heavenly Father knoweth that ye have need of all **these things**.*
>
> *But seek ye first the kingdom of God, and his righteousness; and all **these things** shall be added unto you.* [41]

Notice that the expression "these things" is used three times all of which refers to food, drink and clothing.

Thinking on Mary's pregnancy Joseph had some concerns.

> *Now the birth of Jesus Christ was on this wise: When as his mother Mary was espoused to Joseph, before*

---

[40] D&C 11:23-25.

[41] Matthew 6:31-33.

23

*they came together, she was found with child of the
Holy Ghost.*

*Then Joseph her husband, being a just man, and not
willing to make her a publick example, was minded to
put her away privily.*

*But **while he thought on these things**, behold, the
angel of the Lord appeared unto him in a dream,
saying, Joseph, thou son of David, fear not to take unto
thee Mary thy wife: for that which is conceived in her
is of the Holy Ghost.* [42]

These examples are cited from the Book of Mormon, Doctrine
and Covenants (in the Savior's own words) and the New
Testament. Remember the multiple times this expression is
used in our scriptures:

- New Testament -201 times,
- Doctrine & Covenants - 117 times, and
- Book of Mormon - 366 times.

We conclude that the identification of "these things" always
precedes the expression. Sometimes the exact meaning of the
term "these things" is complex from the language that is used
but the meaning is derived from the preceding language in all
cases.

Suffering "These Things"

The Savior stated,

*For behold, I, God, have suffered these things for all,
that they might not suffer if they would repent;*[43]

[42] Matthew 1:18-20.

[43] D&C 19:16.

24

Where do we look to find the meaning of "these things" that the Savior suffered? We need to look at the preceding language in the revelation (Section 19) itself. If anyone looks elsewhere they are looking in the wrong place. Other scriptures may show relational aspects to his atonement but to understand "these things" he suffered", the preceding language holds the key to understanding.

A casual reading of the previous verses in Section 19, which contains this expression of the Savior's sufferings, does not provide a quick answer about the meaning of "these things." As with other statements by the Savior, we need to study the language carefully.

This revelation (Section 19) was a call to repentance for Martin Harris and deals with God's decreed judgments and punishments of humankind. The verses that are applicable to understanding *these things* he suffered are:

> *And surely **every man must repent or suffer…** "*[44].

> *Wherefore, I revoke not the **judgments** which I shall pass, but **woes shall go forth, weeping, wailing and gnashing of teeth, yea, to those who are found on my left hand.***
> *Nevertheless, it is not written that there shall be no end to **this torment**,* [45]

These verses refer to suffering, judgments and torment and are the only preceding verses that discuss them. The Savior states categorically that every man must repent or there will be suffering. No excuses, repent or suffer. Notice that the Savior

---

[44] D&C 19:4.

[45] D&C 19:4-6.

states that those on his left hand will suffer woes described as weeping, wailing and gnashing of teeth, which the Savior identified as a "judgment". In the last verse, he describes these woes as a torment. The important concept to understand is that this judgment, suffering and torment is what those on the Savior's left hand suffers.

Therefore, when the Savior says "*I, God, have suffered these things for all*", he is saying I have suffered what those people on my left hand suffers. How do those on his left hand suffer? They suffer at the hand of Satan and his host. The Savior suffered directly from the hand of Satan. He subjected himself to suffer at the hand of Satan.

Amulek taught the poor among Zoramites, the following

> *For behold, if ye have procrastinated the day of your repentance even until death, behold, ye have become subjected to the spirit of the devil, and he doth seal you his ; therefore, the Spirit of the Lord hath withdrawn from you, and hath no place in you, and **the devil hath all power over you;** and this is the final state of the wicked.* [46]

There are a number of scriptures that record that the wicked will suffer in hell under the control of Satan and his hosts.[47] This is further substantiated by the Savior's statement

> *And the righteous shall be gathered on my right hand unto eternal life; and the wicked on my left hand will I be ashamed to own before the Father;*

---

[46] Alma 34:25.

[47] 2 Nephi 2:27-29; Mosiah 6:2-5; Alma 9:28; Alma 34:35; See also D&C 29:36-39; D&C 29:40-45.

*Wherefore I will say unto them—**Depart from me, ye cursed, into everlasting fire, prepared for the devil and his angels.*** [48]

This quote seems to state that only those on his right hand will be in the highest degree in the celestial kingdom with the Father and those on his left hand will suffer the buffeting and torment of Satan and his angels or as we say they will suffer in hell. This raises a dilemma for this author.

This is the dilemma. In the discussion on the marriage covenant, the language identifies that those who are faithful in the Church who are married in mortality but not married by the priesthood temple marriage and die, then they will be ministering angels and will not have eternal life. They will suffer everlasting fire which Joseph Smith identifies as knowing they could have had a better eternal position but it will gnaw at them throughout eternity. However, I do not believe that they will suffer in hell. [Read essay "MARRIAGE COVENANT" and section "Everlasting Fire" in essay "JUDGMENTS at MORTAL DEATH"].

The quote above brings to memory the experience of Moses when he commanded in the name of the Savior for Satan to leave him.[49] When Moses commanded Satan to leave, Satan responded with *"weeping, wailing and gnashing of teeth"* and Moses began to fear for he saw the "bitterness of hell.[50] This expression *"weeping, wailing and gnashing of teeth"* is the reaction of those who suffer in hell.

---

[48] D&C 29:27-28

[49] Moses 1:22.

[50] Moses 1:20.

One other person has experienced Satan's power and torment like the Savior while in mortality. That person was Joseph Smith. After he knelt in his first prayer he recorded

> *I had scarcely done so, when immediately I was seized upon by some power which entirely overcame me, and had such an astonishing influence over me as to bind my tongue so that I could not speak. Thick darkness gathered around me, and it seemed to me for a time as if I were doomed to sudden destruction.*

> *But, exerting all my powers to call upon God to deliver me out of the power of this enemy which had seized upon me, and at the very moment when I was ready to sink into despair and abandon myself to destruction— not to an imaginary ruin, but to the power of some actual being from the unseen world, who had such marvelous power as I had never before felt.* [51]

Because the Savior's endured these buffetings and torment, he has already suffered the punishment that we would have to suffer for our sins, if we did not repent. In this process, he suffered for all humankind not just members of his church. This was necessary to become our judge.

Following the gospel summary given to the Lamanites, the Savior said

> *Now this is the commandment: Repent, all ye ends of the earth, and come unto me and be baptized in my name, **that ye may be sanctified by the reception of the Holy Ghost,** that ye may stand <u>spotless before me</u> at the last day[52].*

---

[51] Smith, History of the Church 1:15–16.

When we repent, and are baptized, the Savior gives us forgiveness. When we continue changing our lives by continued repentance and seeking light and knowledge, we draw closer to sanctification through the Holy Ghost and become spotless clean.

There is another important concept relating to this discussion. At the beginning of the Section 19, the Savior stated,

> *I, having accomplished and finished the will of him whose I am, even the Father, concerning me--having done this **that I might subdue all things unto myself**—*
>
> ***Retaining all power**, even <u>to the destroying of Satan and his works at the end of the world</u>, and the last great day of judgment, which I shall pass upon the inhabitants thereof, **judging every man according to his works and the deeds which he hath done**.* [53]

This statement shows he did the will of the Father and that he received and retains all power. With this power, he will destroy *"**Satan and his works at the end of the world**"*. This statement is made to assure us that he is more powerful than Satan from whom he suffered in the Garden.

By fulfilling the will of the Father, he also became our judge and at the end of the world he will pass judgment on all humankind according to their works and deeds.

By this description, we should not conclude that everyone on the Savior's left hand will suffer in hell. For example, Those, who die without law and little children, will not suffer in hell because the Savior's atonement prevents this[54]. Little children

---

[52] 3 Nephi 27:20

[53] D&C 19:2-3.

are sinless and will be in the celestial kingdom. Those without law are guaranteed to be in the terrestrial kingdom

Personal Sins

We have shown that in the Garden, the Savior suffered at the hands of Satan for all humankind. He did this to fulfill the will of the Father for which the Father make him our judge. He did not take upon him our personal sins in the Garden because he suffered for all humankind. So when does he take upon him our personal sins?

Forgiveness after repentance, baptism and receiving the Holy Ghost is the first instance that the Savior takes upon him our personal sins. By giving us forgiveness, he begins taking upon himself our personal sins for the purpose of holding us guiltless before the Father at the final judgment. A further explanation of how this is done is explained in the "ENDURING to the END "essay

His Greater Suffering

There is one difference between mortals suffering from Satan than what the Savior suffered. That difference is that Christ suffered "these things" while in the flesh.

The Savior said,

> *Which suffering caused myself, even God, the greatest of all, **to tremble because of pain, and to bleed at every pore**, and to suffer **both body and spirit**"*[55]

The Savior had both body and spirit pain. There is no way to measure or fully understand this combination of pain except to

---

[54] D&C 76:71-72; D&C 29:45

[55] D&C 19:18.

understand that the Savior bled at every pore from that pain. Man, who is committed to hell will only suffer spirit pain as they are not committed to hell until they die.

ENDURING to the END

Many who might read this essay will already know about most if not all the scriptures relating to this topic. This essay emphasizes the way that the Savior judges our individual sins. The emphasis here is the fact that the Savior is exercising his judgment as he forgives or not forgives sins. As identified in the essay "Christ's Gospel", when the Savior gives forgiveness for individual sin and we are faithful to the end of our lives, he takes upon him our sins and holds us guiltless before the Father.

Enduring in the faith has been a commandment from the beginning. This applies to a person whether they lived prior to Christ's birth or after it.

> *That as many as would believe and be baptized in his holy name, and* **endure in faith to the end**, *should be saved--*

> *Not only those who believed after he came in the meridian of time, in the flesh, but all those from the beginning,* **even as many as were before he came, who believed in the words of the holy prophets**, *who spake as they were inspired by the gift of the Holy Ghost, who truly testified of him in all things, should have eternal life,*

> *As well as those who should come after,* **who should believe in the gifts and callings of God by the Holy Ghost,** *which beareth record of the Father and of the Son;*[56]

31

The prophets have written much about the Savior's atonement for individual sins and about his atonement for the sins of the world. These are related concepts but really have some differences depending on the context of their usage. Sins of the world actually encompass the salvation of all including the salvation of those who will inherit the terrestrial and telestial kingdoms. [Read the subsection "Sins of the World" in the essay "SALVATION OF MAN"].

Individual Sins – Savior's Judgments

When individuals are baptized and receive the Holy Ghost, they become members of his Church. They are forgiven of their sins if they have truly repented[57]. Even after our baptism if we sin and truly repent the Savior gives us forgiveness for those sins. The Lord said,

> *Behold, he who has repented of his sins, the same is forgiven, and **I, the Lord, remember them no more.***[58]

The Savior exercises his judgment powers in giving this forgiveness. What this means is that those sins are no longer a factor in his future judgments. If that individual continues seeking truth and righteousness, then these sins are not remembered at the final judgment when he holds us "guiltless" before the Father.

However, forgiveness is a conditional event until the death of an individual. The Savior said,

> *And now, verily I say unto you, I, the Lord, will not lay any sin to your charge; go your ways and sin no more;*

---

56 D&C 20:25-27; See also D&C 20:29; 2 Nephi 9:23-24.

57 D&C 20:37.

58 D&C 58:42.

but unto that soul who sinneth shall the former sins return, saith the Lord your God.[59]

Therefore, when a person repents and then sins again, the forgiveness for former sins is rescinded and the person is not forgiven of those sins. Stated another way, those sins are then remembered by the Savior at judgment time. The Lord restated this principle in the Kirtland temple dedicatory prayer, which was a revelation to Joseph Smith. Joseph prayed

*Jehovah, have mercy upon this people, and as all men sin forgive the transgressions of thy people, and **let them be blotted out forever.***[60]

To be "blotted out" refers to this concept that the Savior will remember them no more.

Alma gave the most descriptive verse in the Book of Mormon about how the Savior provides the atonement for individual sins.

*Now the Spirit knoweth all things; nevertheless the **Son of God suffereth according to the flesh that he might take upon him the sins of his people, that he might blot out their transgressions according to the power of his deliverance;** and now behold, this is the testimony which is in me.* [61]

His "power of deliverance" is his will and judgment to remember our sins no more at the final judgment. At the final judgment, members of his Church have the assurance that if

---

[59] D&C 82:7.

[60] D&C 109:34.

[61] Alma 7:13.

they truly repent and endure to the end, the Savior blots out their sins and holds them guiltless before the Father.

Our mortal life is a probationary state during which we can repent. Alma in explaining this probationary period said this to Zeezrom and the people of Ammonihah.

> *And we see that death comes upon mankind, yea, the death which has been spoken of by Amulek, which is the temporal death; nevertheless **there was a space granted unto man in which he might repent**; therefore **this life became a probationary state; a time to prepare to meet God**; a time to prepare for that endless state which has been spoken of by us, which is after the resurrection of the dead.*[62]

Nephi explained the same concept.

> *The day should come that they must be judged of their works, yea, even the works which were done by the temporal body **in their days of probation**.*[63]

This last quote refers to the final judgment, which occurs at the end of the millennium. What is being taught in these two scriptures is that we will be judged on the works we performed during our mortal probation and that will determine our eternal destiny. As Church members, our opportunity to repent occurs in this mortal life and not after death.

Even those who are active members need to be careful about their activity and attitudes. The Lord said of those who are slothful,

---

[62] Alma 12:24; 2 Nephi 2:21; 2 Nephi 9:27; 2 Nephi 33:9; Helaman 13:38; Mormon 9:28; D&C 29:43.

[63] 1 Nephi 15:32.

Wherefore, now let every man learn his duty, and to act in the office in which he is appointed, in all diligence.

He that is slothful shall not be counted worthy to stand, and he that learns not his duty and shows himself not approved shall not be counted worthy to stand. *Even so. Amen.* [64]

The Lord further said,

For behold, it is not meet that I should command in all things; for he that is compelled in all things, the same is a slothful and not a wise servant; **wherefore he receiveth no reward.**

But he that doeth not anything until he is commanded, and receiveth a commandment with doubtful heart, and keepeth it with slothfulness, **the same is damned.** [65]

Joseph Smith wrote,

It is impossible for a man to be saved in ignorance. [66]

A slothful person is a lazy person. Those who learn not their duty would include the lazy and would include those who focus on the things of the world to the exclusion of working in the kingdom. Other activities may not be sinful but those who engage in them to the exclusion of active works of righteousness are at high risk of not being found worthy to enter the Father's kingdom. This is not to say that we should

---

[64] D&C 107:99-100; D&C 58:26.

[65] D&C 58:26- 29.

[66] D&C 131:6.

not engage in these other activities, but if it were to the exclusion of works of righteousness, it would be sin.

Those who are "damned" are those who will not inherit the highest degree in the celestial kingdom. As active members, we cannot serve dedicatedly for a while and then take a long vacation because we have previously worked hard in our service to the Savior. We continue to serve whenever and however we can to the end of our mortal lives, which is "enduring to the end."

Perfection and Sin

There is a common notion in the Church that as Church members we continue to sin even up to our death because we are not perfect. Perfection is that elusive status that we can never reach in mortality. We equate non-perfection with sin, but perfection includes learning eternal principles that relate to functioning in eternity.

Working and laboring in the kingdom of God has a positive effect on our relationship with the Savior and our Heavenly Father. There are two scriptures in the New Testament that shed light on this concept.

> *Brethren, if any of you do err from the truth, and one convert him;*
>
> *Let him know, that he which converteth the sinner from the error of his way shall save a soul from death, and shall hide a multitude of sins.* [67]

And also,

---

[67] James 5:19-20.

And above all things have fervent charity among yourselves: for charity shall cover the multitude of sins. [68]

A person who is influential in the conversion of another person is one who furthers the Lord's work. That is, they are sharing the gospel with others as the Lord has commanded us. A person who develops true charity is one whose conduct in this life showing concern and support in various ways for others especially for those in distress.

In connection with this concept, the Savior exercised mercy in giving forgiveness to some elders in Kirtland. Some of these elders had sinned and probably had not fully repented but all were taking active steps to prepare for and fulfill a commandment to travel to Zion (Missouri). This was not a simple task and was taking weeks to prepare. To this group the Lord said,

> *For verily I say unto you, I will that ye should overcome the world; wherefore I will have compassion upon you.*
>
> *There are those among you who have sinned; but verily I say, for this once, for mine own glory, and for the salvation of souls, I have forgiven you your sins.*
>
> *I will be merciful unto you, for I have given unto you the kingdom.* [69]

The Lord in exercising his judgment powers was willing to give them forgiveness for their dedicated activity of preparing to travel to Missouri as the Lord commanded. This seems to

---

[68] 1 Peter 4:8.

[69] D&C 64:2-4.

demonstrate that we are progressing in the character traits needed to become like our Father when we are actively pursuing and implementing activities which further the work of God. As one continues with these activities and traits using introspection to evaluate our conduct to ensure that it complies with the Savior, then we do not have a propensity to sin.

We may not be perfect but our dedicated efforts may be acceptable to the Savior. True perfection is not just the absence of sin but it is the process of gaining further light and truth. Joseph Smith wrote,

> Whatever **principle of intelligence we attain unto in this life, it will rise with us in the resurrection.**
>
> And if a person gains more knowledge and intelligence in this life through his diligence and obedience than another, he will have so much the advantage in the world to come. [70]

Intelligence is light and truth.[71] The Lord explained in the revelations Joseph received,

> And no man receiveth a fulness unless he keepeth his commandments.
>
> **He that keepeth his commandments receiveth truth and light, until he is glorified in truth and knoweth all things.** [72]

Further,

---

[70] D&C 130:18-19.

[71] D&C 93:29.

[72] D&C 93:27-28.

The glory of God is intelligence, or, in other words, light and truth.

Light and truth forsake that evil one. [73]

Our goal in this mortality should be to gain as much knowledge, light, truth and good works as we are able. Moroni wrote in closing his book, entitled "Moroni" in the Book of Mormon, wrote that perfection is possible in this life.

Yea, come unto Christ, and be perfected in him, *and deny yourselves of all ungodliness; and if ye shall deny yourselves of all ungodliness, and love God with all your might, mind and strength, then is his grace sufficient for you, that by his grace ye may be perfect in Christ; and if by the grace of God ye are perfect in Christ, ye can in nowise deny the power of God.*

And again, if ye by the grace of God are perfect in Christ, and deny not his power, then are ye sanctified in Christ by the grace of God, through the shedding of the blood of Christ, which is in the covenant of the Father unto the remission of your sins, that ye become holy, without spot. [74]

Moroni states that it is possible to become perfect or sanctified in Christ because of the grace of Christ.

CHRIST'S LOVE

Probably the most obvious event that demonstrates the Savior's love for humankind is his ministry wherein he performed many miracles of healing. They are obvious

---

[73] D&C 93:36-37.

[74] Moroni 10:32-33

because many witnessed these miracles as he performed them. We have no record of all of these miracles but the Savior's reputation of being a healer was widely known. Many came to him for healing.

One such event, recorded by Matthew, Mark and Luke[75] describes a man who had palsy which confined him to a bed. He was brought to the Savior and the multitude was so great that the Savior could not be reached. They took the afflicted man to the roof of the building, opened the roof and let him down so that the Savior could minister to him. The Savior recognized the faith of the invalid man and stated that his sins were forgiven. Obviously, the man had great faith in the Savior. Upon recognizing the critical thoughts of the scribes that the Savior was committing blasphemy because only God could forgive sins the Savior healed the man and told him to arise and return to his home. This demonstrated that he had the power to forgive sins as well as heal people. This power to forgive sins is the most important aspect of his atonement.

The multitude was astonished at this miracle. All three gospels record that the multitude "glorified God" and had not seen such miracles. This is an example of his reputation. The popularity of Christ with the people was very strong. This is also illustrated by his entry into Jerusalem at Passover time.[76] Matthew, Mark and John describe this event in similar terms. John records that many came to see Lazarus, whom Jesus had recently raised from the dead. All of these people had seen or heard stories about the Savior's healing powers. He was

---

[75] Matthew 9:2-8; Mark 2:1-12; Luke 5:18-26.

[76] Matthew 21:1-111 Mark 11:1-10; John 12:9-15.

recognized by some as did Nicodemus, who said the Savior was a

> *"teacher come from God: for no man can do these miracles that thou doest, except God be with him."*[77]

The Savior ministered and blessed the people because of his great love for them. He did not come to judge during his earthly ministry as he told the adulteress, "Neither do I condemn thee: go, and sin no more."[78] The only criticism that he made was of the works of the Jewish leadership. Verbal condemnation of these Jewish leaders was by way of testifying rather than giving a final judgment. John quoted the Savior as saying,

> *The world cannot hate you; but me it hateth, **because I testify of it, that the works thereof are evil.***[79]

Probably one of the greatest statements of his love for his spirit brothers and sisters is:

> *Greater love hath no man than this, that a man lay down his life for his friends.*[80]

All Christian people quote this statement of the Savior especially as it relates to war and other events when individuals perform some heroic action which preserves the lives of others,

This is true in the military especially when they use their own bodies to absorb the explosive force of a grenade or other such

---

[77] John 3:2.

[78] John 8:11.

[79] John 7:7.

[80] John 15:13.

41

device protecting others within the killing range or in exposing themselves to heavy gunfire to save others. Truly, such an act does signify the love and concern of comrades.

However, when the Savior made this statement, he was referring to his great love for us that he would suffer and die so that he could provide the resurrection and salvation for us. It is true that the Father gave him a commandment but he kept that commandment because of his love for the Father and for us. He said,

> But that the world may know that I love the Father; and as the Father gave me commandment, even so I do.[81]

No person could have this great love for the Father and not have love for the Father's children, which is all of humankind. The commandment to give up his life is recorded as:

> Therefore doth my Father love me, because I lay down my life, that I might take it again.

> No man taketh it from me, but I lay it down of myself. I have power to lay it down, and I have power to take it again. This commandment have I received of my Father. [82] [Read the section "Cause of His Death" in the essay "BLOOD/RESURRECTION – SAVIOR"].

Testimonies of the Prophets
The prophets have taught of this love of the Savior. Moroni recorded in the Book of Ether a conversation he had with the Lord. Moroni expressed concern about his writings and how

---

[81] John 14:21.

[82] John 10:17-18.

42

the gentiles would receive the record, he was finishing. In that conversation Moroni wrote,

> *And again, I remember that thou hast said that thou hast loved the world, even unto the laying down of thy life for the world,* **that thou mightest take it again to prepare a place for the children of men.**
>
> **And now I know that this love which thou hast had for the children of men is charity** ... [83]

In the first verse, Moroni confirms that the Savior loved the world, not just the righteous, but the world to the extent that he laid down his life for the world that he might prepare a place for all of God's children. [Read the section "Sins of the World" in the essay "SALVATION OF MAN"].

When Joseph F. Smith received his revelation, which is now section 138 in the Doctrine and Covenants, he was pondering.

> *And reflecting upon the* **great atoning sacrifice** *that was made by the Son of God,* **for the redemption of the world;**
>
> *And the* **great and wonderful love made manifest by the Father and the Son** *in the coming of the Redeemer into the world;*
>
> *That through* **his atonement, and by obedience to the principles of the gospel, mankind might be saved.**[84]

The "redemption of the world" is the redemption of all humankind except the sons of perdition who are special cases. [Read the essay "SONS OF PERDITION"]. He made special

---

[83] Ether 12:33-34.

[84] D&C 138:2-4.

focus on the "great and wonderful love made manifest by the Father and the Son.

There is one other event that demonstrates the Savior's love for us which occurred in the Garden prior to his suffering from Satan. An angel appeared to him to strengthen him. The following is Luke's account. The Savior prayed,

> *Saying, Father, if thou be willing, remove this cup from me: nevertheless not my will, but thine, be done.*
>
> *And there appeared an angel unto him from heaven, strengthening him.*[85]

Matthew and Mark do not mention the appearance of the angel but record the prayer about the same. The Savior was petitioning the Father that he might not suffer the things he knew that lay ahead. Was it possible for him to not drink of this cup and still become our judge? The cup was the Garden and cross sufferings which he knew would be very painful and difficult but which were the things that were necessary for him to become our judge.

What would the angel say to strengthen him? Undoubtedly the angel would have reconfirmed the Father's love for him and encouraged him to be committed to accept and suffer the agonies so that salvation would be provided to Father's children. The angel would confirm that the Savior could not return to the Father nor could anyone of Father's children return to him without his enduring this bitter cup.

Because of his love for us as his siblings and his love for the Father, he would recognize that he needed to partake of this most painful cup. He willingly did so even though he had the

---

[85] Like 22:42-43.

power to make a different decision. Truly, the Savior suffered and died because of his love of God and us as his brothers and sisters.

Keeping His Commandments

If we keep Christ's commandments we show our love for him and the Father. For he taught his apostles:

> *He that hath my commandments, and kept them, he it is that loved me: and **he that loveth me shall be loved of my Father, and I will love him, and will manifest myself to him.***
>
> *Judas saith unto him, not Iscariot, Lord, how is it that thou wilt manifest thyself unto us, and not unto the world?*
>
> *Jesus answered and said unto him, **If a man love me, he will keep my words: and my Father will love him, and we will come unto him, and make our abode with him.***[86]

Here the Savior is assuring those who keep his commandments that they are loved by him and they will also have the love of the Father and the Savior insomuch that we will abide or dwell with them. He went on to explain,

> *As the Father hath loved me, so have I loved you: <u>continue ye in my love.</u>*
>
> *If ye keep my commandments, ye shall abide in my love; even as I have kept my Father's commandments, and abide in his love.*

---

[86] John 14:21-23. See also D&C 6:20; D&C 124:20, 78.

45

*These things have I spoken unto you, **that my joy might remain in you, and that your joy might be full.***[87]

By keeping his commandments, we will continue to have his love and a fullness of his joy. Those who keep not his commandments and die in their sins will not have this joy but will suffer "everlasting fire" which is a continual knowledge that they could have had a better station in eternity had they lived a different life in mortality. [Read the section "Everlasting Fire" in the essay "JUDGMENTS at MORTAL DEATH"].

We should not conclude that the Savior and the Father do not love the rest of humanity that do not keep his commandments in mortality. We should remember that the Savior will visit those in the terrestrial kingdom throughout eternity. Speaking of those in the terrestrial kingdom,

*These are they **who receive of the presence of the Son**, but not of the fulness of the Father.* [88]

If the Savior had no love for those in the terrestrial kingdom he would not visit them.

Those in the telestial kingdom cannot withstand the glory of the Father or the Savior and cannot be in their presence. They will be servants of the Father and the Savior throughout eternity. As servants, they will do the bidding of the Father and the Savior[89].

---

[87] John 15:9-11.

[88] D&C 76:77.

[89] D & C 76:112

46

The greatest desire of the Father and the Savior is that we would keep their commandments and earn to be in their presence throughout eternity.

-----ATONEMENT EVENTS-----

The Savior outlined the gospel plan to his Nephite disciples in the preceding section. This helps us to understand how the atonement operates in our lives. Some events including his Gethsemane sufferings were detailed. Other important events are covered in this section.

This section begins with concepts of mortality and immortality. This is important because the author discovered an important quote of Joseph Smith in which he stated

> *Therefore Jesus Christ left his blood to atone for the Sins of the world that he might assend into the present of the Father."* [90]

The Savior left his blood in the Garden of Gethsemane, to accomplish two purposes, which were to

- Atone for the sins of the world
- Prepare himself to return to the presence of the Father.

Joseph also made a number of statements regarding the environment in which the Father lives. If anyone is to live in the presence of the Father, their bodies must be changed. This includes the Savior's body.

Also, included in this section are descriptions of the Roman Soldier maltreatments and his sufferings on the cross. They are meticulously presented by describing their intensity and duration. This was included so that a sincere person might feel what the Savior really endured.

There is a general concept that during the Savior's ministry the Savior suffered exactly what we have suffered which is not

---

[90] Ehat, Words of Joseph Smith, 370-371 (Spoken on 10 May 1844).

quite correct. The scriptures that give this impression are explained and also how the Savior understands our suffering, whatever they may entail.

Finally, the notion that the Savior actually used anger to drive the moneychangers out of the temple is challenged. That discussion shows that there was only one temple cleansing event and how the Savior caused the polluters to leave.

MORTALITY

Blood is essential to a living mortal. It performs many functions relating to mortal life including

- carrying oxygen and nutrients to all the body
- carrying carbon dioxide and other waste products back to the lungs, kidneys and liver for disposal
- attacking infections and helping to heal wounds

When a person dies, the heart stops beating and blood ceases to flow through the veins. This starts the decaying process which progresses rather rapidly. In fact, many states have regulations stating that the body needs to be buried or cremated within hours unless it is embalmed. During the embalming process blood is removed from the body and replaced with an embalming fluid.

Generally, our bodies develop until we reach a peak where our body is at its peak performance. Then the body gradually starts to deteriorate, perhaps at different rates but we age. When we are old, our bodies become frail, our skin becomes thin and we bruise easily. We develop ailments such as diabetes, arthritis, atherosclerosis, heart or liver problems, etc. No person is immune from the aging process. Eventually some critical part of our body fails and we die.

At death, there is a separation of our spirit and our mortal body. Our bodies remain with mother earth and our spirits go to the world of spirits.

RESURRECTION

During the millennium, mortal bodies will be changed from a mortal state to a resurrected state in the twinkling of an eye.[91]

> *Wherefore, children shall grow up until they become old; old men shall die; but they shall not sleep in the dust, **but they shall be changed in the twinkling of an eye**.* [92]

Their bodies will become immortal with this change. For those of us who die a mortal death, we will become immortal at our resurrection. When we are resurrected we will have bodies just like we now have only they will be whole and complete in every particular including the hair of our heads. Our bodies will be immortal, that is, not subject to death any more. Amulek taught the people of Ammonihah:

> *Now, <u>this restoration shall come to all</u>, both old and young, both bond and free, both male and female, both the wicked and the righteous; and even there shall not so much as a hair of their heads be lost; **but everything shall be restored to its perfect frame**, as it is now, or in the body.* [93]

Just how our physical bodies are made whole and perfect is not known. We wonder especially for those whose bodies <u>have been cremated or eaten</u> by animals. We know that God

[91] D&C 43:32; 63:51; 101:31.

[92] D&C 63:51.

[93] Alma 11:44.

the creator has all power and will make bodies for our spirit to inhabit. Nephi quoted Jacob as saying,

> *And because of the way of deliverance of our God, the Holy One of Israel, this death, of which I have spoken, which is the temporal, shall deliver up its dead; which death is the grave.*
>
> *And this death of which I have spoken, which is the spiritual death, shall deliver up its dead; which spiritual death is hell; wherefore, death and hell must deliver up their dead, and hell must deliver up its captive spirits, and the grave must deliver up its captive bodies, and the bodies and the spirits of men will be restored one to the other; and it is by the power of the resurrection of the Holy One of Israel.*
>
> *O how great the plan of our God! For on the other hand, the paradise of God must deliver up the spirits of the righteous, and the grave deliver up the body of the righteous; and the spirit and the body is restored to itself again, and **all men become incorruptible, and immortal.*** [94]

The terms incorruptible and immortal mean that our bodies will not suffer disease and afflictions like in mortality and that our bodies with our spirits united will live forever. When the scriptures talk about corruption putting on incorruption, it refers to our mortal bodies becoming immortal not subject to death.

IMMORTALITY

---

[94] 2 Nephi 9:11-13; Alma 11:42-43.

In the Resurrection essay, we wrote about the resurrection of the physical body. We ask this question: "What causes a body when it is resurrected to not die again? We know that our physical bodies will be resurrected and will be complete and whole. In this essay, we will explain what makes it immortal.

The prophet Ezekiel was shown a valley of dry bones in vision and the Lord continued,

> *And he said unto me, Son of man, can these bones live? And I answered, O Lord God, thou knowest.*
>
> *Again he said unto me, Prophesy upon these bones, and say unto them, O ye dry bones, hear the word of the Lord.*
>
> *Thus saith the Lord God unto these bones; Behold, I will cause breath to enter into you, and ye shall live:*
>
> *And I will lay sinews upon you, and will bring up flesh upon you, and cover you with skin, and put breath in you, and ye shall live; and ye shall know that I am the Lord.*[95]

Then Ezekiel was shown in vision the bones connecting together, then flesh covering the bones and skin covering the flesh. They received breath and lived. Then the Lord continued,

> *Therefore prophesy and say unto them* [Israel], *Thus saith the Lord God; Behold, O my people, I will open your graves, and cause you to come up out of your graves, and bring you into the land of Israel.*

---

[95] Ezekiel 37:3-6.

And ye shall know that I am the Lord, when I have opened your graves, O my people, and brought you up out of your graves,

*And **shall put my spirit in you, and ye shall live.**[96]*

This revelation to Ezekiel was about the resurrection of physical bodies. The Lord specifically states that he will *"put my spirit in you"* or into the physical bodies that these bodies will live. This spirit is not the Holy Ghost. It is something different and will be in the bodies of all resurrected beings. What is this spirit in resurrected bodies?

On Sunday 20 March 1842 Wilford Woodruff recorded in his journal quoting Joseph Smith

> *As concerning the resurrection, I will merely say that all men will come from the grave as they lie down, whether old or young; there will not be "added unto their stature one cubit," neither taken from it; **all will be raised by the power of God, <u>having spirit in their bodies</u>, and not blood.***[97]

Joseph taught that resurrected bodies had spirit in them and not blood. This spirit replaces blood and will flow throughout our bodies like blood does now. We can conclude that this spirit makes the difference between resurrected persons and mortal persons. There is a reason why blood is absent from a resurrected person. The following quotes give the answer.

In his King Follett sermon Joseph describes the environment in which God dwells:

---

[96] Ezekiel 37:11-14.

[97] Smith, History of the Church, 4:556.

***Some shall rise to the everlasting burnings of God;
for God dwells in everlasting burnings*[98]**

Thomas Bullock on Sunday May 12, 1844 recorded the
Prophet as saying,

> <u>*God Almighty himself dwells in eternal fire;*</u> **flesh and
> blood cannot go there, for all corruption** [bodies with
> blood] **is devoured by the fire.** *Our God is a
> consuming fire.* **When our flesh is quickened by the
> Spirit, there will be no blood in this tabernacle,**[99]

In Oct 1843, Willard Richards recorded the prophet as saying

> **Flesh and blood cannot go there** [presence of God]*;*
> **but flesh and bones, quickened by the Spirit of God,
> can.** [100]

These last three quotes teach us that God lives in eternal
burnings. We do not know exactly what these eternal burnings
are but flesh with blood cannot go there for the flesh and
blood would be consumed which probably means destroyed.
For bodies of flesh and bones to exist in the presence of the
Father there must be spirit flowing through the veins of that
body.

When we are resurrected, we are resurrected with spirit
flowing through the veins of our bodies as described by
Ezekiel and verified by these quotes. This spirit flowing
through our bodies is what makes our bodies immortal.

George Laub recorded Joseph's address of May 12, 1844 as

---

[98] Smith, History of The Church of the Church, 6:317.

[99] Smith, History of the Church, 6:366 (Spoken on 10 May 1844).

[100] Smith, History of the Church, 6:52 (Spoken on 9 Oct, 1843).

we could not abide his [Father in Heaven] *presents unless pure Spirits in us.* **for the Blood is the corruptible part of the tabernacles.** [101]

Blood is the corruptible part of our mortal bodies. What this means is that blood is what causes our bodies to deteriorate, age and eventually die. Spirit is the replacement for blood. It flows through our bodies just like blood. When one reads the scriptures that talk about being corruptible, they refer to bodies with blood in them. When they refer of incorruption, they refer to resurrected bodies with spirit and not blood in them. When they refer to corruption putting on incorruption they refer to the resurrection of all with spirit flowing through their bodies and not blood.

When the Savior returned to the Father, he had to have all blood out of his body leaving only spirit flowing through his veins. This occurred in the Garden of Gethsemane as will be shown in the next essay.

BLOOD/RESURRECTION – SAVIOR

We know from the above essays that blood flowing through the veins of mortal man causes the body to age and die. The question is "What was flowing through the veins of the Savior from his birth to his death?"

We know that the Savior had blood in his veins because he shed blood in the Garden of Gethsemane. However, there could not be only blood in his veins, for if he had only blood, he would have been mortal just like any other mortal on this earth. He would be subject to aging and death just like us.

---

[101] Ehat, Words of Joseph Smith, 370.

God, the Father, was the natural father of the Savior and Mary was his mother. The Father was immortal and had spirit flowing through his veins. Mary was mortal having blood in her veins.

The Father passed onto the Savior spirit to be in the Savior's veins at his birth. The fluid going through the Savior's body was a mixture of blood and spirit. The blood came from his mortal mother and spirit came from his immortal Father.

Concerning the blood in the Savior's body, George Laub recorded on 12 May 1844 Joseph Smith as saying,

> *Concerning Resurrection Flesh and Blood cannot inherit the kingdom of god or the kingdom that god inherits or inhabits.* But the **flesh without the blood and the Spirit of god flowing in the vains in Sted of blood** *for blood is the part of the body that causes corruption.* *therefore we must be changed in the twinkle of an Eye or have to lay down these tabernacles and leave the blood vanish away* **Therefore Jesus Christ left his blood to atone for the Sins of the world that he might assend into the present of the Father.** "[102]

Here Joseph states that we must get rid of our blood and get it replaced with spirit. He says

> *therefore we must be changed in the twinkle of an Eye or have to lay down these tabernacles and leave the blood vanish away*

Joseph refers to two ways in which spirit replaces blood in our bodies. The expression "*to lay down these tabernacles and*

---

[102] Ehat, Words of Joseph Smith, 370-371 (Spoken on 10 May 1844).

leave the blood vanish away" refers to our current state that we must die, the blood vanishes away. Then we are resurrected with spirit in our veins. The expression *"changed in the twinkle of an Eye"* refers to becoming immortal during the millennium

In referring to the millennium, the Lord stated

> *children shall grow up until they become old; old men shall die; but they shall not sleep in the dust, but they shall be changed in the twinkling of an eye.*[103]

This instantaneous change will probably occur through a priesthood ordinance. When this happens the blood in their bodies will be changed instantly to spirit flowing through their veins because the spirit is what makes their bodies immortal.

The following expression from George Laub's above quote needs to be explained,

> **Therefore Jesus Christ left his blood <u>to atone for the Sins of the world</u> that he <u>might assend into the present of the father.</u>**

To atone for the sins of the world Jesus suffered directly at the hands of Satan. [Explained in the essay "GETHSEMANE"]. Satan caused Jesus to suffer extreme physical and spirit pain. This pain was so intensive that the Savior bled at every pore. By this suffering he suffered what we would suffer if we do not repent.

What was accomplished by this suffering? By this suffering, he was made our king, judge and advocate with the Father in accordance with the Father's plan or will. In a sense, he took

---

[103] D&C 63:51

upon him our sins by suffering what we would have suffered, if we do not repent. However, all of humankind is commanded to repent and when we repent, he gives us forgiveness. If we continue to learn, repent and keep his commandments then he remembers our sins no longer making us clean and holds us worthy to be in God's presence.

The second part of this quote states that the Savior shed his blood "that he might *ascend into the presence of the Father*". To be in the presence of the Father he could not have any blood in his body. He had to shed all of his blood from his body at the time that he was shedding his blood to atone for the sins of the world. This happened in the Garden of Gethsemane. Several scriptures describe the Savior eliminating his blood from his body.

King Benjamin stated that the Savior bled from **every pore** of his body.[104] Luke describes that the Savior as sweating **"great drops of blood"** and places this event in the Garden of Gethsemane.[105] The Savior gave his own statement of his suffering,

> *Which suffering caused myself, even God, the greatest of all, to tremble because of pain, and **to bleed at every pore**, and to suffer both body and spirit.*[106] .

The blood the Savior lost was not a small amount. He could not have any blood left in his body and be able to return to the presence of the Father. What was left in the veins of the Savior after this experience was pure spirit, which came from his

---

[104] Mosiah 3:7.

[105] Luke 22:44.

[106] D&C 19:18.

Father. Having pure spirit and no blood, he was immortal just as those during the millennium who are changed in the twinkling of an eye resulting in only spirit in their bodies. Having done this, he could return to the presence of the Father EXCEPT that he had to complete his atonement by suffering Roman soldier maltreatment and crucifixion on the cross.

Two scriptures concerning the blood of the Savior need to be addressed. The Gospel of John does contain a statement that a spear was thrust in the side of the Savior and blood and water came out. [107] What really happened here was that when the spear pierced his body, spirit came out which is stated as water. There was no blood left to expunge from his body.

Some scribe, being mortal, thought he knew that when a body is pierced blood comes out, added the term blood later. He did not understand the body of the Savior. This is the only reasonable explanation for this passage knowing that there was no blood left in his body.

The other scripture is,

> And, having made peace through the **blood of his cross**, by him to reconcile all things unto himself; by him, I say, whether they be things in earth, or things in heaven. [108]

This expression is not clear. Perhaps the translation is not correct. However, Joseph Smith taught that all the Savior's blood was eliminated at the time that he suffered for the sins of the world, which occurred in the Garden. Following the

---

[107] John 19:34.

[108] Colossians 1:20.

Garden experience there was no blood in the Savior's body and therefore no blood was shed on the cross.

When Joseph translated the New Testament, he did not address these concepts in his translation. He never completed the translation and, at the time, he did not understand that the Savior had to eliminate all blood "*to assend to the presence of the Father*". These statements concerning blood and spirit by Joseph Smith were given in the last two years of his life. Joseph had this to say about the things that he revealed to the members.

> *Immortality dwells in everlasting burnings. I will from time to time reveal to you the subjects that are revealed by the Holy Ghost to me.* [109]"

We should not be concerned that this concept is not included in his translation of the New Testament as they were revealed in the last days of his life.

Being Immortal - Suffering Pain
The next question that needs to be discussed is "If the Savior's body was immortal, how did he suffer physical pain?"

He suffered pain because of the physical abuse of the guards, the scourging and wounds from the nails on the cross. We need to recognize that pain in any body is generated by the disturbance of nerve cells, which are part of the nervous system. The Savior's nervous system is just like ours. Any time a guard would strike him with his fist, he would feel it just like we would. When they put a crown of thorns on his head and beat those thorns into his head, he would feel those thorny points piercing his skin and cranium just like we

---

[109] Smith, History of the Church, 6:366.

would. When they scourged him making his body raw, he would feel the full intensity of pain just like we would. However, his body was not subject to natural death because spirit and not blood was flowing through his veins.

Cause of His Death

Since there was no blood in his body and his body had only spirit flowing through his veins thus making him immortal, "How could he die?"

Death for the Savior was different than for mortal people. In his case death was the separation of his spirit from his body not the failure of the functioning of his body as happens to man.

Many writers have written and speculated about what caused the Savior to die. Failure of some body function is often identified. Some have felt that the Savior died of a broken heart, which from their descriptions have been interpreted as a ruptured heart causing death. They reason that with a ruptured heart, blood would flow into the chest cavity and be released from his body along with water (spirit), when the spear was thrust into his side. Some have adopted this view as showing the great compassion of the Savior for humankind and because of that compassion he died of a broken heart. Some discount this concept saying that it is medically impossible for the heart to rupture.

Here are some of the proposed causes of the death of the Savior either individually or in combination:

> cardiac rupture
> asphyxiation
> hypovolemic shock
> pulmonary embolism

> arrhythmia
> dehydration

(See the essay "HISTORICAL CRUCIFIXION" for more information). Such speculations about how the Savior died because of the failure of the body are misplaced because he was immortal. These writers did not have the knowledge of what the Prophet Joseph Smith has revealed.

Following Gethsemane, the Savior had only spirit running through his veins. At that time, his body could have returned to the presence of the Father because there was no blood left in his veins. However, he had to finish his atonement. He was required by the Father to be crucified.[110] The Savior had this to say about his death:

> *Therefore doth my Father love me, because I lay down my life, that I might take it again.*
>
> *No man taketh it from me, but I lay it down of myself. I have power to lay it down, and I have power to take it again. This commandment have I received of my Father.* [111]

The Savior could not return to the Father's presence at this time for he had to fulfill this commandment so that he could provide the resurrection for all humankind. It is important to note that humankind could not take his life from him. Only he could cause his own death. His Gethsemane experience did not change his power to lay down his life and take it again. Joseph said

---

[110] 3 Nephi 27:14.

[111] John 10:17-18.

62

What did Jesus say? (Mark it, Elder Rigdon!) The scriptures inform us that Jesus said, as the Father hath power in himself, even so hath the Son power-to do what? Why, what the Father did. The answer is obvious-in a manner to lay down his body and take it up again. Jesus, what are you going to do? To lay down my life as my Father did, and take it up again. Do you believe it? [112]

Decision to Die

As stated above the Savior was required by the Father to be crucified. Following his scourging and his public display in the royal robe, the Savior was put upon the cross. His body was not subject to natural death because of the spirit flowing through his veins. He was commanded to give up his life but he could not cause his death until he was certain that his suffering on the cross was acceptable to the Father.[113] Any mortal person would naturally die at some point under the same conditions. The Savior suffered his pains longer than any mortal could suffer because he would not die until he knew that his suffering was acceptable to the Father. The following discussion will show this statement to be true.

Since Christ was commanded to give up his life by crucifixion,[114] the questions are "How long did he have to suffer on the cross before he caused his death? Was the decision left to the Savior to determine that his suffering on the cross was sufficient for the Father? How would he know

---

[112] Smith, History of the Church, 6:306.

[113] 3 Nephi 27:13-16; John 10:17-18.

[114] John 10:16-17; 3 Nephi 27:13-16.

when he had completed the Father's command?" No scriptures clearly answer these questions.

However, there are two scriptures when analyzed together will help us understand the answers to these questions.

> *And about the ninth hour Jesus cried with a loud voice saying... My God, my God, why hast thou forsaken me?*[115]

James E. Talmage and Bruce R. McConkie confirmed this cry of great physical pain. (See the section "Final Moments" in the essay "MALTREATMENT")

John tells us that the Savior arrived at the point of knowing *"Jesus knowing that all things were now accomplished."*[116] This was followed by a drink of vinegar and then the Savior died.

The meaning of "all things were now accomplished" is that the Savior knew his sacrifice and suffering were acceptable to his Father and he could will his death.

The Savior did not know at the time of his cry of pain that his suffering was acceptable to the Father. This is a critical understanding. If he knew that "all things were now accomplished" he would not be making his cry of pain to the Father. He would will his death because it was his decision to make.

It is a very important concept to understand that when the Savior petitioned the Father with his cry of physical pain that

---

[115] Matthew 27:46; JST Matthew 27:59; Mark 15:34-37.

[116] John 19:28.

he did not know whether his suffering was acceptable to the Father.

What the Savior was really communicating by his cry of physical pain was, "I am really hurting Father. I cannot bear this any longer. I have not heard from you. How much more do I need to suffer?" The two scriptures above describe the Savior's last moments. They describe the same sequence of time. The time between the Savior's cry of pain and him knowing that "all things were now accomplished" was immediate.

Joseph Smith translated Matthews's account of the Savior's last moments.[117] In this account, the Savior made his cry of physical pain to the Father following which he was given a drink on a sponge. Then in a loud voice the Savior said,

> *Father, it is finished, thy will is done and he yielded up the ghost.* [118]

This translated account by Joseph Smith also shows an immediate change from his cry of physical pain to knowing it was completed. He then willed his death. Luke records the following about his death:

> *And when Jesus had cried with a loud voice, he said,* **Father, into thy hands I commend my spirit: and having said thus, he gave up the ghost.** [119]

Death was his spirit leaving his body by his command and not by the malfunction or trauma of his body. The Savior's spirit

---

[117] Matthew 27:50-54.

[118] Matthew 27:54.

[119] Luke 23:46.

left his body to visit the world of spirits to finish the Father's command by ministering in the world of spirits. (For full information read the essay "JOSEPH F. SMITH REVELATION")

How did the Savior come to know that the will of the Father was done? It seems obvious that the Father communicated to him following his cry of pain that his suffering was sufficient. The method of communication is not known but the communication had to have happened.

It is important to understand that during the Savior's ministry the Father had communicated directly with the Savior. We do not have a record of these communications but we know they happened. In fact, the Father is the one who commanded the Savior to suffer on the cross and to give up his life. It was the Father who determined when his suffering was sufficient.

The suffering of the Savior on the cross was some six or so hours. Remember that he had been scourged prior to the cross. That scourging was probably extended because there was no blood showing because his blood was gone. Remember also as he was on the cross his pains would increase just like ours would increase with time. He would not die until he had confirmation from the Father to command his death. When you look at these facts, it shows that the Savior suffered more intense pains far longer than any mortal man. This explains how the Savior suffered greater pains than any mortal and he is now able to judge us righteously.

State of His Body
We ask this question "What was the state of his body which had the fluid "spirit" in its veins after his spirit left his body?"

66

In trying to understand how his body would react to his spirit leaving his body, we have to reorient our thinking away from our mortal bodies. The Savior's body being immortal would be different.

When mortal man's spirit leaves his body, or dies, his heart stops pumping, his body quickly begins to decay. After death, one of the first functions performed is to preserve the body for burial by replacing the blood with a preservative fluid. It seems reasonable to believe that the Savior's body would not decay since his body had all spirit in it. His body was immortal. It would probably continue to function. One thing is certain: his body would be preserved until he returned for his spirit to re-inhabit his body.

When a person has open-heart surgery, the physicians set up a process that keeps the blood flowing through the patient's body. The body does not begin decaying because the cells and organs are receiving nourishment through the circulating blood. The heart stops pumping and the physicians repair that heart. The heart is then stimulated to beat and pump the blood through the veins. Many people talk of seeing themselves on the surgery table and listening to the conversations of the medical personnel during the surgery. The fact that they can look upon their own bodies and hear the conversations of the medical personnel shows that the sprit has left the body. Their spirits can leave their bodies and then return after the heart is stimulated to pump.

In the Savior's case, his heart and organs were functioning properly at the time he commanded his death. (See the section "Decision to Die" in the preceding section). However, his back was raw from the scourging and he had wounds in his hands and feet. At the time of his death, he had very severe pain. The Savior's relief from pain was to have his spirit leave the body.

When his spirit left his body, it is entirely possible that his body would continue to function with the heart pumping spirit through the veins and the organs. What would cause his body to not function? Mortal man's body stops functioning, forcing the spirit to leave the body. However, the Savior's body was functioning normally when he commanded his spirit to leave. Again, what would cause the body to not function?

By continuing to function with the spirit flowing through the veins, the wounded areas would heal so when the Savior re-inhabited his body he would feel no pain. His immortal body would have healed itself.

Whether or not one believes that his body would continue to function with his heart beating is not material. This author believes that it did. When he repossessed his body his wounds were healed, leaving scar tissue and he had no pain.

HISTORICAL CRUCIFIXION and SCOURGING

Corporal punishment has existed from ancient times until today. When trying to find specifics on ancient corporal punishment using the internet, few written articles were found. However, several gave some generalities. For example, the New World Encyclopedia recorded this,

> *While the early history of **corporal punishment** is unclear, the practice was certainly present in classical civilizations, being used in Greece, Rome, Egypt, and Israel, for both judicial and educational discipline. Practices varied greatly.* [120]

120

Corporal punishment has been used from ancient to modern times. This was recorded in England describing medieval punishments.

In England the Whipping Act of 1530 authorized the whipping of thieves, blasphemers, poachers, men and women guilty of minor offenses, and even the insane. Victims were tied to the end of a cart until the 1590s, when the whipping post was introduced.

*During the 19th century, imprisonment gradually replaced corporal penalties as a punishment for crime, but the courts retained the power to order whippings in cases involving violent crimes (**see** prison). This power was terminated in England, Scotland, and Wales by the Criminal Justice Act of 1948, although corporal punishment for mutiny incitement to mutiny, and gross personal violence to an officer of a prison when committed by a male person was permitted in England and Wales until 1967.* [121]

The last floggings in the United States, were carried out in the state of Delaware in 1952. They were abolished in 1972 by the governor commuting a sentence of flogging and then making a public case of repealing the law.

Corporal punishments have been given using a large number of different practices. However, we are mainly interested in two, which are scourging and crucifixion. These two practices

---

http://www.newworldencyclopedia.org/entry/Corporal_punishment, under History of corporal punishment. Last visited July 2016

[121] https://en.wikipedia.org/wiki/Flagellation#Antiquity, Last visited July 2016

are of great interest to Christianity because they are the major corporal punishments, which the Savior suffered.

Scourging

The tool used was a whip with several leather straps sometimes laced with bone and metal with small lead balls at the end. The victim was tied low to a post so that they were bent over or tied high to stretch them up. There was no limit to the number of lashes. The contemporary historians, Livy, Suetonius and Josephus, have written of scourging cases where victims died while still bound to the post. Scourging was referred to as "half death" [122]

Although the Jewish law restricted the lashes to 40, the Romans inflicted the punishment. The effects of the scourging would make a massive wound with bruises from the shoulders to buttock or sometimes lower. Any mortal person who suffered scourging that did not die would be near death and if a person were crucified following scourging they would only live a very short time. Criminals and slaves were mainly the ones to whom this punishment was given.

Authors are divided as to whether scourging commonly preceded crucifixion. It was the common practice for the condemned to carry their own cross as the Savior was supposed to have done but was unable. The soldiers enlisted Simon to carried it for him. Joe Zias quoted Plutarch (AD 46-120), a Greek historian and biographer,

> ...*each criminal condemned to death bears his cross on his back*[123]

---

[122] https://en.wikipedia.org/wiki/Flagellation#Antiquity. Last visited July 2016

The part that was carried is the patibulum or crosspiece. If scourging preceded crucifixion, the person, who was scourged, would not be physically able to carry his cross being "half dead". Consequently, the common practice of carrying his cross would not seem to be compatible with a practice of scourging prior to their crucifixion. In addition, the Romans wanted the victims to live as long as possible to act as a deterrent. Scourging would cause a very early death on the cross.

The two thieves crucified with the Savior were not scourged. If they had been scourged, they would have died prior to the Savior's death and would not have had their legs broken to cause their death. [Read "Final Moments" in essay "MALTREATMENT".

Crucifixion
Several different ancient civilizations punished people with crucifixion. The Romans began using crucifixion about 600 BC and was probably borrowed from the Carthaginians. The crosses that were used consisted of the post, patibulum and sometimes a sedile or seat. The patibulum or crosspiece was rested on the top of the post or down from the top a very short distance. Various other support mechanisms were used but not by the Romans.

The Romans often prolonged the death of a victim because they wanted the victim's suffering to act as a deterrent to others. Providing a "sedile" or a place to sit would give the victim rest and would lengthen the time to die. The Romans used crucifixion as a deterrent for others that might wish to

---

[123] Crucifixion in Antiquity – The Evidence: p. 2-3.

conduct themselves as those who were crucified. Zias quotes Quintilian who wrote that,

> *whenever we crucify the guilty, the most, crowded roads are chosen, where most people can see and be moved by this fear. For penalties relate not so much to retribution as to their exemplary effect'* "[124]

Many people are generally knowledgeable about Spartacus, a slave gladiator, who escaped with about 70-80 other gladiators. Eventually they raised an army estimated from 80,000 to over 100,000 men who were mostly slaves. After a number of successes this army was defeated about 71 BC. Most were killed but about 6,000 of the army was captured and crucified. They lined the apian way and were left on their crosses for a long period of time. It was an example to others who disobeyed Roman law.

Other large groups were also crucified. Zias makes this statement with his reference,

> *Alexander the Great had 2,000 survivors from the siege of Tyre crucified on the shores of the Mediterranean[4] In addition, during the times of Caligula – AD 37-41 – Jews were tortured and crucified in the amphitheater to entertain the inhabitants of Alexandria.[125]*

---

[124] Zias, Crucifixion in Antiquity – The Evidence, 7; Zias Ref: [18] Quintilian [AD 35-95) Decl 274

https://web.archive.org/web/20110615201341/http://www.centuryone. org/crucifixion2.html. Last visited July 2016.

[125] Zias, Crucifixion in antiquity – The Evidence, 1; Zias ref: 4 Curtius Rufus, *Hist. Alex. 4.4.17*

A number of ancient authors have described crucifixion as being an extremely torturous and painful death. The following quote illustrates this.

Cicero called crucifixion the **'extreme and ultimate punishment of slaves'** *(*servitutis extremum summumque supplicium, Against Verres 2.5.169), and the *'cruelest and most disgusting penalty.'* (crudelissimum taeterrimumque supplicium, ibid. 2.5. 165.)* [126]

Josephus writes of an incident when the Romans surrounded Jerusalem about 55 AD. A highly respected Jewish fighter named Eleazar often showed much boldness in the face of their enemy during battle and by being the last to leave a battle. In his last battle, he stayed outside the Jerusalem walls and talked with those on the walls. He was captured. The Roman general caused that he was stripped naked and placed where those in the city could see him. He was *"sorely whipped before their eyes."* Josephus further stated

The city, with one voice, sorely lamented him, and the mourning proved greater than could well be supposed, upon the calamity of a single person

The Roman general recognized this and commanded that a cross be posted before the city as if they were going to crucify Eleazar. The city was horrified by this prospect. Eleazar

---

https://web.archive.org/web/20110615201341/http://www.centuryone. org/crucifixion2.html. Last visited July 2016.

[126] Bible history online: The Roman Scourge; Link is http://www.bible-history.com/past/flagrum.html

- quote is beneath the picture "Flagellum, Symbol of Sol." Last visited July 2016

apparently convinced the city to save themselves and him from this "most miserable death" by giving themselves up to the Romans, which they did.[127] This most miserable death was the whipping or scourging followed by crucifixion.

Josephus describes an event about 169 BC where King Antiochus IV (called Epiphanies) of Syria conquered the Jewish people, pillaged the temple treasury, disallowed their sacrifices, decreed their sons could not be circumcised and sacrificed swine on the temple altar. Some refused to obey these rules restricting their religious practices. They were beaten and then crucified. Josephus wrote,

> *But the best men, and those of the noblest souls, did not regard him, but did pay a greater respect to the customs of their country than concern as to the punishment which he threatened to the disobedient; on which account they every day underwent great miseries and bitter torments; **for they were whipped with rods, and their bodies were torn to pieces, and were crucified, while they were still alive, and breathed.** They also strangled those women and their sons whom they had circumcised, as the king had appointed, **hanging their sons about their necks as they were upon the crosses.*** [128]

This is one of the most brutal accounts of whipping and crucifixion. Notice that Josephus identifies that crosses were used by the crucifiers.

Authors have questioned how the Savior was attached to the patibulum. Sometimes rope was used to attach the victims to the patibulum. We know with certainty that the Savior was nailed to the wood in his hands and feet for he said to the Nephites

> *Arise and come forth unto me, that ye may thrust your hands into my side, and also that ye may feel the prints of the nails in my hands and in my feet, that ye may know that I am the God of Israel, and the God of the whole earth, and have been slain for the sins of the world.*

> *And it came to pass that the multitude went forth, and thrust their hands into his side, and **did feel the prints of the nails in his hands and in his feet;*** [129]

The two thieves would be nailed in the same fashion as the Savior. Mr. Zias in his article made note of an important understanding that relates to attaching victims to the Patibulum. He wrote

> *Eyewitness accounts by prisoners of war in Dachau during WWII reported that victims suspended from beams by their wrist, which were tied, expired within ten minutes if their feet were weighted or tied down and within one hour if their feet were unweighted and the victim was able to raise and lower himself to*

---

[129] 3 Nephi 11:14-15.

permit respiration. Death in this manner, which is one form of crucifixion, was the result of suffocation.[17] " [130]

The soldiers were undoubtedly taught much about crucifixion. They knew how to nail the Savior and two thieves to their patibulum to accomplish their death. Nailing their arms near the perpendicular and with broken legs and a fatigued body, death would occur in a short time. The Soldiers knew that they could break the legs of the victims and they would die prior to the Sabbath as the Jewish people required. Roman soldiers knew that death occurring on the Sabbath, which started at dusk would bring extremely strong complaints.

---

[130] Crucifixion in Antiquity – The Evidence: p. 6-7.

MALTREATMENT

The Savior suffered intensely in the Garden of Gethsemane, but it was of short duration. Immediately following his Garden ordeal, he was arrested and his physical sufferings began. These trials challenged his willpower and his love and commitment to the Father and to us as his brothers and sisters. These were the tests that would determine whether he would remain sinless and fulfill his atonement or fail.

During his maltreatments, he suffered physical pain that is not commonly understood. We have tried to examine the events carefully trying to ascertain what pains he really suffered.

Arrest, Trial and Maltreatments

There were significant testing events following Gethsemane. These events were mostly provocative. He was arrested, tried and found guilty of blasphemy by those who were sons of perdition. (See the section "Knowing God's Power" in the essay "SONS OF PERDITION.") They were agents of Satan. The maltreatment events that followed his guilty verdict was Satan-directed. They were provocative and intended to get the Savior to react and sin. If Satan could get the Savior to react to these maltreatments, Satan would win his battle by getting the Savior to sin.

Anger or hatred would be the most likely sins if the Savior had reacted to his maltreatment. Throughout his ministry, he had been faithful to his calling and ministry. We know that the Savior suffered grief beginning at the Garden and lasting to his death. [Read the section "Emotion" in the essay "WHAT the SAVIOR SUFFERED"]. If he changed from that feeling of grief to anger or hatred, Satan would win and all of us would lose for we would not have a redeemer. But the Savior gave "no heed"[131] to these temptations.

77

These provocative maltreatments occurred after his arrest. First, he was taken to Annas[132] where the first maltreatment occurred. Annas and the people who were there knew what was going on and why the Savior was arrested. Annas "asked Jesus of his disciples, and of his doctrine." [133] This was intended to see if the Savior would admit directly that he was the Son of God. The Savior did not respond directly to Annas but told him to ask those that heard him and that he taught no secrets. An officer did not like the way the Savior responded to Annas and struck him with the palm of his hand. Knowing that this was against Jewish law the Savior verbally challenged the officer saying

> *If I have spoken evil, bear witness of the evil: but if well, why smitest thou me?*[134]

This is the only recorded response or complaint that the Savior made during all the maltreatments he received. He silently endured the rest of the maltreatments.

Without any more discussion Annas sent the bound Savior to Caiaphas. [135] Since Judas had previously agreed to deliver the Savior to them, Caiaphas had assembled others so that a council could be convened as soon as the Savior arrived. The council was convened and witnesses called and nothing was found that could be used to condemn the Savior. Finally, Caiaphas asked the Savior whether he was the Son of God.

---

[131] D&C 20:22.

[132] John 18:19-24.

[133] John 18:19.

[134] John 18:23.

[135] Matthew 26:63-66; Mark 14:61-64; Luke 22:66-71.

Matthew, Mark and Luke record the same answer given with some slight differences. All three recorded Caiaphas as saying that the Savior's answer was an admission that he was the Son of God and this was blasphemy. The council agreed and they declared that the Savior was worthy of death.

Matthew and Mark wrote that the maltreatments were delivered following the verdict. Luke records the maltreatments and then the verdict. John does not comment on the trial, verdict or the maltreatments.

Luke records that the verdict declaring the Savior was worthy of death was given at the council meeting held "as soon as it was day." John records that the council took Jesus to Pilate "early" [136] on the same morning. Luke's record that the council was held at daylight could not be accurate for several reasons. If the council met early and had witnesses, it would delay the meeting with Pilate which would make the meeting with Pilate more toward midday. That would make all the following events impossible to be completed at the times that are mentioned in other scriptures. Luke also records the maltreatments happening prior to the council trial. It is unlikely that the maltreatments would occur prior to his guilty verdict. Matthew and Mark's accounts are more accurate on this point.

The verdict was given several hours prior to dawn as recorded by Matthew and Mark. (See the essay "DETERMINING PASSOVER EVENTS.")

The maltreatments began as soon as the verdict was given. Luke records the maltreatments

---

[136] John 18:28, Luke 22:66.

And the men that held Jesus mocked him, and smote him.

And when they had blindfolded him, they struck him on the face, and asked him, saying, Prophesy, who is it that smote thee?

And many other things blasphemously spake they against him. [137]

Nephi prophesied of these maltreatments when he recorded

And the world, because of their iniquity, shall judge him to be a thing of naught; wherefore they scourge him, and he suffereth it; and they smite him, and he suffereth it. Yea, they spit upon him, and he suffereth it, because of his loving kindness and his long-suffering towards the children of men. [138]

These maltreatments lasted for some time. It appears that it was not one person who issued the maltreatments but each one coming forward perhaps with another taking their turn to inflict spitting, mocking, slapping, buffeting (using their fist) and ridicule to break his will. Undoubtedly, they repeated these actions many times.

There was one event that surely happened but was not recorded in the New Testament. Isaiah prophesied of this event.

*I gave my back to the smiters, and **my cheeks to them that plucked off the hair**: I hid not my face from shame and spitting.*[139]

---

[137] Luke 22:64-65.

[138] 1 Nephi 19:9.

Removing the hair from his face was an act to shame the Savior in the public view. Though not recorded in our New Testament, it nevertheless happened. But the worst was yet to come. The council took the Savior to Pilate early in the morning who, after a short discussion, sent him to Herod. Herod questioned the Savior but got no answer. Herod and his men *"set him at naught, and mocked him, and arrayed him in a gorgeous robe, and sent him again to Pilate."* [140]

Pilate now had to deal with the council and their cry to crucify the Savior. The exchange between Pilate and the Jewish council and other assembled people is described in all four gospels.[141]

The next event that happened was the scourging. Luke records that an offer to scourge the Savior was made but does not record that it happened. Matthew and Mark show that Pilate had him scourged. Then he was released to be crucified. The Savior felt the pain from this scourging just as we would feel it. (See the essay "BLOOD/RESURRECTION – SAVIOR" for complete information). Remember that some mortal men died while being scourged and that Josephus described those that were scourged as half dead. (See the section "Scourging" in the essay "HISTORICAL CRUCIFIXION and SCOURGING" for more information)

Because spirit flowed through the veins of the Savior and he was immortal, he may have been scourged more harshly than mortals because he would not die from the scourging due to his immortality. There would be no blood showing on his back

[139] Isaiah 50:6.

[140] Like 23:11.

[141] Matthew 27:11-26; Mark 15:1-16; Luke 23:1-7, 13-25; John 19:1-16.

81

because all the blood was shed in Gethsemane. The spirit that flowed through his body would show like water. (See the essay "BLOOD/RESURRECTION – SAVIOR" for justification for this statement). Those making the strikes would probably continue longer than normal because no blood would be showing.

Following the scourging the Savior's back would be raw. The nerves were severely impacted giving a terrible, burning, highly intensified pain and would weaken the Savior significantly. His clothes were put back on to intensify the back pain even more. Any person who has had a painful wound such as a badly sunburned back that has had cloth dragged across it understands how that pain can intensify.

The soldiers took Jesus to the common hall called the Prætorium with all the soldiers present. Matthew then records the next event

> *And they **stripped him**, and put on him a scarlet robe.*
>
> *And when they had platted a crown of thorns, they put it upon his head, and a reed in his right hand: and they bowed the knee before him, and mocked him, saying, Hail, King of the Jews!*
>
> *And **they spit upon him, and took the reed, and smote him on the head**.*
>
> *And after that they had mocked him, they took the robe off from him, and put his own raiment on him, and led him away to crucify him.* [142] *.*

The action of stripping him and putting on the scarlet robe would again cause him to feel the intensified back pain. The

[142] Matthew 27:28-31, Mark 15:16-20, John 19:1-3.

robe and the mocking were intended for humiliation. Picture the Savior sitting with the robe on, a crown of thorns and the reed as a mock scepter, and the soldiers kneeling in front of him and in mocking tones saying "Hail King of the Jews", and his back burning in pain. Then the soldiers rising and taking the reed to beat him about the head with the crown of thorns still there.

These soldiers were trained to inflict pain and humiliate their victims. A crown of thorns is not a customary torture instrument. Since he was the King of the Jews the soldiers used this crown to not only ridicule him but also to cause him more pain. The more pain, the more deterrent the example would be. The thorns would be chosen to inflict as much additional pain as possible. The pounding of the thorns would drive the thorns into the skin and cranium. The attendant pain would be very sharp. Anyone who has had a syringe needle poke a bone or had a sharp pointed instrument pierce the skin and bone would understand how painful that can be. These thorns were not just touching the bones but were driven into the bone with the force from the reed. The soldiers would swing it hard to create as much pain as possible. The reed would be disintegrated when the act was completed but nevertheless it would drive the thorns through the skin into the cranium. Even if the thorns were removed, the pain would continue.

Consider this scene. The Savior was being mocked. He had great powers. He was in a much-weakened condition having no sleep and enduring the trial throughout the night. His body was increasingly weakened by the physical beatings. The physical pain was very intense coming from the back with the robe weighing on the damaged nerves. The fact that Simon was enlisted to carry the Savior's cross shows his weakened condition. The crown of thorns was causing intense pain at every thorn that pierced his scalp and especially those that pierced the bone.

Yet his self-control was firm. Silently he endured the mockings and maltreatment. As Nephi said he suffered it *"because of his loving kindness and his long-suffering towards the children of men.* "[143] Remember that these events following his scourge caused continued pain throughout the rest of the ordeal.

John records that in this condition Pilate displayed him to the mob saying "Behold the man!" Pilate was hoping that the mob would agree to release the Savior. But the cries were to crucify him. So Pilate relented and crucified the Savior. During this process the robe was removed and his own garments put on him intensifying his back pain as the cloth dragged across the wounded back.

It is unknown whether the crown of thorns was removed prior to crucifixion. The scriptures do not say one way or the other. Some early Christian paintings show the Savior on the cross with the crown of thorns. It is likely that it was left to continue as much pain as possible as he was crucified. This would be compatible with the soldiers training. That would be additional pain concurrent with the scourging pain and the attendant pains from the cross.

His Cross Pains
After the Savior was nailed to the cross he had to contend with multiple pain and body issues. There would be the back pain

---

[143] 1 Nephi 19:9.

from the scourging, pain from the nails, pain from the thorny crown, thirst and extreme fatigue.

It is unknown how the Savior's body would have reacted to the difficulty of breathing while on the cross because his body was immortal with spirit flowing through the veins. Not being able to breathe properly probably would cause him some physical discomfort but not death. Breathing would be affected by the position of his body. If he relaxed his legs to ease the pain from the nails in his feet, it would create a strain on his diaphragm making it more difficult to breath. The closer to the vertical that the hands and wrists were nailed would cause more difficulty in breathing. We do not know this so we really do not know how difficult breathing was. But it is believed that breathing was difficult.

However, his nervous system would react just like ours. The strains, fatigue and possibly cramping, would all contribute to the Savior's physical pain. The bruises, torn skin and muscles of the back would be very inflamed. The pain from the back, nail holes, thorn s would grow stronger with time.

While this physical pain was increasing, the verbal abuse continued. Matthew wrote,

> *And they that passed by reviled him, wagging their heads,*

> *And saying, Thou that destroyest the temple, and buildest it in three days, save thyself. If thou be the Son of God, come down from the cross.*

> *Likewise also the chief priests mocking him, with the scribes and elders, said,*

He saved others; himself he cannot save. If he be the King of Israel, let him now come down from the cross, and we will believe him.

He trusted in God; let him deliver him now, if he will have him: for he said, I am the Son of God. [144]

This was the strongest maltreatment that could be mustered by Satan. The Savior's physical pain was at its most severe point and the charges given were as biting as could be generated. However, the Savior gave "no heed" to their biting remarks.

Nephi gives the true motivation of the Savior in conducting himself in the manner that he did.

And the world, because of their iniquity, shall judge him to be a thing of naught; wherefore they scourge him, and he suffereth it; and they smite him, and he suffereth it. Yea, they spit upon him, and he ***suffereth it, because of his loving kindness and his long-suffering towards the children of men.*** [145]

All of these maltreatments and pains were designed by his persecutors to get the Savior to lose his self-control and react as the "natural man" would react. The most common mortal reaction would be to replace his love with anger, a tool of Satan. The Savior never did knowing that all humankind would be lost to Satan if he did. The Savior truly loved us by enduring what he did!

To illustrate the Savior's perfect self-control and love for us, remember the Roman soldiers who were men of war and were taught to make punishments cruel and painful as a deterrent to

---

[144] Matthew 27:39-43, Mark 15:29–32, Luke 23:39-43.

[145] 1 Nephi 19:9.

others. Remember that they were the ones who took the reed and pounded the crown of thorns into his head, the pain of which was probably still being felt. In the final stages of his crucifixion as he hung on the cross, he demonstrated that there were no "natural man" characteristics in him for he said *"forgive them Father for they know not what they do"*[146]. The word "them" refers to the soldiers. This was a sincere genuine prayer given out of concern for the soldier's eternal welfare, who were unknowing in what they did.

We should note the soldier's reaction to the Savior's death. Matthew records

> *Now when the centurion, and they that were with him, watching Jesus, saw the earthquake, and those things that were done, they feared greatly, saying,* **Truly this was the Son of God.** [147]

There is one last point that needs to be stressed and should be remembered. Though the Savior never succumbed to the maltreatments in keeping with his perfect character and his great love, he nevertheless suffered. One of the definitions of the word suffer is to "undergo or experience."[148]

Notice that experience is a term used to define suffers. This brings again to mind the Savior's response to Joseph Smith's Liberty Jail prayer. The Lord in his response to that prayer describes the many trials that Joseph had already experienced and some that he could possibly face and then the Lord says

---

[146] Luke 23:34; JST Luke 23:35.

[147] Matthew 27:54, Mark 15:39, Luke 23:47.

[148] http://www.merriam-webster.com/dictionary/suffer. Last visited July 2016.

*know thou, my son, that **all these things shall give thee experience**, and shall be for thy good.*[149]

Then the Savior said his now famous statement

The Son of Man hath descended below them all.[150]

The Savior's experience or sufferings far exceeded that of Joseph's or Job's experience. The expression "them all" refers to any and all experiences suffered by man and having that experience puts him in the position that the Father planned from the beginning. That is to be our judge. These experiences gave the Savior experiences where he could provide a "righteous" judgment by the experience he had.

These experiences are sufficient for him to understand all trials that humankind faces. He can provide perfect mercy and give succor to help humankind so that at the final judgment he can provide the best possible kingdom and glory.

Final Moments
James E. Talmage places the time of nailing to the cross as occurring between 9am and 10am. He wrote,

> *Jesus was nailed to the cross during the forenoon of that fateful Friday, **probably between nine and ten o'clock**. At noontide the light of the sun was obscured, and black darkness spread over the whole land. The terrifying gloom continued for a period of three hours,*[151]

The Savior finally arrived at his pain threshold. The scriptures state,

---

[149] D&C 122:7.

[150] D&C 122:8.

[151] Talmage, Jesus the Christ: p. 660.

And about the ninth hour Jesus cried with a loud voice saying ... My God, my God, why hast thou forsaken me?[152]

Up until this point the Savior had patiently endured all physical pain. His physical pain had been building in intensity as he suffered on the cross. This quoted statement made to the Father was definitely a cry of great physical pain. Of this event James E. Talmage wrote,

> At the **ninth hour, or about three in the afternoon**, a loud voice, surpassing the most anguished **cry of physical suffering** issued from the central cross, rending the dreadful darkness. It was the voice of the Christ: ... 'My God, my God, why hast thou forsaken me?' What mind of man can fathom the significance of that awful cry? It seems, that in addition to the fearful suffering incident to crucifixion, the agony of Gethsemane had recurred, intensified beyond human power to endure. [153]

From Talmage we learn that the Savior was on the cross between five (5) and six (6) hours before he willed his death. This is an extremely long time to last for any mortal person, who has suffered scourging and then crucifixion. Because of this the Savior suffered longer and more intensely than any mortal.

Talmage confirms that Christ's cry to the Father resulted from the great physical pain he was experiencing. Because of that intense pain, Talmage suggests that Christ re-suffered his

---

[152] Matthew 27:46; JST Matthew 27:59; Mark 15:34-37.

[153] Talmage, Jesus the Christ: p. 660-661.

Garden pains as he could not account for the pain intensity other than that.

Bruce R. McConkie also recognized this as a cry of great physical pain. He suggests that Christ re-suffered the pains of Gethsemane during the three (3) hours of darkness. He quoted James E. Talmage.[154] Both recognized the Savior's cry as a cry of great pain and couldn't account for the pain intensity other than suggesting that he re-suffered the pains of Gethsemane.

Re-Suffering the Pains of Gethsemane?
Both Talmage and McConkie believe that Christ re-suffered his Garden sufferings while on the cross. This question of re-suffering the Garden pains needs to be addressed.

The purpose of Christ's suffering in the Garden is by his own words as follows:

> *I, God, have suffered these things for all, that they might not suffer if they would repent;*[155]

The sufferings referred to in this quote are his Garden sufferings. The Savior fulfilled this stated purpose in the Garden. He shed all of his blood during his suffering in the Garden. There was no more blood to shed. (See the essay "BLOOD/RESURRECTION – SAVIOR" for complete information).

Everything the Savior did was done according to the will of the Father. Why would the Father require the Savior to re-suffer his pains in the Garden when he had already

---

[154] McConkie, The Mortal Messiah: Vol. 4, p. 225.

[155] D&C 19:16.

accomplished the purpose of his Garden ordeal? The Savior could not bleed at every pore as he did in the Garden because at this time Christ's blood had been eliminated from his body. It seems obvious that the Father would not require this. The great pain suffered on the cross resulted from something different. The Savior did not re-suffer his Garden sufferings while on the cross.

His pain from the various body parts, his head, cranium, back, nail holes with his body weakness was growing in intensity.

From the section "Decision to Die" in the essay "BLOOD/RESURRECTION – SAVIOR" we identified that the Savior could not will his death until he was certain that his suffering was sufficient according to the Father's will. As the Savior suffered on the cross, his pain intensified with time. He suffered from the multiple pains longer than any mortal could suffer without succumbing to death. It was the multiple pains for a longer period that caused the Savior to suffer more than any mortal. In the opinion of this author it was hours longer.

WHAT the SAVIOR SUFFERED

There is a belief that is common in the Church that the Savior suffered exactly what we have suffered or will suffer in mortality and having done that, he knows how to judge and succor us. We will challenge the concept that the Savior suffered "exactly" what we suffer.

Considerable effort has been spent detailing what the Savior suffered in and after the Garden of Gethsemane. The idea that he suffered exactly what we suffer comes from the following scripture or some like it.

> *And he shall go forth, **suffering pains and afflictions and temptations of <u>every kind</u>**; and this that the word*

*might be fulfilled which saith he will take upon him **the pains and the sicknesses of his people.***

*And he will take upon him **death**, that he may loose the bands of death which bind his people; and he will take upon him **their infirmities**, that his bowels may be filled with mercy, according to the flesh, that he may know according to the flesh how to succor his people **according to their infirmities.*** [156]

Some people feel that when the scriptures say that the Savior has suffered the pain of all men that it includes every physical or mental pain that man has suffered including severe emotional trauma and mental illnesses.

We take exception to this concept of his suffering exactly what man has suffered. We can test this concept by asking a few simple questions:

- Did the Savior experience the pains of child birth?
- Did the Savior suffer diseases such as typhoid fever, bubonic plague, tuberculosis, cancer, small pox leprosy and the like?

He healed people with these but did not suffer them.

- Did the Savior suffer what amputees or those who were born with no limbs suffer? Nothing in the scriptures even suggests this.
- Did the Savior suffer from mental deficiencies?

Nothing in the scriptures even suggests this. His mind was clear and active.

---

[156] Alma 7:11-12 see also D&C 18:11.

- Did the Savior suffer the health issues that many of us experience such as diabetes, heart problems, arthritis or broken bones?

He suffered none of these as his body functioned perfectly.

Other questions could be posed in a similar fashion. The whole point is that the Savior did not experience "exactly" what we suffer. What needs explanation is how the Savior's sufferings relate to humankind's sufferings of pains, sicknesses and infirmities that gives him the understanding of our sufferings.

Man's physical conditions display common physical characteristics. It is a matter of looking at man's ailments that are suffered and comparing that with what the Savior suffered to determine how the Savior's suffering experiences relate to man's ailments.

The quoted scripture above lists the following ailments of man

- Pains
- sicknesses
- death
- infirmities

The Savior will take upon him man's pains, sicknesses, death and infirmities by suffering pains, afflictions and temptations of every kind including death. What this statement amounts to is that it can be shown that the Savior has suffered the kinds of ailment characteristics suffered by man. He has not suffered exactly what man has suffered but what he has suffered matches the characteristics of man's ailments.

Pain

We will examine how the physical pain of child birth compares to the Savior's pain. Has a woman, who suffered the most severe birth pains and even suffered death, suffered greater physical pain than the Savior prior to his death? The answer to this question is no. Suffering pain in one part of the body is not much different than suffering pain in another part of the body. Pain is pain! Intensity is the key to this understanding. The Savior suffered greater intensity of pain because he suffered past the point that a mortal would die. His continued suffering past the threshold of mortal death created him greater intensity of pain. As for pain, it occurred in the Garden and throughout the maltreatments he suffered.

Other scriptures state that he suffered the "pain of all men." For example Nephi recorded Jacob's message

> *And he cometh into the world that he may save all men if they will hearken unto his voice; for behold, he **suffereth the pains of all men, yea, the pains of every living creature, both men, women, and children, who belong to the family of Adam.***
>
> *And he **suffereth this that the resurrection might pass upon all men, that all might stand before him at the great and judgment day.*** [157]

Christ had this to say

> *For, behold, the Lord your Redeemer suffered death in the flesh; wherefore he **suffered the pain of all men,** that all men might repent and come unto him.* [158]

---

[157] 2 Nephi 9:21-22.

[158] D&C 18:11.

Some might feel that these scriptures are evidence of the Savior suffering exactly what we have suffered. From the questions, we posed earlier in this essay, we can see that he did not suffer exactly what we suffer. It is a matter of comparing man's sufferings and what the Savior suffered.

In a real sense the pains of all men are the pains of death itself. This includes suffering physical pain leading up to death. This would also include the loneliness and grief of loved ones when a person dies. Christ suffered alone.

The resurrection provided by the Savior cures the pain of death itself. We have shown the greater physical pain experienced by the Savior prior to his death is greater than what man suffers leading up to man's death regardless of the pain intensity of man's death. The Savior suffered the equivalent of the loneliness of love ones when he suffered his atonement alone. Remember he complained to the Father "Why hast thou forsaken me?

Sickness and Infirmities
The term sicknesses would refer to all kinds of bodily ailments some of which result in death. Humankind has suffered numerous sicknesses such as small pox, typhoid, bubonic plague, polio, and from body malfunctions such as diabetes, cancers, leukemia, blood clots, strokes and the like. The persons experiencing these sicknesses experience common symptoms of physical pain, weakness, body aches and discomfort. These symptoms increase until death or some recovery is felt.

The Savior did not suffer from disease. It is likely that he was immune to these diseases due to some spirit fluid flowing through his body which he inherited from his Father. He understands the human body. He healed a good many people

95

of their infirmities during his ministry. He even raised Lazarus from the dead.[159]

The key symptoms of these diseases should be compared to the state of the Savior's body as he tried to carry his cross to the place of execution. He suffered weakness, fatigue, severe pain, which are equivalent to suffering any of these disease type ailments.

He felt the weakness of his body after having been up all night and being scourged. In fact, he could not carry his cross for his own crucifixion. Simon carried it for him. Instead of lying on a bed to recover as the majority of people do, he was nailed on a cross for hours. Was he not suffering more pain, fatigue and discomfort in his position on the cross than those with illness who lay on beds, straw, dirt or, for that matter, stones as they neared death?

Now we will discuss infirmities. Mortal infirmity normally occurs as age progresses. This often happens in old age especially when the individual is suffering from diabetes, arthritis and other health issues. The applicable definition of infirmity is

> a: the quality or state of being infirm or weakness lacking vitality

> b: the condition of being feeble: FRAILTY[160]

The weakness that the Savior suffered would give him the experience to fully understand our issues of aging. [Read the

---

[159] John 11:1-45.

[160] http://www.merriam-webster.com/dictionary/infirmity. Last visited July 2016.

essay "Arrest, Trial and Maltreatments" to understand more fully his weakened body as he hung on the cross].

He knows what it means to suffer from sickness and infirmities.

Affliction

The term affliction is defined as

> 1: the state of being afflicted
>
> 2: the cause of persistent pain or distress
>
> 3: great suffering [161]

The maltreatment suffered by the Savior certainly describes this definition. The following scripture describes the Savior's condition during his atonement.

> *He is despised and rejected of men; a man of sorrows, and acquainted with grief: and we hid as it were our faces from him; he was despised, and we esteemed him not.*
>
> *Surely he hath borne our griefs, and carried our sorrows: yet we did esteem him stricken, smitten of God, and **afflicted.***
>
> **But he was wounded for our transgressions, he was bruised for our iniquities: the chastisement of our peace was upon him; and with his stripes we are healed.** [162]

---

[161] http://www.merriam-webster.com/dictionary/affliction. Last visited July 2016.

[162] Isaiah 53:3-5.

The first verse reinforces the understanding that the Savior suffered the emotion, sorrow, during his atonement. In the last verse, Isaiah describes his affliction as wounded, bruised and suffering stripes. He was wounded by the scourging, crown of thorns and the nails in his hands and feet. He was bruised by the buffetings (with fists), slapping, scourging and the reed pounding. The stripes specifically refer to the scourging. The Savior suffered afflictions and knows how to take that into account when he judges us with our afflictions.

Emotion

The online Reference dictionary[163] defines emotion as

> **1.** an affective state of consciousness in which joy, sorrow, fear, hate, or the like, is experienced, **as distinguished from cognitive and volitional states of consciousness.**

> **2.** any of the feelings of joy, sorrow, fear, hate, love, etc.

> **3.** any strong agitation of the feelings actuated by experiencing love, hate, fear, etc., and usually accompanied by certain physiological changes, as increased heartbeat or respiration, and often overt manifestation, as crying or shaking.

The key word in these definitions is feeling. An emotion is what you are currently feeling. Notice that the online Reference dictionary defines emotion as the "affective state of consciousness" as compared to the cognitive and volitional

---

[163] http://dictionary.reference.com/browse/emotion?s=t. Last visited July 2016.

states of consciousness. The three states of consciousness of every person are defined as:

> Cognitive - pertains to those mental processes that use memory, judgment, perception and reasoning
> Volitional - pertains to the power to exercise choice or the act of making a choice.
> Affective – is our experiencing joy, sorrow, fear, hate or the like, which we call emotions.

Obviously these functions have an interactive role with each other. What we chose to do will affect our abilities in the cognitive and emotional functions. If we chose to study our abilities in the cognitive area will increase especially in those areas we study. If we choose to watch certain movies, that can stir our emotions or feelings in various ways. Anger can affect our ability to make choices and our ability to exercise judgment.

One Emotion

One important aspect of emotion is that only one emotion can be felt at any one time. When a person experiences an emotion it is their current feeling. A person does not feel anger and love at the same time. A person may alternate between feelings but only one is felt at any one point in time. Some emotions are associated with each other. A person who is angry can become hateful. But not all angry people are hateful people.

Nephi and his brothers, Laman and Lemuel, provide two examples showing how emotions change. Laman first approached Laban for the brass plates. Laban was angry and called Laman a robber and was going to slay Laman. He fled and joined his brothers. After discussing the situation, it was decided that they would go to their father's house and gather all of their valuables. These were to be offered to Laban for the brass plates. Laban drove them out and they left their valuables behind as they fled for their lives. Then Laman and Lemuel were angry and beat Nephi and Sam with rods. An angel appeared, rebuking Laman and Lemuel and gave the group a charge to go back and get the brass plates and the Lord would deliver Laban into their hands.[164] After the angel left, Laman and Lemuel did not want to go back because of the following

> *How is it possible that the Lord will deliver Laban into our hands? Behold, he is a mighty man, and he can command fifty, yea, even he can slay fifty; then why not us?*[165]

So Laman and Lemuel were feeling anger which subsided and then were fearful at the thought that they needed to go back. They did not experience anger and fear at the same time.

On another occasion, Nephi and his brothers took a journey back to visit Ishmael and his family. They agreed to join the group and travel back to join Lehi. During the journey back Laman and Lemuel and others rebelled against Nephi. They wanted to return to Jerusalem so they bound Nephi with cords and were planning to kill him and leave him in the desert. Nephi prayed to the Lord that he might break the cords. After he was free from the cords he spoke to them.

> *And it came to pass that **they were angry with me again**, and sought to lay hands upon me; but behold, one of the daughters of Ishmael, yea, and also her*

---

[164] 1 Nephi 3:25-31.

[165] 1 Nephi 3:31.

mother, and one of the sons of Ishmael, did plead with my brethren, insomuch that they did soften their hearts; and they did cease striving to take away my life.

*And it came to pass that **they were sorrowful, because of their wickedness**, insomuch that they did bow down before me, and did plead with me that I would forgive them of the thing that they had done against me.*

And it came to pass that I did frankly forgive them all that they had done, " [166]

In this instance Laman and Lemuel with others were still extremely angry with Nephi. Their motivation and desire was to return to Jerusalem. After the pleading of others in the group their anger subsided and they became sorrowful and asked for forgiveness which they received. These examples illustrate how only one emotion is felt at any one time.

Another example is when the people of Limhi were released from bondage to the Lamanites and traveled to Zarahemla[167].

After the arrival of Limhi and Alma's groups, King Mosiah received records that these groups carried and delivered to him. He had these records read to his people.[168] Their emotional response was recorded

And now, when Mosiah had made an end of reading the records, his people who tarried in the land were struck with wonder and amazement.

---

[166] 1 Nephi 7:19-21.

[167] Mosiah Ch. 22.

[168] Mosiah 25:5-6.

For they knew not what to think; for when they beheld those that had been delivered out of bondage they were filled with exceedingly great joy.

And again, when they thought of their brethren who had been slain by the Lamanites they were filled with sorrow, and even shed many tears of sorrow.

And again, when they thought of the immediate goodness of God, and his power in delivering Alma and his brethren out of the hands of the Lamanites and of bondage, they did raise their voices and give thanks to God.

And again, when they thought upon the Lamanites, who were their brethren, of their sinful and polluted state, they were filled with pain and anguish for the welfare of their souls.

And it came to pass that those who were the children of Amulon and his brethren, who had taken to wife the daughters of the Lamanites, were displeased with the conduct of their fathers, and they would no longer be called by the names of their fathers, therefore they took upon themselves the name of Nephi, that they might be called the children of Nephi and be numbered among those who were called Nephites. [169]

The emotional reactions were "*wonder and amazement*", "*sorrow*" to the point of tears, gratitude as expressed by "*giving thanks to God*", "*pain and anguish*" and "*displeased.*" Notice that these responses were related to their thoughts.

---

[169] Mosiah 25:11-12.

Can an angry parent feel love for their children at the same time? A parent's response could be a whipping giving vent to that anger. But the parent may have adopted a deep value system based on love for their children and they exercise the cognitive function to act according to that value system even though they are angry with their children. A person may be feeling one emotion but using the cognitive abilities may act differently.

The Prophet Joseph Smith wrote an epistle from Liberty Jail on March 25, 1839 in which he wrote,

> received some letters last evening-one from Emma, one from Don C. Smith, and one from Bishop Partridge-all breathing a kind and consoling spirit. We were much gratified with their contents. We had been a long time without information; and when we read those letters they were to our souls as the gentle air is refreshing, **but our joy was mingled with grief, because of the sufferings of the poor and much injured Saints**. And we need not say to you that <u>the floodgates of our hearts were lifted and our eyes were a fountain of tears</u>, but those who have not been enclosed in the walls of prison without cause or provocation, can have but little idea how sweet the voice of a friend is.[170]

In this quote, it appears that those in the jail were experiencing both joy and grief. The emotion that they were experiencing was joy as expressed by "*the floodgates of our hearts were lifted and our eyes were a fountain of tears.*" But Joseph and the others previously experienced heartfelt grief and concern for the suffering saints as they received reports of their

---

[170] Smith, History of the Church, 3:294.

suffering. When Joseph wrote of mingling grief with joy he was exercising the "cognitive" functions and remembering the grief they had previously felt while feeling the joy of the letters. As he focused on those events he might have felt that grief very briefly but temporarily. When returning to read the letters, he would feel joy. It is difficult to believe he was emotionally and deeply grieving for the injured saints when at the same time being so joyous on receiving the letters. We need to remember that emotion is what one is currently feeling. We can remember and talk about other emotions that we have experienced but not be feeling those emotions at the moment.

Savior's Emotion

Did the Savior truly suffer emotional trauma or severe emotional trauma during his ordeal as some believe?

What do we really know about the emotions that the Savior suffered through his atonement sufferings? When Christ was in the Garden, he took Peter, James and John with him a bit further than the others and prior to his prayer, he said

> *My soul is exceeding **sorrowful, even unto death**: tarry ye here, and watch with me.*[171]

By his own words, he deeply felt this sorrow and he would suffer this until he died, for that sorrow was unto death. Being sorrowful is not experiencing severe emotional trauma as we might interpret this expression. When sorrow is felt deeply we call it grief. The Savior is known as a man of sorrow and grief. Isaiah even prophesied of his grief.

---

[171] Matthew 26:38; Mark 14:34.

*He is despised and rejected of men; **a man of sorrows,
and acquainted with grief**"*[172]

There is no scriptural evidence that the Savior changed his
sorrow to any other emotion. His statement indicates that he
will experience this sorrow "unto death." The one event that
needs explanation is his prayer on the cross to the Father about
forgiving the soldiers because they did not know what they
were doing. His perfect character was able to recognize that
the soldiers were not to be blamed for what he was
experiencing. He recognized that the soldiers were not acting
on their own initiative, but were trained and ordered to do the
things they did. It does show his great control in not giving
way to anger against them because they executed these severe
maltreatments.

Sorrow is an emotion that is felt by those in heaven. The
Savior visited the Nephites and foretold that the fourth
generation of Nephites would fall into sin. He said

> *But behold, **it sorroweth me** because of the fourth
> generation from this generation, for they are led away
> captive by him even as was the son of perdition; for
> they will sell me for silver and for gold, and for that
> which moth doth corrupt and which thieves can break
> through and steal.* [173]

Sorrow is an emotion that is also felt by our spirits. We had
that emotion prior to coming to earth. In the revelation given
to Joseph Smith and Sidney Rigdon they confirmed

---

[172] Isaiah 53:3.

[173] 3 Nephi 27:32.

*And this we saw also, and bear record, that an angel of God **who was in authority** in the presence of God, who rebelled against the Only Begotten Son whom the Father loved and who was in the bosom of the Father, was thrust down from the presence of God and the Son,*

*And was called Perdition, for **the heavens wept over him**—he was Lucifer, a son of the morning.* [174]

When Satan fell from his station "in authority" we "wept" because of our love for him had turned to sorrow over his failure.

When the Savior granted the three Nephites their desire that they remain on earth to continue their mission, they became changed and not subject to mortal frailties. The Savior said this to them:

*And again, ye shall not have pain while ye shall dwell in the flesh, **neither sorrow save it be for the sins of the world;** and all this will I do because of the thing which ye have desired of me, for ye have desired that ye might bring the souls of men unto me, while the world shall stand* [175]

The prophet Mormon experienced sorrow for his wicked people,

*And wo is me because of their wickedness; for **my heart has been filled with sorrow** because of their wickedness, all my days; nevertheless, I know that I shall be lifted up at the last day.* [176]

---

[174] D&C 76:25-26.

[175] 3 Nephi 28:9.

Sorrow is a righteous emotion and can be felt in heaven and on the earth.

There are some members that feel that the Savior suffered severe emotional trauma or severe mental distress. If the Savior was suffering sorrow throughout his ordeal, he could not have suffered severe emotional trauma or severe mental distress.

Suffering Alone

One of the things that people suffer is the challenge of being afflicted in some way and being alone to endure it. Older people, after losing a spouse, deeply feel this loneliness. The Savior suffered this more deeply than any mortal man.

When all is finished, the Savior will present the Father with the kingdom.

> *When he shall deliver up the kingdom, and present it unto the Father, spotless, saying: I have overcome and **have trodden the wine-press alone**, even the wine-press of the fierceness of the wrath of Almighty God.* [177]

From this scripture, we see that the winepress is symbolic of the "fierceness of the wrath of almighty God" or the fiercest judgment ever given of God. The wine-press represents the sufferings in the Garden of Gethsemane and on the Cross which were the major components of his atonement. He overcame them **alone**. It is true that an angel appeared to him strengthening him.[178] This strengthening undoubtedly reminded him of the importance that all humankind was

---

[176] Mormon 2:19.

[177] D&C 76:107.

[178] Luke 22:43.

dependent upon his fulfilling the atonement and the will of the Father. Because of his love for God and his spirit siblings, he did not withdraw. The angel left after he encouraged the Savior to fulfill his atonement. The Savior was alone during his atonement

Humankind has experienced some things the Savior has not experienced. These are sinful thoughts and actions. Obviously if he had experienced these things he would not have been a perfect example but would have been sinful himself. The Savior has experienced all he needs to know to judge and succor us. He will be able to apply justice and mercy accordingly.

ANGER – SAVIOR'S PERFECTION

One of the most challenging and misunderstood events was the Savior cleansing the temple. It is misunderstood because of the conclusion of most people who read of this event believes the Savior in his anger used strong force to remove the polluters from the temple. Many paintings depict the Savior with raised arm with whip in hand standing in majesty above cowering men.

Nephi was extremely angry with his brothers following his father's death. Many terrible acts have been committed by persons who are angry. We have addressed anger as it relates to the Savior's perfection and anger in humankind.

Consulting several dictionaries, anger or being angry is defined as,

> a **strong feeling** of displeasure and belligerence aroused by a wrong. [179]

---

[179] http://dictionary.reference.com/browse/anger?s=t. Last visited July

The wrong in this definition could be a perceived wrong but not actually in fact.

The difference between feeling displeasure and anger is the intensity with which the emotion is felt. A person can feel displeasure and not have anger. Anger is an emotion that can cause people to lose self-control and consequently cause great misery, injury, damage, destruction and even death. It is an emotion that must be controlled and eliminated from us.

Tool of Satan

There are a number of examples from the scriptures of how Satan uses anger to accomplish his purposes.

In the Book of Mormon Ammon and his brethren traveled to the Lamanites to teach and convert as many as they possibly could. King Lamoni and a number of his people were converted. They became known as the people of Anti-Nephi-Lehi.

The Amalekites appear to be a group of Nephites that developed a deep hatred of the Nephites but lived among the Lamanites. This conclusion is drawn from the fact that the Amalekites and their associates, the Amulonites, were largely of the religion called the "Nehors." This religion was practiced by the people of Ammonihah, who were Nephites and mostly destroyed by the Lamanites. Also, they are listed separately from the Lamanites as opposed to be included as Lamanites.[180]

Because the Amalekites had a hatred of the Nephites and wanted to destroy them, they stirred up the Lamanites to go to war against the Nephites. The Amalekites and Lamanites were

---

2016.

[180] Alma 21:2-5

defeated in battle. Their anger was turned against the Anti-Nephi-Lehi people.

> *And it came to pass that the Amalekites, because of their loss, were exceedingly angry.* And when they saw *that they could not seek revenge from the Nephites,* **they began to stir up the people in anger against their brethren, the people of Anti-Nephi-Lehi; therefore they began again to destroy them.** [181]

Ammon petitioned the Lord to determine whether King Limhi and his people should go with Ammon and return to Zarahemla. The Lord responded,

> *Get this people out of this land, that they perish not; for* **Satan has great hold on the hearts of the Amalekites, <u>who do stir up the Lamanites to anger</u> against their brethren to slay them;** *therefore get thee out of this land; and blessed are this people in this generation, for I will preserve them.* [182]

Another example of Satan's power to influence people to anger is described in Mormons letter to his son, Moroni describing the Nephites of his time.

> *And now behold, my son, I fear lest the Lamanites shall destroy this people; for they do not repent, and* **Satan stirreth them up continually to anger one with another.**
>
> *Behold, I am laboring with them continually; and* **when I speak the word of God with sharpness they tremble and anger against me;** *and when I use no*

---

[181] Alma 27:2.

[182] Alma 27:12.

*sharpness they harden their hearts against it;
wherefore, I fear lest the Spirit of the Lord hath ceased
striving with them.* [183]

Notice above that when Mormon presses his people to change
their ways, they respond with anger and never changed their
ways.

The Lord had this to say about the people who stole the 117
pages of manuscript of the first translation of the Book of
Mormon.

*For, behold, they shall not accomplish their evil
designs in lying against those words. For, behold, if
you should bring forth the same words they will say
that you have lied and that you have pretended to
translate, but that you have contradicted yourself.*

*And, behold, **they will publish this, and Satan will
harden the hearts of the people to stir them up to
anger against you, that they will not believe my
words**.* [184]

The Lord did not have Joseph retranslate that part which was
taken but substituted the translation of the small plates of
Nephi to replace that which was lost. Consequently, those who
made the changes were prevented from causing anger against
the Prophet. In speaking of purchasing lands in Zion the Lord
said,

*Wherefore, I the Lord will that you should purchase
the lands, that you may have advantage of the world,*

---

[183] Moroni 9:3-4.

[184] D&C 10:31-32.

111

*that you may have claim on the world, **that they may
not be stirred up unto anger.***

***For Satan putteth it into their hearts to anger against
you, and to the shedding of blood.*** [185]

The Savior taught in the Sermon on the Mount and also to the
Nephites the following about anger

> *But I say unto you, that **whosoever is angry with his
> brother shall be in danger of his judgment,**[186]*

However, the Savior said this about anger to the Nephites
when he appeared to them

> *Behold, this is **not my doctrine, to stir up the hearts of
> men with anger,** one against another; but this is <u>my
> doctrine, that such things should be done away.</u> [187]*

Nephi's Anger

Nephi's anger with his brothers Laman and Lemuel is a good
example of how anger interferes with having the spirit of the
Lord. This is illustrated in Nephi's psalm.[188] It is alleged to be
written in a chiasmic form which has been discussed more in
our classrooms than the reason why he was so distraught.
Most people are puzzled by the depth of despair and the sins
described by Nephi. Some use it as a justification that if so
great a prophet as Nephi has great sins they are not so bad off.
In order to understand Nephi's psalm, we need to understand

---

[185] D&C 63:27-28.

[186] 3 Nephi 12:21–22, Matthew 5:20-21.

[187] 3 Nephi 11:30.

[188] 2 Nephi 4:17-35.

112

his situation at the time of his writing. This writing occurred right after his father's death. He recorded,

> *And it came to pass after my father, Lehi, had spoken unto all his household, according to the feelings of his heart and the Spirit of the Lord which was in him, he waxed old. And it came to pass that he died, and was buried.*
>
> *And it came to pass that not many days after his death, Laman and Lemuel and the sons of Ishmael were angry with me because of the admonitions of the Lord.*
>
> *For I, Nephi, was constrained to speak unto them, according to his word; for I had spoken many things unto them, and also my father, before his death; many of which sayings are written upon mine other plates.*[189]

While Lehi was alive he was a measure of protection to Nephi. By their Jewish custom, they needed to obey their father. Although they obeyed their father by leaving Jerusalem with him, they complained bitterly and even threatened Nephi's death at times. Nephi further recorded after his father's death,

> *Behold, it came to pass that I, Nephi, did cry much unto the Lord my God, because of the anger of my brethren.*
>
> *But behold, their anger did increase against me, insomuch that they did seek to take away my life.*
>
> *Yea, they did murmur against me, saying: Our younger brother thinks to rule over us; and we have had much trial because of him; wherefore, now let us slay him, that we may not be afflicted more because of his*

---

[189] 2 Nephi 4:12-14.

*words. For behold, we will not have him to be our
ruler; for it belongs unto us, who are the elder
brethren, to rule over this people.*[190]

Nephi was the object of Laman and Lemuel's hatred to the
point of wanting to kill him. We will now turn to Nephi's
psalm to understand his feelings. He wrote,

> *O wretched man that I am! Yea, my heart sorroweth
> because of my flesh; my soul grieveth because of mine
> iniquities.* [191]

Nephi then recounts many dreams, visitations of angels,
mercies and visions some of which he was commanded not to
write. Then he says,

> *And why should I yield to sin, because of my flesh?
> Yea, why should I give way to temptations, that the evil
> one have place in my heart to destroy my peace and
> afflict my soul?* **Why am I angry because of mine
> enemy?** [192]

Nephi was angry with his enemy? And who was his enemy?
His enemy was his brothers Laman and Lemuel who wanted
to kill him. In fact, Nephi referred to his brothers and those
that followed them as his enemy or enemies some seven (7)
times during his psalm.[193] He had been in control of his
emotions and forgiving throughout their trials in arriving at the
Promised Land. At this time, Nephi's emotional response was
that he was very angry with his brothers.

---

[190] 2 Nephi 5:1-3.

[191] 2 Nephi 4:17.

[192] 2 Nephi 4:27.

[193] 2 Nephi 4:22,27,28,29,31,33.

We need to address the expression which is quoted above,

Yea, why should I give way to temptations, that the evil one have place in my heart to destroy my peace and afflict my soul?

In this expression, he speaks of an *"evil one"* having a place *"in his heart"*. What Nephi was feeling was anger. We feel anger in our chest area or heart. Nephi knows that feeling anger is wrong and destroys his peace. He further writes of his solution or of his repentance

*Awake, my soul! No longer droop in sin. Rejoice, O my heart, and give place no more for the **enemy of my soul**.*

*Do not **anger again because of mine enemies**.*[194]

And what was the "enemy of my soul"? It was anger against his brothers which was destroying Nephi's peace. Notice that Nephi again refers to his brothers as his enemy and not his brethren. This describes what has happened to his relationship with his brothers. Nephi's solution (or repentance) was *"Do not anger again."* He knows he has to control this anger by eliminating it.

Nephi wrote so negatively about his anger calling it his sins. In the beginning verses Nephi was lamenting his sin but talked about it in the plural, sins. This is what is generally confusing to readers. His writing sounds like he has committed many serious sins but he has only one. Nephi lamented his anger because it was destroying his peace and his ability to have the spirit of God with him. This would prevent any more visions, dreams or communications from God until it is removed.

---

[194] 2 Nephi 4:28-29.

This was a huge challenge to Nephi. After Lehi died and was buried, Nephi gave counsel to his brothers and they rejected his teachings. They took the position that they were the elder sons and the leadership belonged to them by right of seniority and custom. They completely ignored the angel's message to them that Nephi would be their leader. They no longer followed Nephi's leadership and counsel and wanted to kill him.[195] Nephi's reaction in this case was anger. In all the offenses that Laman and Lemuel committed against Nephi, this was the first time that Nephi was angry with his brothers. He had been so long-suffering and patient and put forth a great deal of effort to help his brothers to be righteous. But they would have none of it.

There were five major incidents[196] where Laman and Lemuel were angry with Nephi (and Sam). In all cases Nephi was full of the spirit, patient and concerned about his brothers. He had no anger. Note how angry the brothers were in each situation. They acted on that anger in each situation and threatened Nephi with death except for the first instance when they beat Nephi and Sam. They sinned because of their anger and were brought to repentance by various means in every case.

But this last time was different. Their father, Lehi, had died. Laman and Lemuel's attempts to kill Nephi were increasing and more serious. Shortly after this Nephi was inspired to separate from his brothers, which he did.

The one lesson that we should learn from Nephi's experience is that the spirit and peace of God cannot dwell in a person who is angry regardless of the reason for that anger. If you

---

195 2 Nephi 4:13-14; 2 Nephi 5:1-4.

196 1 Nephi 3:28-30; 7:7-21; 16:34-39; 17:7-55; 18:10-20.

have anger in your heart it interferes with the spirit or Holy Ghost and his potential communications.

Savior's Anger?

Did the Savior exercise anger during his earthly ministry? There are two things that need to be addressed. One is a scripture and the other is the temple cleansing.

The Savior entered a synagogue on the Sabbath day. A man with a withered hand was there. Pharisees were also there to see if the Savior would heal the man on the Sabbath day.

> *And he saith unto them, Is it lawful to do good on the sabbath days, or to do evil? to save life, or to kill? But they held their peace.*
>
> *And when he had looked round about on them **with anger, being grieved** for the hardness of their hearts, he saith unto the man, Stretch forth thine hand. And he stretched it out: and his hand was restored whole as the other.* [197]

The scripture states that the Savior looked on them "with anger, being grieved." The Savior was capable of emotions just as we are. An emotion is what one currently feels. It is impossible for us to have anger while feeling deep sorrow or grief at the same instant. [Read the section "Emotion" in the essay "WHAT the SAVIOR SUFFERED" for confirmation of this statement]. So it would be impossible for the Savior to feel both of these emotions at the same time. Think of your own personal experience of when you were angry. Could you have felt deep sorrow at the same instant? Sorrow may follow

---

[197] Mark 3:4-5.

anger but not felt at the same time. This is demonstrated by Laman and Lemuel in their relationship with Nephi.

Several times Laman and Lemuel became angry with Nephi and strived to take away his life. When they repented, they became sorrowful demonstrating that anger and sorrow or grief cannot be felt at the same time.

This scriptural expression saying that the Savior had "anger, being grieved" could not have happened because you can only feel one emotion at a time as illustrated above.

Temple Cleansing Issue
The temple cleansing now needs to be addressed as some feel that the Lord had intense anger during the cleansing of the temple.

All four gospels recorded cleansing temple events. Matthew, Mark and Luke record a temple cleansing as occurring at the end of the Lord's ministry. John's record states that Jesus travelled to Jerusalem for the Passover following his first miracle. This would be his first ministerial visit to Jerusalem. This was three years prior to his last supper and the subsequent events. It was also three years prior to the temple cleansing event recorded by Matthew, Mark and Luke.

Scholars have questioned whether the recorded temple cleansing was two separate events or one. This was a major issue some years past and continues as there are people that hold both views. Church members hold both views and have expressed such in classes heard by this author. This author has concluded that there was only one event.

John's Record
Following the cleansing of the temple as recorded by John, the Jewish leadership questioned his purpose. Remember that

previous language in John's record places this soon after his first miracle.

> *Then answered the Jews and said unto him, What sign shewest thou unto us, seeing that thou doest these things?*
>
> *Jesus answered and said unto them, Destroy this temple, and in three days I will raise it up.*
>
> *Then said the Jews,* **Forty and six years was this temple in building, and wilt thou rear it up in three days?**
>
> *But he spake of the temple of his body.* [198]

The concerns about John's record being at the beginning of the Savior's ministry are,

- The purpose and effect of the Savior's cleansing the temple at this early date.

- The Savior's reply to the Jewish leaders which was "Destroy this temple, and in three days I will raise it up." [199]

Issue One

The Gospel of John has no wording that would give us a clue as to the purpose of cleansing of the temple at this early date. It is well conceded that the temple was polluted by the things that were going on. If the temple were cleansed at this early date it was polluted again soon thereafter. It had to be cleansed again in three years. To cleanse the temple, then leave to minister to the people letting it be polluted again does not

---

[198] John 2:18-21.

[199] John 2:19.

make sense, particularly when he had to come back and cleanse it again.

The reason that the temple became polluted was that the Jewish leadership used it to provide significant income for them. Any interruption to this income would not be tolerated. The Jewish leaders would take punitive action immediately if this event happened early in the Savior's ministry because there would be no fear of the people. The Savior was unknown. This would complicate his ability to perform his ministry which was still to be done.

Why would the Savior take steps to antagonize the Jewish leadership by cleansing the temple at this early stage when he took steps to avoid them later in his ministry? In fact, near the end of his ministry the Savior declined to attend the Feast of the Tabernacle in Jerusalem with his disciples, whom he encouraged to attend. John records this statement regarding the Jewish leadership attitude to act.

> *After these things Jesus walked in Galilee: for he would not walk in Jewry, because the Jews sought to kill him.* [200]

The Savior was avoiding contact with the Jewish leadership because they would complicate his activities. The Savior encouraged his disciples to go and mingle with those at the feast telling them that they would be OK but he declined to go. In explaining his decision, he said,

> **My time is not yet come.**
> *The world cannot hate you; but me it hateth, because I testify of it, that the works thereof are evil.* [201]

---

[200] John 7:1.

In this refusal to attend the feast, the Savior was avoiding confrontation with the Jewish leaders before the time he was ready to fulfill his atonement.

Following the vision of Moses and Elijah on the Mount of Transfiguration, the Savior told this to Peter, James and John as they were returning from the Mount

> *And as they came down from the mountain, he charged them that they should tell no man what things they had seen,* ***till the Son of man were risen from the dead.***[202]

It was acceptable to tell of the visitation of Moses and Elias (Elijah) and not keep it confidential but it needed to wait until his resurrection. If the story was told immediately prior to that time, it was likely to become wide spread. If it came to the ears of the Jewish leadership and being as evil as they were, they likely would have taken earlier steps to try to kill the Savior before his ministry was completed. This would make it more difficult for the Savior to complete his ministry.

After the cleansing of the temple at the end of his ministry, the Savior asked his disciples to find a place for the Passover meal and say to the owner,

> ***My time is at hand****; I will keep the passover at thy house with my disciples.*[203]

This is a different mindset than when the Savior did not attend the Feast of the Tabernacle because his time was "not yet." It demonstrates an attitude of being ready to proceed with the

---

[201] John 7:6-7.

[202] Mark 9:9.

[203] Matthew 26:18.

things that he had to experience at the hands of the Jewish leadership. Cleansing the temple at the end of his ministry allowed him to teach, heal and minister at the temple.

Issue 2

John's record states that the Savior made this response to the Jewish leadership at the beginning of his ministry *"Destroy this temple, and in three days I will raise it up."* [204]

Take note of the response of the Jewish leadership that they assumed he was talking about the temple being destroyed when the Savior spoke of his body. Since he was speaking of the body, he was saying "Kill me and in three days I will live again." This was a challenge to kill him. The major question is, "Why would the Savior make this statement at the beginning of his ministry." His atonement events were three years away. To suggest that they should kill him at this point in time makes no sense.

The likely antagonism of the Jewish leadership, the lack of a genuine purpose and the statement to kill him and in three days he would be resurrected makes John's record <u>unlikely</u> to have happened at the beginning of his ministry. We should point out that when John wrote his gospel, he had copies of Matthew, Mark and Luke. He was encouraged to write his gospel because these other gospels were lacking explanations about some things he knew.

One Event

Consider now how the "Destroy this temple" statement fits <u>into the events described by</u> Matthew, Mark and Luke.

[204] John 2:19.

Throughout this discussion, we must remember the writings of Matthew, Mark and Luke did not record the "Destroy this temple" statement. Only John's gospel recorded it. The current version of John places it at the beginning of his ministry, which is highly suspect.

After the temple cleansing near the end of his ministry, he taught and healed people daily in the temple. The Jewish leadership came to him at the temple and asked him by what authority he did "these things"[205] meaning the cleansing of the temple. John's record contained a similar request. According to Matthew, Mark and Luke the Savior did not respond to their query because they did not respond to his question which was:

The baptism of John, was it from heaven, or of men?

They failed to respond because they were afraid of the people and could not express their true feelings about John's ministry.

And Jesus said unto them, Neither tell I you by what authority I do these things. [206]

It is totally uncharacteristic of the Savior to say nothing further when such a question is posed. This retort is very sharp. He was always teaching. Undoubtedly when he stated the above response he would have added

Destroy this temple, and in three days I will raise it up"

This was a challenge to kill him and in three days he would be resurrected. Remember that John's current record records that the Jewish leadership believed that the Savior referred to the

---

[205] Matthew 21:23; Mark 11:27-28; Luke 20:1-2.

[206] Luke 20:4,8; See Luke 20:2-8; Matthew 21:23-27; Mark 11:27-33.

temple building which was supposed to have occurred at the beginning of his ministry. Matthew, Mark and Luke record that they were at the temple when they posed their question about his authority to cleanse the temple. John records no location. They were at the temple when Jesus made this statement.

Events following this exchange with the Jewish leadership as recorded by Matthew, Mark and Luke demonstrate that this challenge was made by the Savior at this later time. At the trial before Caiaphas, witnesses were called to testify against the Savior. Two testified that

> *This fellow said, I am able to destroy the temple of God, and to build it in three days.* [207]

Mark records the witnesses as saying,

> *I will destroy this temple that is made with hands, and within three days I will build another made without hands.* [208]

When the Savior was suffering on the cross he was reviled by some saying,

> *Thou that destroyest the temple, and buildest it in three days, save thyself. If thou be the Son of God, come down from the cross.* [209]

These witnesses and revilers would never have remembered this "Destroy this temple" statement made three years early as he began his ministry. They had classified this statement as a

---

[207] Matthew 26:61.

[208] Mark 14:58.

[209] Matthew 27:40; Luke 15:2930.

boastful statement and not of much consequence. It was only remembered because it was recently stated at the end of his ministry.

It is important to remember that Matthew, Mark and Luke did not record the "Destroy this temple" statement yet they recorded other people as having heard the Savior make that statement at the end of his mission. Only John recorded it but it fits perfectly in the factual descriptions of Matthew, Mark and Luke.

Why John's Gospel records it early in the Lord's ministry is not readily known. If we had John's original writing, we would probably understand. It is the author's opinion that the language in John was altered. It is the author's opinion that John, having access to Matthew, Mark and Luke, he wrote of events that gave clarification to some events and included other events not contained in those writings and gave no time frame for them. This author believes that others added such language making it appear as an early ministry statement.

The only reasonable conclusion is that there was only one event of cleansing the temple.

Savior's Temple Cleansing
In order to understand the real motivation of the Savior undertaking this cleansing, we need to understand the true purpose of the temple and why it should be a reverent and prayerful place. The Savior came to fulfill the Law of Moses and to restore that which was taken away when the Law of Moses was instituted. In addition, the restoration of priesthood sealing keys occurred when Elijah appeared at the Mount of Transfiguration. At that time the full temple ordinances were restored allowing all men and women to "see the face of God" which the temple ordinances provide. These principles would

be taught by the Savior's apostles. The Savior needed to cleanse the temple to demonstrate the sacredness of the temple and the ordinances that belonged therein.

Most everyone views this scene of cleansing the temple as the Savior going up to those in the temple and with anger and majesty swinging his recently made scourge and whipping the polluters to drive them out. This is illustrated by artists and their creations some of which can be viewed on the internet.[210] You can go directly by clicking on the link in the footnote[211] or by internet searching using the phrase "temple cleansing pictures".

Most all of these paintings depict cowering men with the Savior's arm raised ready to strike. This is suggested by John's record that the Savior made a scourge and then drove them out. This is not an accurate understanding. John writes that the Savior drove them out of the temple and then told some to leave which is an inconsistent statement. How could he tell them to leave when they were already out?

All descriptions[212] of this event in the New Testament are cryptic. Matthew, Mark and Luke mention nothing about oxen or sheep. Matthew, Mark and John mention the dove sellers. Matthew states that the money changers table was turned over.

---

[210] Use Bing or Yahoo search engines; Enter "pictures Jesus cleansing temple.

[211] Last visited December 2016.
http://www.bing.com/images/search?q=picture+christ+cleansing+tem ple&qpvt=picture+Christ+cleansing+temple&qpvt=picture+Christ+cle ansing+temple&qpvt=picture+Christ+cleansing+temple&FORM=IGR E.

[212] John 2:13-20; Matthew 21:12-13; Mark 11:15-17; Luke 19:45-46.

Matthew and Mark state that the seats of the dove sellers were upset whereas John stated that the tables were upset but told the dove sellers to remove their birds. John's record identifies oxen and sheep as being driven out.

The gospel records are incomplete on this event. None of the accounts specifically describe how the events developed to rid the temple of the polluters. However, John's description is the most complete and includes the activities contained in the other gospels except for the statement of Matthew and Luke who recorded that the Savior upset the seats of the dove sellers. John's record will be used as the model to explain this event because of its completeness and description. John records that Jesus

> *found in the temple those that sold oxen and sheep and doves, and the changers of money sitting:*
>
> *And when he had made a scourge of small cords, he* **drove them all out of the temple, and the sheep, and the oxen; and poured out the changers' money, and overthrew the tables;**
>
> **And said unto them that sold doves, Take these things hence; make not my Father's house an house of merchandise.**[213]

The sequence of events described in this quote from John could not have happened in the way that it is recorded. John's record shows that the Savior made a scourge and then drove "them all out." This statement is the one that gives the impression that the Savior used the scourge on men. John's record states the Savior,

---

[213] John 2:14-16.

- drove out the sheep and the oxen
- poured out the changers' money
- overthrew the tables
- told them that sold doves" to remove the doves from the temple

This list shows the activities that the Savior used to cleanse the temple. However, it does not specifically show the order or how the events developed.

First of all, we need to understand that the Savior would not just walk in and start swinging the scourge and demanding that they leave. He would never do that! This is not compatible with the Savior's character as demonstrated in other New Testament events and it is not compatible with the principle that man has his agency and force will not be used. However, many artists illustrate the Savior in great majesty swinging his scourge of cords driving men away from the temple. This is the reaction that many readers have.

The Savior would not do anything until he gave the polluters an opportunity to correct their sinful conduct. His ministry clearly demonstrates this.

Also, we need to understand that the Savior's mission during his ministry was to teach, minister and not judge. The Savior's purpose was to get those who polluted the temple out so that he could teach, minister and heal in this sacred place. He had a firmness of purpose and he needed to have these polluters gone.

This description that follows is the likely course of events.

When the Savior first entered the temple with his scourge, he would have told the money changers and those that bought and sold the oxen and sheep that they would have to leave.

They would be surprised because that is the kind of command they were not accustomed to hear. Holding true to their charge they would probably refuse to obey thinking that no one should give them such a command except the Chief Priests who ran the temple. Who was this man telling them to leave? Strong language probably followed.

To demonstrate his firmness of purpose, the Savior would then turn over the tables which scattered the money. He would tell them that they were polluting his Father's house and to take their money and leave. Then he would turn to the dove sellers and tell them that they were polluting the temple and to leave. While the money changers and the sellers were picking up their money he would use his scourge to drive the oxen and sheep out of the temple grounds.

This would be a startling event to these polluters. These people had never been challenged in this manner. Once the polluters had gathered their money they would leave, having no purpose to remain. Their merchandise, the oxen and sheep, were out of the temple. They were out of business with the animals gone. The sellers of doves would take their doves out of the temple with them fearing that the Savior would open their cages and let the doves escape as they witnessed him driving out the oxen and sheep.

There is a painting by William Brassey Hole which demonstrates this scenario. William Brassey Hole, 1846-1917, painted many Bible scenes, 80 watercolor pictures of which were displayed in a book entitled "Life of Jesus of Nazareth." From his work, he came to know the character of the Savior. This painting does show the absence of anger typically depicted by other painters. His painting shows a table being picked up by one person and a second person picking up money, with the Savor pointing the way to leave the temple.

His right arm is at his side holding the scourge and is not active. The animals were in the background not having been driven out. His painting can be viewed on the internet using Bing or Yahoo search engines using the expression "William Brassey Hole cleansing temple."[214]

Do a left click on the painting to enlarge it.[215]

The Savior had total and complete self-control. The Savior did no physical harm or damage to the men personally. He did not use the scourge on the men. He used just enough force to turn over the tables. Then with both his verbal chastisement and his driving the oxen and sheep out of the temple, he accomplished his purpose. This was necessary and acceptable to the Father.

This author believes that his displeasure did not rise to the level of anger as we mortals know it. Cleansing the temple was a necessary act and was accomplished with a very minimal amount of force. After the polluters were gone the Savior taught, blessed and healed in the temple. We do not have a record of all his teachings but undoubtedly he taught of the sacredness of the temple and the sacred ordinances that belong therein. It was his purpose to restore these things by fulfilling the Law of Moses and restoring all that was lost.

James E Talmage View

James E. Talmage wrote of two temple cleansings whereas we have made the case that there was only one. In his book, Jesus

---

[214] Other search engines may work but Bing and Yahoo have been verified.

[215] Last visited December 2016.
http://www.bing.com/images/search?q=william+brassey+hole+cleansing+temple&id=26906AC92819493C60AF2475BE4F5065F3D1DE5F&FORM=IQFRBA.

the Christ, Talmage made this statement when writing about the second temple cleansing.

Within the temple grounds Jesus was filled with indignation at the scene of tumult and desecration which the place presented. Three years before, at Passover time, **He had been wrought up to a high state of righteous anger** *by a similar exhibition of sordid chaffering within the sacred precincts, and had driven out the sheep and oxen, and* **forcibly expelled the traders and the money-changers and all who were using His Father's house as a house of merchandise.**[216]

This is the response that most people have because they read that Jesus made a scourge and then drove them all out. The assumption is that the scourge was used as the tool to drive the people out. That kind of action would reflect anger. But we have provided a different view of the use of the scourge. It was not used on people but on cattle to drive them out. We have taken that position because we do not believe the Savior would use the scourge on people. That would be using force to impose his will. He would not act in that manner. It is contrary to Father's giving us our agency to make choices. In fact, this author does not believe that "righteous anger" exists. As previously shown anger as we know it prevents us from having the spirit as Nephi experienced when he was anger with his enemies (his brothers).

Talmage used this phrase "righteous anger" to describe the Savior's actions. I believe that Talmage thought that the Savior used the whip on men as most view this scene. He coined the term "righteous anger" because he knew that the

---

[216] Talmage, Jesus the Christ, 490.

Savior had not sinned and he visualized the Savior as having intensive anger. So his anger was righteous. However, in viewing the scene as we have described, that anger is missing.

To Nephi his anger was an enemy to his soul and prevented him from having the spirit with him. His anger was sinful. To say that the Savior was angry in the same way and used a whip to physically drive the polluters out would make the Savior sinful and not our example. To say that the Savior had anger which is a tool of Satan is not describing the Savior's emotion accurately. The Savior was in complete control and had displeasure but not anger.

----- ATONEMENT RESULTS -----

In this section we address the concept of the infinite atonement as explained in the Book of Mormon. It seems to this author that some have made it more complicated than it really is. In addition, we address the marriage covenant. On examining section 132 carefully and consulting Joseph Smith's record in the History of the Church, it seems conclusive that the new and everlastng covenant is the marriage covenant and only the marriage covenant.

The eternal status and destiny of humankind is also addressed.

INFINITE ATONEMENT

Jacob, Nephi's brother, is the first person in the Book of Mormon to use the expression "*infinite atonement*". He went into considerable depth to explain the fall in the Garden of Eden and the atonement. Jacob's sermon is perhaps the best explanation in the scriptures of the basic plan of salvation.[217]

Jacob's sermon according to Nephi's record begins

> *For as death hath passed upon all men, to fulfil the merciful plan of the great Creator, <u>there must needs be a power of resurrection</u>, and the resurrection must needs come unto man by reason of the fall; and the **fall** came by reason of transgression; and because man became fallen they were cut off from the presence of the Lord.*
>
> *Wherefore it must needs be an <u>**infinite atonement**</u>— save it should be an infinite atonement this corruption* [mortal body] *could not put on incorruption* [immortal body]*. Wherefore, the first*

---

[217] 2 Nephi 9:6-15

judgment which came upon man must needs have
remained to an endless duration. And if so, this flesh
must have laid down to rot and to crumble to its
mother earth, to rise no more.[218]

Jacob states that because Adam and Eve transgressed all men became subject to death and were *"cut off from the presence of the Lord"*. Because of this fall *"there must needs be a power of resurrection"*. Then he directly links the expression *"infinite atonement"* to the resurrection with his statement that when there is no *"infinite atonement"* then *"this corruption could not put on incorruption."* What Jacob is really saying is that the *"power of the resurrection"* is this *"infinite atonement"* and resurrected humankind will live forever.

The word *"corruption"* when used in the scriptures refers to our mortal bodies and when they *"put on incorruption"* they are resurrected and live forever.

So when we read the expression *"infinite atonement"* or *"infinite sacrifice"* without which there would be no resurrection, it refers to the attribute of the resurrection that our lives will be without end or infinite upon our resurrection.

Jacob goes on to describe what our eternal status would be if no atonement or resurrection were provided. We would become subject to Satan throughout eternity as spirits suffering his same fate. [219] Following that he describes the resurrection of the wicked and then the righteous [220] which the *"infinite atonement"* or *"infinite sacrifice"* provides.

---

218 2 Nephi 9:6-7.

219 2 Nephi 9:8-9.

220 2 Nephi 9:10-13.

MARRIAGE COVENANT

We will discuss the principles and laws pertaining to the celestial marriage covenant. Joseph Smith recorded the revelation in his diary and history in Nauvoo, Illinois, July 12th 1843. The title to this revelation was approved by Joseph Smith and recorded as

> ***Revelation on the Eternity of the Marriage Covenant Including the Plurality of Wives.*** [221]

This revelation is Section 132 in the current version of the Doctrine and Covenants. According to the wording this revelation is about the "eternity of the marriage covenant" and plural marriage. This essay will not address any questions or issues relating to plural marriage as later prophets have received revelation declaring that Church members must not continue this practice. Our current prophets continue to teach and support that change.

This essay will demonstrate that the "new and everlasting covenant" is a single covenant and refers to the "marriage covenant" as revealed to Joseph Smith. Joseph records the following at the beginning of the revelation:

> *For behold, I reveal unto you **a new and an everlasting covenant**; and if ye abide not that covenant, then are ye damned; for no one can reject this covenant and be permitted to enter into my glory.*[222]

The expression bolded above which is "*a new and an everlasting covenant*" is found in one other place in the scriptures. That is in section 22 verse one. All other references

---

[221] Smith, History of the Church, 5:501.

[222] D&C 132:4.

135

to this covenant are recorded in the scriptures as the "new and everlasting covenant". In fact the first occurrence of the expression *"new and everlasting covenant"* is in two (2) paragraphs following the expression *"a new and an everlasting covenant."* This expression is very commonly used in the Church but the Lord introduces this covenant as "a new and an everlasting covenant." Two key words in this expression are "a" and "an." These words are singular in form. This covenant is "a new covenant" and it is "an everlasting covenant". It is a single covenant which is new and everlasting but not multiple covenants.

The word "new" has the meaning of "replacing existing one". This covenant replaces the old man made marriage covenants and is the only one recognized by the Father past death.

Structure of Section 132
We will begin with the structure and wording contained in the revelation.

Verses 1-3 - The Savior acknowledged Joseph's petition to understand why Abraham, Isaac and Jacob as well as Moses, David and Solomon (whom the Savior called "his servants") had many wives. The Savior's revelation deals with the marriage of these faithful servants to their many wives.

Verses 4-6 – It should be noted that if a person rejects or does not receive this covenant they will not

be permited to enter into my glory. "[223]

If we are not being permitted to enter into Heavenly Father's and the Savior's glory we will not be married, have children and participate in these heavenly blessings. This means that

---

[223] D&C 132:4.

we will not inherit the highest degree of the celestial kingdom. We will see in the following verses that if while in this life we have the availability of partaking of this marriage covenant and do not do so, we reject this covenant and lose its promise.

Verse 7 - The law governing the new and everlasting covenant is partially quoted

> *the conditions of **this law** are these: <u>All covenants, contracts, bonds, obligations, oaths, vows, performances, connections, associations, or expectations,</u> that are not made and entered into and **sealed by the Holy Spirit of promise, of him who is anointed**...*

> *are of no efficacy, virtue, or force in and after the resurrection from the dead; for **all contracts that are not made unto this end have an end when men are dead.** [224]*

As one reads this revelation and carefully examines this list one might believe that this list includes the full gospel ordinances. This list of words describes potential relationships, feelings and expectations that may exist between people. It does not refer ordinances. The list of words is

- Covenants   between people
- Contracts   between people
- Bonds   between people
- Obligations   between people
- Oaths   between people or individually
- Vows   between people
- Performances   between people

---

[224] D&C 132:7.

- Ceremonies   between people
- Connections   between people
- Associations   between people
- Expectations   between people or individually

The revelation refers to this list of terms by using the term "contract" which requires two or more parties. This list of terms represents ways in which people might adopt or claim they are married even after this life. From the quote above these associations must be by "him who is anointed" which means a sealing ordinance by the holy priesthood. The Lord said *"All contracts* (referring to the list above) *that are not made unto this end have an end when men are dead."* Unless marriage is properly administered it will not last past death. More will be said as we progress in this writing.

It should be noted that this list does not describe the ordinances of the gospel required to be able to go to the temple to have this marriage ordinance performed. Other ordinances of the gospel such as baptism are not included or suggested in this list of words.

Marriage must be performed by "*him who is anointed*". The prophet and President of the Church is the one who has that power. Joseph Smith had that authority at the time this revelation was recorded. We understand now that the President of the Church does not directly perform these sealings. Currently marriage is performed by those who have been given authority for this special purpose as authorized by the President.

Verses 8-14 - The important points contained in these verses are:

- *no man shall come unto the Father but by me or by my word, which is my law, saith the Lord.* (Verse 12)
- the Lord states that whatever man creates will be destroyed when men are dead and that only those things that remain will have been made by him by the priesthood.

Verse 15-17 reads,

> *Therefore, if a man marry him a wife in the world, **and he marry her not by me nor by my word, and he covenant with her so long as he is in the world and she with him, their covenant and marriage are not of force when they are dead,** and when they are out of the world; therefore, they are not bound by any law when they are out of the world.*

> *Therefore, <u>when they are out of the world they neither marry nor are given in marriage; but are appointed angels in heaven,</u> **which angels are ministering servants,** to minister for those who are worthy of a far more, and an exceeding, and an eternal weight of glory.*

> *For these angels did not abide my law; therefore, <u>they cannot be enlarged, but remain separately and singly, without exaltation, in their saved condition, to all eternity; and from henceforth are not gods, but are angels of God forever and ever.</u>*

The verses begin:

> *Therefore if a man marry him a wife ...*

This marriage is described as a man and wife making a covenant between them that their marriage is for time but they

139

were not married according to the Lord's way. The Lord's way is being married in the temple by one holding the proper priesthood authority. Consequently, their marriage has no effect after they are dead. When they die they are foreclosed from an eternal marriage and if otherwise faithful, will be a ministering angel to those who are exalted.

If their parents were married in the temple and faithful to the end of their lives, then by their marriage covenant, that child will be a ministering angel to them. As a ministering angel they will not be in the highest degree of the celestial kingdom.

Should their marriage later be performed later by proxy, the proxy marriage will not be valid because they did not follow the law which requires their marriage to be sealed in the temple during their mortality if it is available to them.

For example, my grandfather was a "priest" in the Aaronic Priesthood. He had a very close bond with his wife nicknamed "Rit" who died at an early age. My mother states that grandfather was approached many times to prepare himself to go to the temple and to be sealed to his wife. He had an expectation that he would be with his wife without that. He never accepted this counsel. He will not have her in eternity even as much as I would like it to be different. However his Father and Mother were married in the temple and were faithful.

In doing our genealogy we perform all marriages for deceased relatives. We do no judge as there may be circumstances that may make a difference.

Verse 18 - This verse discusses a marriage where the couple makes a covenant between themselves that their marriage is for time and all eternity. This described marriage is the same as that described in verses 15-17 except for the covenant between them. The fact that they made this covenant between themselves and not by the Lord's priesthood does not make a difference for them. Since their marriage is not sealed by priesthood authority the marriage is not effective beyond death.

This verses also state those not married as described will not be able to pass by the angels and gods who are appointed to guard the entry into the highest degree in the celestial kingdom even though they may have learned how to do this in their temple endowment. Only faithful couples, married in the marriage covenant will pass by the angels. This principle would also apply to those described in verses 15-17.

Verse 19-20 - This describes a marriage properly made in the new and everlasting covenant and by the sealing by the special authority of the prophet and describes the blessings thereof. They shall:

1. inherit thrones, kingdoms, principalities, and powers, dominions, all heights and depths
2. pass by the angels and the gods which are set there to determine their worthiness to enter.

I had a discussion with one of my wife's roommates. She was perplexed because in her patriarchal blessing she was counseled to not marry out of the temple or the marriage covenant. I had no knowledge of why that was in her patriarchal blessing. She expressed a very strong desire to be married. She did not have any offers of marriage from temple worthy men. She could not understand why she was counseled to marry in the temple. Several years following our marriage she married but not in the temple. She still continued to attend

Church and go to the temple. Her husband often attended Church with her but did not join the Church.

Then she developed cancer and died. My belief is that her husband never joined the Church. Whether he did or did not is immaterial to the point of including this story. If he did not join the Church then this good sister will be a ministering angel to her faithful parents in the celestial kingdom, much to our sadness. She had rejected the new and everlasting covenant or marriage covenant as specified in verses 19-20. She had not rejected the gospel. She was faithful in all but the marriage covenant. By not being married in the marriage covenant her situation is described in verses 15-17.

Section 131
This revelation states that there are three heavens or degrees in the celestial kingdom. This is important to understand as other things are explained about the marriage covenant.

> *In the celestial glory there are three heavens or degrees;*
>
> *And in order to obtain the highest, a man must enter into this order of the priesthood [meaning the new and everlasting covenant of marriage];*
>
> *And if he does not, he cannot obtain it.*
>
> **He may enter into the other, but that is the end of his kingdom;** *he cannot have an increase.* [225]

It is a man's responsibility to propose marriage and to qualify to enter into the marriage covenant. If he does not, he will not obtain the highest degree. A sister is not obligated to accept

---

[225] D&C 131:1-4.

any marriage proposal which she deems not suitable for her. If she dies without marriage and is otherwise faithful she will be entitled to have that priesthood marriage covenant performed for her when she identifies the companion she wishes to have for eternity. This will happen at a time in which further revelations and commandments are revealed. But it will happen. She will not be denied that blessing if she endures to the end.

Section 22 and Marriage Covenant

This section contains the exact language as written in Section 132. It identifies a covenant as *"a new and an everlasting covenant"* and is identical to the expression describing the covenant in section 132. As previously discussed this phrase has two important words. They are *"a"* and *"an."* Both of these words are singular in form. They show that it is a single covenant and the same covenant identified in Section 132 which is the marriage covenant and only the marriage covenant.

In studying this section this author had difficulty reconciling the head notes identifying baptism as a "new and everlasting covenant" and stating that verses 2, 3 and 4 are referring to baptism. Verse three is the troublesome verse. In it the Lord uses the expression *"this last covenant"* to refer to the covenant in verse one recorded as *"a new and an everlasting covenant"* which is identical to a reference in Section 132, which Joseph Smith wrote was a "revelation on the marriage covenant."

How can baptism be identified as *"this last covenant?"* The following will analyze the language and show that this expression refers to the marriage covenant.

Section 22 was recorded in April 1830 and was a response to some who wanted to affiliate with the Church without being re-baptized having already been baptized in another faith. This section reads,

> *Behold, I say unto you that all old covenants have I caused to be done away in this thing; and **this is a new and an everlasting covenant**, even that which was from the beginning.*
>
> *Wherefore, although a man should be baptized an hundred times it availeth him nothing, for you cannot enter in at the strait gate by the law of Moses, neither by your dead works.*
>
> *For it is because of your dead works that I have caused this last covenant and this church to be built up unto me, even as in days of old.*
>
> *Wherefore, enter ye in at the gate, as I have commanded, and seek not to counsel your God. Amen.* [226]

The head notes of this section read

1. Baptism is a new and everlasting covenant;

2–4. Authoritative baptism is required.

It seems clear that verses two and four assert that "Authoritative baptism is required." It is the understanding of verse three that that is the troublesome verse. Does it really refer to baptism?

Baptism is the very first covenant that we make and by baptism we enter the path that will lead to eternal life. Clearly verses 2 and 4 refer to baptism.

---

[226] D&C 22:1-4.

At baptism a covenant is made to attend Church to partake of the sacrament and renew our commitment to keep God's commandments. In the temple we receive the ordinances of initiatory and endowment with their associated covenants and promises. The very last and most important covenant that we make which will lead us to eternal life is the New and an Everlasting Covenant which is the marriage covenant as explained above.

How can baptism be referred to as "this last covenant"? The term "this last covenant" contained in verse 3 is singular in form and refers to a single covenant that is described as "last." This phrase refers to the covenant referred to in verse 1 which is *"a new and an everlasting covenant"* which is the marriage covenant.

At the time of this revelation (Section 22) we knew all about baptism. The Church was organized on 6 April 1830 and on that day Joseph recorded section 20 in the Doctrine and Covenants. In section 20 the Lord specified the exact date that the Church was to be organized showing that section 20 was given prior to the actual organization. In this revelation baptism is confirmed as necessary for salvation.[227] It describes the mode of baptism by one who has the priesthood and authority[228] and provides entry into his Church. The Lord said,

> *And again, by way of commandment to the church*
> *concerning the manner of baptism—All those who*
> *humble themselves before God, and desire to be*
> *baptized, and come forth with broken hearts and*
> *contrite spirits, and witness before the church that they*

---

[227] D&C 20:25-27.

[228] D&C 20:72-74.

145

have truly repented of all their sins, and are willing to take upon them the name of Jesus Christ, having a determination to serve him to the end, and truly manifest by their works that they have received of the Spirit of Christ unto the remission of their sins, **shall be received by baptism into his church.** [229]

The Book of Mormon was published in 1829 and contained many scriptures showing that baptism was necessary for salvation. It showed the Savior was baptized[230] and that he commanded Nephite people to be baptized when he appeared to them beginning with his disciples.[231] The Book of Mormon and section 20 show that the Church had full and complete knowledge of baptism when the Church was organized. What more needed to be revealed or "built up" about baptism? The Church is "built up" by new members being added by baptism.

Building Up the Church & Covenant

What does the Lord mean when he says in verse three **"I have caused this last covenant and this church to be built up unto me"**?

We will begin to answer this question by addressing the expression "to be built up." If you say to your child before going on a business trip "I want you to be good" then you mean that while you are gone you want this child's conduct and activities to conform to your notion of good. This expression "to be" is a reference to future events from the time the statement is made.

---

[229] D&C 20:37.

[230] 2 Nephi 31:4-6.

[231] 3 Nephi 19:10-13.

By the expression "*to be built up unto me*" the Lord is saying that in the future he has many more revelations, events and keys to restore to build up "*this last covenant*" and "*this church.*" Section 22 was given in New York State immediately following the organization of the Church.

Subsequently the Church headquarters was moved to Kirtland, Ohio where many more revelations and instructions by the Prophet on how the Church was to be organized and managed were given. Also a commandment was given to build a temple at Kirtland where additional authority, keys and ordinances were to be given. However, the temple ordinances were not taught to the Church in general at that time. It was not until the Nauvoo Temple was built that the Church members were instructed in temple ordinances including the marriage covenant. In fact section 132 was not recorded until July 1843 even though Joseph Smith knew the revelation long before that.

When the Lord says "*I have caused*" he means I have started or have initiated things. That starting or initiation was the restoration of the priesthood and the creation of his Church on April 6, 1830. Section 22 was given after the Church was organized but in the same month.

The question that arises is: "At the time of this revelation what more needed to be revealed about baptism?" What had "*to be built up*" about baptism? As discussed above all had been revealed about baptism except to give a second witness of its necessity. Section 22 does this in verses 2 and 4.

The next question to be answered is "Why did the Lord couple "*this last covenant*" with "*this church*" to the expression "*to be built up unto me*"? The Church needs to be built up because it is the entity that provides the new and everlasting covenant or marriage covenant in the temple. The marriage covenant needed *"to be built up"* at the time of the revelation because many things needed to be revealed to implement it.

It is the last and most important covenant in the sequence of covenants that are made. Without the marriage covenant we do not have exaltation and cannot have an increase (or children) in eternity. This ordinance provides the sealing between couples to be able to return to the presence of the Father in the highest degree of the celestial kingdom with their children and to have children in the eternities. This is the ultimate goal of the Savior and the Father.

In fact "*this last covenant*" and the Church are still being built up unto the Lord by the Church growing in numbers by new couples entering into the marriage covenant and members providing the temple covenants for our dead.

Baptism is not "this last covenant" The last covenant that is made in the temple is the marriage covenant and is the covenant that exalts people. The expression "*this last covenant*" refers to the marriage covenant.

Marriage Covenant Children

The First Presidency and Quorum of the Twelve Apostles of the Church of Jesus Christ of Latter-day Saints issued a proclamation entitled "The Family: A Proclamation to the World." In it is the statement

> *The divine plan of happiness enables family relationships to be perpetuated beyond the grave. Sacred ordinances and covenants available in holy temples make it possible for individuals to return to the presence of God and for **families to be united eternally**.*

Being united eternally comes from the sealing powers of the marriage covenant. The Prophet Joseph Smith recorded the following in his journal dated August 13, 1843 when making comments about Judge Elisa Higby's passing:

> *Four destroying angels holding power over the four quarters of the earth <u>until the servants of God are sealed in their foreheads</u>, which signifies sealing the blessing upon their heads, <u>meaning the everlasting covenant, thereby making their calling and election sure.</u> When a seal is put upon the father and mother,* ***it secures their posterity, so that they cannot be lost, but will be saved by virtue of the covenant of their father and mother.*** [232]

It is important to understand the full significance of these two quotes. The first quote is from the Family Proclamation and authorized by the First Presidency and the Quorum of the Twelve Apostles. The second quote is by Joseph Smith. When Joseph spoke he had a clerk record his message. Upon receiving the notes he would review them and put them in his journal. Willard Richards was his clerk. Joseph made changes to Willard Richards' notes which included the bolded part of the above quote. We know that Joseph made these changes by comparing Willard Richard's journal entry[233] for this talk with Joseph's record. The bolded part of the above quote is exactly Joseph's words.

Joseph's quote is about the sealing powers of the marriage covenant. If the parents abide by this covenant their posterity will be saved with them by virtue of their marriage covenant.

---

[232] Smith, History of the Church, 5:530.

[233] Ehat, Words of Joseph Smith, 238.

This statement by Joseph Smith does not say what the salvation of their posterity will be but they will not be lost. The First Presidency and the Quorum of the Twelve Apostles confirm this concept when they stated in their Proclamation that "families will be united eternally." This is independent of the righteousness of their children because their children "cannot be lost." The marriage covenant and faithfulness of the parents will bind the family together.

There is one significant difference between the Family Proclamation and Joseph's statement. The Proclamation identifies children can be with parents whereas Joseph's statement is "*It secures their posterity.*" The word posterity is a broader group than "*children.*" It probably includes descendants up to the third or fourth generation as is commonly expressed in the scriptures. If we are true and faithful to our temple marriage covenant we will have our posterity with us in the celestial kingdom.

Our posterity does not always accept what we teach and their lives vary in righteousness.

They may

- accept the gospel principles through repentance then marry faithfully in the temple and endure to the end
- accept the gospel principles either initially or after repentance and be married but not married in the temple by the time both are dead.
- not accept or live the gospel principles and die in their unrepentant state.

If at the death of a posterity member they have been faithful and have entered the marriage covenant keeping it faithfully to the end of their lives they are not wayward. They will be with the faithful covenant parents in the highest degree of the celestial kingdom because they received and followed the marriage covenant law. They qualify by their own conduct and that close family relationship will continue in the celestial kingdom.

If a posterity member is faithful and marries but does not accept the marriage covenant by the time both are dead he cannot inherit the highest degree but will be a ministering angel. We repeat the marriage standard.

> *Therefore, **if a man marry him a wife in the world, and he marry her not by me nor by my word, and he covenant with her so long as he is in the world and she with him, their covenant and marriage are not of force when they are dead,** and when they are out of the world; therefore, they are not bound by any law when they are out of the world.*

> *Therefore, **when they are out of the world they neither marry nor are given in marriage; but are <u>appointed angels in heaven, which angels are ministering servants</u>, to minister for those who are worthy of a far more, and an exceeding, and an eternal weight of glory.***

> *For these angels did not abide my law; therefore, they cannot be enlarged, but remain separately and singly, without exaltation, in their saved condition, to all eternity; and from henceforth are not gods, but are angels of God forever and ever.* [234]

---

[234] D&C 132:15-17.

151

It should be emphasized that if a couple marries they must be married in the marriage covenant during their mortality. Performing the marriage covenant for them after both are dead will not be valid unless there are extenuating circumstances. This is because they previously rejected this covenant by their non-conformance during mortality. We are encouraged to do these marriages by proxy because we are not judges. If they were otherwise faithful they become ministering angels.

Ministering angels minister for those who have a greater glory who are in the highest degree in the celestial kingdom. If they were sealed to their parents and their parents were faithful they will minister for their parents because of their parent's marriage covenant.

Our Wayward Posterity
Elder Orson F. Whitney made this statement about what Joseph Smith taught

> *The Prophet Joseph Smith declared and he never taught more comforting doctrine that the eternal sealings of faithful parents and the divine promises made to them for valiant service in the Cause of Truth, would save not only themselves,* **_but likewise their posterity_**. **Though some of the sheep may wander, the eye of the Shepherd is upon them, and sooner or later they will feel the tentacles of Divine Providence reaching out after them and drawing them back to the fold.** *Either in this life or the life to come, they will return.* **They will have to pay their debt to justice; they will suffer for their sins.** [235]

---

[235] Whitney, Church Conference Report, April 1929, 110.

Several general authorities have quoted this passage from Elder Whitney and the principle has been taught by others. This statement confirms that posterity and not just children are saved. There are two other primary principles in this statement.

- The Savior will reach out to those who are wayward to draw them back into the fold of the family.

- If they die in their sins they will have to pay their debt to justice. They will suffer for their sins.

It is comforting to faithful parents to know that the Father and the Savior will provide events which will encourage wayward children to return to full fellowship. We must remember that our children have their agency and may choose not to respond to those promptings.

If wayward posterity responds to the "tentacles of Divine Providence" and sincerely repent they will be forgiven. Depending on their marital status they will be in the highest degree of the celestial kingdom or a ministering angel.

That wayward posterity that do not respond to the "tentacles of Divine Providence" and die in their sins will have to "pay their debt to justice." They will pay for their sins in the same way that every other mortal pays for their sins.

Amulek taught the Zoramites

> *For behold, if ye have procrastinated the day of your repentance even until death,* **behold, ye have become subjected to the spirit of the devil, and he doth seal you his ; therefore, the Spirit of the Lord hath withdrawn from you, and hath no place in you, and**

the devil hath all power over you; *and this is the final*
state of the wicked. [236]

Unrepentant children will become subject unto Satan when
they die. They suffer in hell and will suffer the buffetings and
torment of Satan in hell. They will suffer everlasting fire
which is their dreading the final judgments of the Savior. Both
of these judgments will be severe. [Read the essay
"JUDGMENTS at MORTAL DEATH"]. When they are
resurrected they have paid for their sins and receive
forgiveness. They will no longer suffer the buffetings of Satan
but will feel that "fire" knowing they could have had a better
position in eternity than the one they have.

The question that needs to be answered is "If our posterity dies
in their sins where will these wayward children be consigned
and what glory will they have?" If they are consigned to the
telestial kingdom they would be lost to their parents because
telestial people will not be where their parents will be. Faithful
parents are promised that none of their posterity will be lost.

Wayward children will be with their faithful parents according
to the promises and so will be consigned to the celestial
kingdom. They will not be co-equals with their parents nor as
co-equals with ministering angels because they are judged by
their works during mortality. Their works do not merit the
same as their parents or ministering angels. They will be
consigned to the lowest degree in the celestial kingdom. They
will be helpful to their parents in some capacity that will
probably be directed by their parents.

The Lord has not revealed all of the qualifications and the full
extent of the laws governing those who might inherit the two

---

[236] Alma 34:35.

lower degrees of the celestial glory. These laws may have broader implications for people other than posterity of faithful marriage covenant parents.

Revelation to William E. McLellin

There is a scripture in the revelation to William E. McLellin that relates to this concept of having the promise of the marriage covenant or everlasting covenant even though it had not been revealed.

> *Behold, thus saith the Lord unto my servant William E. McLellin—Blessed are you, inasmuch as **you have turned away from your iniquities, and have received my truths**, saith the Lord your Redeemer, the Savior of the world, even of as many as believe on my name.*

> *Verily I say unto you, blessed are you for **receiving mine everlasting covenant, even the fulness of my gospel**, sent forth unto the children of men, **that they might have life and be made partakers of the <u>glories which are to be revealed in the last days</u>**, as it was written by the prophets and apostles in days of old.* [237]

The expression "everlasting covenant" refers to the new and everlasting covenant or marriage covenant. This revelation also states that the "glories" of this covenant were yet to be revealed. At that time the Church was building the Kirtland Temple.

The question is: "Why did the Savior say that by "turning away from your iniquities" and "receiving my truths" that William was "receiving mine everlasting covenant" when it had not yet been implemented?"

---

[237] D&C 66:1-2.

At the time of this revelation for William in 1831 Joseph and Oliver had not yet received the sealing keys from Elijah which occurred in the Kirtland Temple in April 1836. Joseph Smith recorded the new and everlasting covenant in 1843 which he identifies as the "marriage covenant" in his history. The everlasting covenant was not made available to the Church members until 1846. A few had been sealed prior to that time but the sealings were not available to the general membership.

The answer to the question is every married couple who will enter into the presence of the Father will have a temple marriage performed for them in person or by proxy. At the time the revelation was given to McLellin temple marriage was not available.

On May 11, 1838, a bishop's court was held for William E. McLellin at Far West Missouri. Joseph Smith wrote this in his history

> *I attended the trial of William E. McLellin and Dr. McCord, for transgression, before the Bishop's court .*

> *William E. McLellin stated about the same as McCord, and that he had no confidence in the heads of the Church, believing they had transgressed, and had got out of the way, consequently he quit praying and keeping the commandments of God, and indulged himself in his lustful desires, but when he heard that the First Presidency had made a general settlement, and acknowledged their sins, he began to pray again. When I interrogated him, he said he had seen nothing out of the way himself, but he judged from hearsay.* [238]

---

[238] Smith, History of The Church 3:31.

There is no existing record of that court but B. H. Roberts wrote this as a footnote in the history of the Church.

It will be observed that the text is silent in relation to what action was taken respecting William E. McLellin, and the Far West Record is silent upon the subject also. In fact the minutes of the trial before the Bishop are not written in that record at all. It is known, however, from other sources that William E. McLellin was finally excommunicated from the Church at Far West. Thence forward he took an active part in the persecution of the Saints in Missouri, and at one time expressed the desire to do violence to the person of Joseph Smith, while the latter was confined in Liberty prison. [239]

Not having endured to the end William lost his rights to the everlasting covenant.

Today the Church is under the marriage covenant requirements. Members who marry must be married in the temple by the priesthood sealing keys while in mortality. To do otherwise rejects this covenant and after their death their marriage is not valid and if they are otherwise faithful they will be ministering angels for those who did not reject this covenant.

SALVATION OF MAN

The atonement of the Savior provided salvation for all humankind not just those who will be worthy of the celestial kingdom. When the Savior appeared to the Nephites the first words uttered to them were:

---

[239] Smith, History of The Church 3:33.

Behold, I am Jesus Christ, whom the prophets testified shall come into the world.

*And behold, I am the light and the life of the world; and I have drunk out of that bitter cup which the Father hath given me, and **have glorified the Father in taking upon me the sins of the world**, in the which I have suffered the will of the Father in all things from the beginning.*[240]

And further he demonstrated his resurrection.

*Arise and come forth unto me, that ye may thrust your hands into my side, and also that ye may feel the prints of the nails in my hands and in my feet, **that ye may know that I am the God of Israel, and the God of the whole earth**, and have been **slain for the sins of the world.***[241]

The Savior verifies that he is the "God of Israel and the God of the whole earth." By feeling the scarred wounds in his hands, feet and side these would know who he was. He also states that he was "slain for the sins of the world" and by so doing has taken "upon me the sins of the world."

Sins of the World

Generally, this expression "sins of the world" is a broader concept than his judgments for individual sin. When the Savior makes judgments on individual sin he is judging for qualifications for the celestial kingdom.

---

[240] 3 Nephi 11:11.

[241] 3 Nephi 11:14.

There are eight (8) scriptures that say that Christ was "slain" or crucified for the "sins of the world."[242] There are nine (9) others that say that Christ will take away, atone for or bear the "sins of the world" or that Christ will take upon him the "sins of the world."[243] To take away, atone for, bear or take upon him the sins of the world means that the Savior is responsible to the Father to provide the resurrection for all and salvation of some kind for all of Father's children according to the plan we accepted before the world was. The one exception is those who become sons of perdition who will receive no salvation. [Read the essay "SONS OF PERDITION" for detailed information]. However, the Savior will be responsible to see that the sons of perdition are placed where there will be no power or influence on the rest of humankind.

A voice declared to Joseph Smith and Sidney Rigdon in their revelation of the kingdoms of glory about the full mission of the Savior.

> *And this is the gospel, the glad tidings, which the voice out of the heavens bore record unto us*
>
> *That he came into the world, even **Jesus, to be crucified for the world, and to bear the sins of the world, and to sanctify the world, and to cleanse it from all unrighteousness;***
>
> ***That through him all might be saved whom the Father had put into his power and made by him;***

---

[242] D&C 76:40–44; 1 Nephi 11:33; Alma 30:26; D&C 21:9; D&C 35:2; D&C 46:13; D&C53:2; D&C 54:1.

[243] 1 Nephi 10:10; Alma 5:48, 7:13, 34:8, 36:17, 42:12; Mosiah 26:23; 3 Nephi 11:11; D&C 76:41.

Who glorifies the Father, and saves all the works of his hands, except those sons of perdition who deny the Son after the Father has revealed him. [244]

This scripture verifies that his atonement is to provide a salvation of some kind for all who are not sons of perdition.

He further states that his purpose is to "sanctify the world and to cleanse it from all unrighteousness." To sanctify the world means to make the earth holy. This earth will be made holy to become a celestial world and the place where those worthy of being in the celestial kingdom will dwell. This cleansing will occur by eliminating all unrighteous beings or things from it. The Savior made a covenant with the church members in which he said

> *And this shall be my covenant with you, ye shall have it for the land of your inheritance, and for the inheritance of your children forever, while the earth shall stand, and **ye shall possess it again in eternity, no more to pass away.*** [245] *Emphasis added.*

This scripture establishes that worthy members of the Church will inhabit the earth in eternity. But those of the telestial and terrestrial kingdoms do not have this promise and will not be on the earth. The earth is only for those worthy of the celestial kingdom. It is well established that the resurrection of all will be the reuniting of our physical bodies with our spirits. Since our resurrected bodies are physical there must be a physical place for these physical bodies to reside. Nothing has been revealed about where these other kingdoms will be. Since the

---

[244] D&C 76:39–43.

[245] D&C 38:20.

Savior has taken upon him the "sins of the world" he is responsible to provide the places where these other kingdoms will be located. Those in the telestial kingdom will be:

> *as innumerable as the stars in the firmament of heaven, or as the sand upon the seashore.* [246]

Whatever planet or place the Savior will provide must be very large to accommodate this group

Forgiveness and Glory

When the final resurrection occurs at the end of the millennium those who are resurrected from hell will be forgiven of their sins for they will have suffered the buffetings of Satan as punishment for their sins. Those who are sons of perdition will not receive forgiveness. Joseph Smith said,

> *All sins shall be forgiven, except the sin against the Holy Ghost; for Jesus, will save* ***all except the sons of perdition.*** [247]

And again, he said,

> *All sins, and all blasphemies, and every transgression, except one, that man can be guilty of, may be forgiven; and* ***there is a salvation for all men, either in this world or the world to come****, who have not committed the unpardonable sin "*[248]

Joseph does not state when that forgiveness is given. The issue is the timing of when forgiveness is given. In this second quote is the expression "in this world or in the world to come"

---

[246] D&C 76:109.

[247] Smith, History of the Church, 6:314.

[248] Smith, History of the Church, 6:313-314.

This world refers to our earth life and the world to come refers to our life in eternity. So forgiveness in this life is given when we repent and are baptized. If we sin in this life and are already baptized then forgiveness is given upon our repentance in this life.

For those who are committed to the control of Satan then forgiveness is given when they are resurrected and released from the control of Satan. At that time they will have suffered for their own sins and will be forgiven. At some point all but the sons of perdition will be forgiven. That forgiveness allows them to receive a salvation either in the celestial, terrestrial or telestial kingdoms in accordance with the plan given to us. It should be noted that our wayward children will be with us in the celestial kingdom but they have to pay for their own sins.

When we are consigned to one of these kingdoms our bodies will be given a glory commensurate with the kingdom to which we are consigned. Consider these quotes from Doctrine and Covenants and Joseph Smith,

> These are they **whose bodies are celestial**, whose glory is that of the sun, even the glory of God, the highest of all, whose glory the sun of the firmament is written of as being typical.[249]

> Wherefore, they are **bodies terrestrial**, and not bodies celestial, **and differ in glory** as the moon differs from the sun.[250]

> And again, we saw the glory of the telestial, which glory is that of the lesser, even as the glory of the stars

---

[249] D&C 76:70.

[250] D&C 76:78.

differs from that of the glory of the moon in the firmament.[251]

And Joseph said,

Some dwell in higher glory than others. [252]

When comparing the three kingdoms we recognize that all who have salvation will have a glory albeit at different levels. However, the sons of perdition will not be in any of these kingdoms and hence will have no glory. They will be in darkness.

When Joseph Smith saw the Father and Savior he saw a light brighter than the sun emanating from them. It appears that our bodies may radiate this glory. Just what this glory may be is not known definitively but might relate to the level of light our spirits radiate following our resurrection.

Kingdoms, Dominions and Glory

During the final preparations for the Savior to complete his atonement he said to his apostles,

In my Father's house are many mansions: if it were not so, I would have told you. I go to prepare a place for you.[253]

Joseph in explaining this scripture said,

My text is on the resurrection of the dead, which you will find in the 14th chapter of John- 'In my Father's house are many mansions.' It should be- 'In my

---

[251] D&C 76:81.

[252] Smith, History of the Church, 6:366.

[253] John `14:2.

Father's kingdom are many kingdoms,' in order that ye may be heirs of God and joint-heirs with me.

Here Joseph is saying that the Savior's statement is referring to kingdoms in the highest degree of the celestial kingdom. A kingdom is ruled by a king. Those who inherit the highest degree in the celestial kingdom will have a kingdom and are priests/priestesses and kings/queens[254] and will dwell in the presence of the Father and Christ[255]. There are many kingdoms in the celestial kingdom each ruled by a king.

These are equal in power, might and dominion[256]. Notice that glory is not mentioned in this list. The glory of individuals in the celestial kingdom will be different but will grow as worlds are created and inhabited. Their glory grows just as the glory of our Father in Heaven grows when some of his children qualify to be with him in the celestial kingdom.

Joseph further said this about mansions:

*There are mansions for those who obey a celestial law, and **there are other mansions for those who come short of the law, every man in his own order.*** [257]

The question is: "What are these mansions of which Joseph spoke?" According to Section 76 all individuals in the terrestrial and telestial kingdoms will have a "dominion."[258] The term dominion as defined in dictionaries refers to ruling

---

[254] D&C 76:56.

[255] D&C 76:62.

[256] D&C 76:95

[257] Smith, History of the Church, 6:365.

[258] D&C 76:95,91, 111.

power, authority or control. Joseph was referring to these dominions as mansions. Each person will have a mansion or dominion "in his own order." These scriptures indicate that each person will have a glory related to that mansion.

How does glory relate to these dominions? A scripture relating to telestial inhabitants gives us a clue to this question. Each person in the telestial kingdom will have his own dominion. The scriptures record the following quote of those in the telestial kingdom:

> *And the glory of the telestial is one, even as the glory of the stars is one;* ***for as one star differs from another star in glory, even so differs one from another in glory in the telestial world.*** [259]

And continuing about those in the telestial kingdom,

> *For they shall be judged according to their works, and every man shall receive according to his own works,* ***his own dominion, in the mansions which are prepared***[260]

This states that each person will have a dominion and a glory and this will be dependent on the good works they perform in mortality. All souls are not equal in the telestial kingdom. This principle is often overlooked. For example, we would expect there would be a big difference between King David should he inherit the telestial kingdom and a random killer who takes life without justification. [Read the section "Murder – Shedding Innocent Blood" in the essay SONS OF PERDITION for more information on King David]. David having done much good

---

[259] D&C 76:98.

[260] D&C 76;111.

prior to his fall of having murdered Uriah will have a brighter glory than a random murderer. Both have committed murder without justification but we know of the great good that David accomplished prior to his murder.

A further note of those in the telestial kingdom is:

> *And **they shall be servants of the Most High**; but where God and Christ dwell they cannot come, worlds without end.* [261]

Being a servant during mortality is far different than being a servant to the Father in eternity which will never change. They will always be servants doing the Father's bidding.

What about those in the terrestrial kingdom? Joseph Smith and Sidney Rigdon saw those in the terrestrial or middle kingdom.

> *we saw the glory of the terrestrial which excels in all things the glory of the telestial, even in glory, and in power, and in might, and in dominion.* "[262]

Those in the terrestrial kingdom have a higher status but are judged on the same basis, being good people and doing good works. It would seem that they would differ in their works of righteousness just like those in the telestial kingdom. Each person's works will be different. It would seem that there would be a difference in glory and dominion for those in the terrestrial kingdom just like those in the telestial kingdom. This is suggested by Joseph when he said each person would have a mansion *"each in his own order."*

---

[261] D&C 76:112.

[262] D&C 76:91.

There is one other thing that should be mentioned about those in the terrestrial kingdom. It is that the Savior will visit those in the terrestrial kingdom.

These are they who receive of the presence of the Son, but not of the fulness of the Father. [263]

However, the administration of the terrestrial will be done by angels appointed to do that function, undoubtedly by directions coming ultimately from the Savior.[264]

The Lord said this about kingdoms:

All kingdoms have a law given;

And there are many kingdoms; for there is no space in the which there is no kingdom; and there is no kingdom in which there is no space, either a greater or a lesser kingdom.

And unto every kingdom is given a law; and unto every law there are certain bounds also and conditions. [265]

Every individual except the sons of perdition will have a dominion, kingdom or mansion of some kind following the final judgment.

JOSEPH F. SMITH REVELATION

President Smith received a revelation on how the gospel was preached to those in the world of spirits or to the dead. Remember that the world of spirits is near us. [Read the

---

[263] D&C 76:77.

[264] D&C 76:86-88.

[265] D&C 88:36-38.

section "World of Spirits" in the essay "JUDGMENTS at MORTAL DEATH"].

Immediately following the Savior's death his spirit went to the world of spirits and there he met and taught the prophets and righteous people. President Smith recorded,

*And there were gathered together in one place an innumerable company of the spirits of the **just, who had been faithful in the testimony of Jesus while they lived in mortality**.*[266]

*While this vast multitude waited and conversed, rejoicing in the hour of their deliverance from the chains of death, the Son of God appeared, declaring liberty to the captives **who had been faithful**.*[267]

President Smith identifies many of the prophets in attendance at the Savior's arrival. He identified all the prophets of the Old Testament and the deceased prophets in the Book of Mormon. Undoubtedly there were prophets from the descendants of those that were lead from the Tower of Babel under the leadership of Jared and his brother although not specifically mentioned

Just Men Made Perfect

Also in attendance were just men made perfect. It should be noted that Joseph Smith identified Gabriel as Noah[268]. President Smith specifically mentions that Noah[269] and Elias[270]

---

[266] D&C 138:12.

[267] D&C 138:18.

[268] Smith, History of the Church, 3:385.

[269] D&C 138:41.

were two of those in attendance at the Savior's coming to the world of spirits. They were just men made perfect and were in the presence of God prior to the Savior visiting the world of spirits. Joseph Smith said,

> *There are **two kinds of beings in heaven**-viz., angels, who are resurrected personages, having bodies of flesh and bones. ... 2nd. The spirits of just men made perfect- they who are not resurrected, but inherit the same glory.*[271]

What are the qualifications of a person to be a "just man made perfect"? The Lord said about those who inherit the celestial kingdom

> *These are they who are just men made perfect through Jesus the mediator of the new covenant, who wrought out this perfect atonement **through the shedding of his own blood**.* [272]

The martyred prophets and teachers who were martyred as recorded in the Old and New Testaments are just men made perfect. These will be with the Father until they are resurrected. They are not the only ones who will become just men made perfect. Righteous men who live perfect lives will also become just men made perfect. Noah also known as Gabriel and Elias are such men. Noah was never martyred yet Noah or Gabriel appeared to Mary to announce that she would bear the Son of God.

---

[270] D&C 138:45.

[271] Smith, History of the Church, 5:267.

[272] D&C 76:69.

*And in the sixth month the **angel Gabriel was sent
from God** unto a city of Galilee, named Nazareth,*

*To a virgin espoused to a man whose name was
Joseph, of the house of David; and the virgin's name
was Mary. "*[273]

Gabriel then announced that Mary would bear the Son of God
and told her of her mission. He had to have been sent from the
presence of God to deliver this message which Mary accepted.
Noah fits the description that Joseph Smith described and was
a just spirit made perfect who came from the presence of God.
He had no body of flesh and bones when he made this
announcement to Mary. No one from this world had yet been
resurrected.

Although the angel that appeared to Zacharias, the father of
John the Baptist, is recorded in Luke as Gabriel, the Lord
states in a latter-day revelation that it was the prophet Elias
who lived at the time of Abraham that appeared to Zacharias
and not Gabriel. [274] However, the messenger said that he stood

*in the presence of God; and am sent to speak unto
thee, and to shew thee these glad tidings"* [275]

Though the identity of the messenger was incorrect there is no
reason to doubt that the messenger came from the presence of
God to deliver such an important message. This supports the
understanding that Elias was the spirit of a just man made
perfect and was in the presence of God. We have no record as
to whether he was martyred or not.

---

[273] Luke 1:26-27.

[274] D&C 27::6-7.

[275] Luke 1:19.

At the time that the Savior visited the world of spirits Noah, Elias and martyred men including Stephen[276], probably the first martyr following Christ, had to have come from the presence of God to this world of spirits to greet the Savior when he came.

Savior's Teaching and Organization
The Savior preached to these faithful the important fundamental doctrines which included

> *the everlasting gospel, the doctrine of the resurrection and the redemption of humankind from the fall, and from individual sins on conditions of repentance.*[277]

In addition to the teachings the Savior presented he gave these faithful spirits the power to be resurrected after he left the world of spirits.

> *These the Lord taught, and **gave them power to come forth**, after his resurrection from the dead, to enter into his Father's kingdom, there to be crowned with immortality and eternal life"*[278]

The "power to come forth" was the power to be resurrected. When the Savior left the group to complete his own resurrection, many others exercised this power of resurrection. Matthew wrote,

> *The graves were opened; and many bodies of the saints which slept arose,*

---

[276] Acts 7:55-60.

[277] D&C 138:18-19.

[278] D&C 138:51.

171

And came out of the graves after his resurrection, and went into the holy city, and appeared unto many. [279]

The Savior organized the faithful spirits to preach the gospel in the world of spirits. President Smith recorded,

*But behold, from among the righteous, he **organized his forces** and **appointed messengers**, **clothed with power and authority**, and **commissioned them to go forth** and carry the light of the gospel to them that were in darkness, even to all the spirits of men; and thus was the gospel preached to the dead.* [280]

Since these spirits who were appointed messengers were faithful during their mortality they would have been ordained to the priesthood during mortality and would have the inherent authority to perform their commission but it required one in authority to designate or call them to perform this commission. It is by the priesthood that the gospel is taught in the world of spirits and exercised when the resurrection occurs. Remember that when vicarious ordinances are performed, ordination to the Melchizedek Priesthood for men follows baptism & confirmation.

President Smith records that the Savior "organized his forces." This means that someone was placed in authority to preside over the work of proselyting in the world of spirits. There are many and various groups in the world of spirits that are entitled to hear the truth and to accept it if they choose. Undoubtedly some priesthood holders were chosen to administer the proselyting activities associated with each of

---

[279] Matthew 27:52-53.

[280] D&C 138:30.

172

these groups. Then there were those who did the actual proselyting. New faithful spirits arrive in the world of spirits to add to the number of commissioned elders to preach the gospel.

> *I beheld that the faithful elders of this dispensation, when they depart from mortal life, continue their labors in the preaching of the gospel of repentance and redemption, through the sacrifice of the Only Begotten Son of God, **among those who are in darkness and under the bondage of sin** in the great world of the spirits of the dead.* [281]

The commissioned elders do not preach to everyone in the world of spirits. The specific groups to whom they preach are identified in the following verses:

> *And the chosen messengers went forth to declare the acceptable day of the Lord and proclaim liberty to the captives who were bound, even unto all who would repent of their sins and receive the gospel.*

> *Thus was **the gospel preached to those who had died in their sins, without a knowledge of the truth, or in transgression, having rejected the prophets.***

> *These were taught faith in God, repentance from sin, vicarious baptism for the remission of sins, the gift of the Holy Ghost by the laying on of hands,*

> *And all other principles of the gospel that were necessary for them to know in order to qualify themselves that they might be judged according to men in the flesh, but live according to God in the spirit.* [282]

---

[281] D&C 138:57.

The two groups to whom the gospel is taught are

> those who "died in their sins without a knowledge of the truth"
> those who were "in transgression having rejected the prophets"

The Wicked

The wicked is the group in the world of spirits that is not included in the description just quoted above. They do not have the opportunity to repent in the world of spirits. These are they who had the gospel teachings and willfully disobeyed them in mortality. Nephi recorded Jacob's teachings about this group of people.

> *But wo unto **him that has the law given, yea, that has all the commandments of God, like unto us, and that transgresseth them**, and that wasteth the days of his probation, for awful is his state!*[283]

Jacob made this statement about 50 years after Lehi first left Jerusalem and not long after the death of Lehi. All of the people were descendants of Lehi or Ishmael. Following Lehi's death and Nephi's separation from his brothers Nephi kept the brass plates of Laban containing the writings of the previous prophets. Nephi and Jacob were prophets. The Nephites had the records and prophets. This people certainly had the "law" as described in the quote above. The law was certainly available to the Nephite generations following this quote.

Alma and Amulek taught the poor among the Zoramites. Amulek said,

---

[282] D&C 138:31-35.

[283] 2 Nephi 9:27.

For behold, if ye have procrastinated the day of your
repentance even until death, behold, <u>ye have become</u>
<u>subjected to the spirit of the devil, and he doth seal you</u>
<u>his</u> ; therefore, **the Spirit of the Lord hath withdrawn**
from you, and hath no place in you, and the devil
hath all power over you; and this is the final state of
the wicked.[284]

Abinadi taught King Noah and his priests,

But behold, and fear, and tremble before God, for ye
ought to tremble; **for the Lord redeemeth none such**
that rebel against him and die in their sins; yea, even
all those that have perished in their sins ever since
the world began, **<u>that have wilfully rebelled against</u>**
<u>God, that have known the commandments of God,</u>
<u>and would not keep them; these are they that have no</u>
<u>part in the first resurrection.</u>

Therefore ought ye not to tremble? For salvation
cometh to none such; for the Lord hath redeemed none
such; yea, neither can the Lord redeem such; for he
cannot deny himself; for he cannot deny justice when it
has its claim.[285]

Those who have no part in the first resurrection are those who
are committed to hell suffering the buffetings of Satan and his
host. There is no repentance available to them for they had
their opportunity to repent in mortality. These will be
resurrected at the time of the final judgment.

The Rebellious

---

[284] Alma 34:35.

[285] Mosiah 15:26-27.

President Smith saw that the rebellious was one of the groups to whom the gospel would be preached. They are described as those who were *"in transgression, having rejected the prophets."*

President Smith saw in his vision the wicked and the rebellious together. He wrote,

> *But unto the **wicked** he did not go, and among the ungodly and the unrepentant who had defiled themselves while in the flesh, his voice was not raised;*
>
> *Neither did the **rebellious** who rejected the testimonies and the warnings of the ancient prophets behold his presence, nor look upon his face.*

Where these were, darkness reigned, *but among the righteous there was peace;* [286]

This scripture identifies two groups. The first group is the wicked who had the teachings and died in their sins and has already been discussed. The second group is the rebellious who rejected the message of the prophets. Both groups were in darkness together.

The rebellious had an opportunity to receive the gospel in mortality by authorized messengers from God. They are therefore responsible for their sins. The authorized representatives who hold the priesthood were described by President Smith as "ancient prophets" who preached to them and bore testimony of the Savior but they did not receive it.

Some of the rebellious were identified as having lived in the days of Noah. Noah did attempt to teach the people but they

[286] D&C 138:20-22.

did not receive his message.[287] When the floods came he and his family were the only ones that had a temporal salvation.[288] All other died in the flood.

It seems that the law which the Nephites had was not had among these people because they are not classified in the same group as the wicked. Enoch and his people had been taken from the earth. This apparently left few if any righteous people behind. With Noah preaching to them they then became responsible for their sins and perished in the flood.

However, the rebellious had the gospel preached to them. They will be able to repent and receive the testimony of Jesus Christ but will not have the full blessings of the gospel. Joseph Smith and Sidney Rigdon saw in vision that those who will inherit the terrestrial kingdom are the rebellious.

> *And also they who are the spirits of men kept in prison, whom the Son visited, and preached the gospel unto them, that they might be judged according to men in the flesh;*
>
> *Who received not the testimony of Jesus in the flesh, but afterwards received it.[289]*

The rebellious who receive the testimony of Jesus in the world of spirits are able to improve their eternal destiny from being consigned to the telestial kingdom to being consigned to the terrestrial kingdom conditioned upon their repentance in the world of spirits.

---

[287] Moses 7:16, 23-24.

[288] Moses 7:23-43.

[289] D&C 76:73-74.

No Knowledge of Truth

President Smith recorded an interesting statement

> *Thus was **the gospel preached to those who had died in their sins, without a knowledge of the truth,***

It identifies a group of people who have no "*knowledge of the truth*" meaning knowledge of God, Jesus Christ or his atonement. Then it identifies "their sins". It seems a little odd in the lexicon. Obvious it is referring to conduct which we identify as sins, in which they have participated. The key element that is important is that they had no knowledge.

Paul *said,*

> *sin is not imputed when there is no law.*[290]

It seems obvious the justice could not be delivered to those who do not know what their conduct represented. They can't be held accountable for something that they did not know or been taught. Nephi wrote of Jacob's teachings

> *Wherefore, he has given a law; and **where there is no law given there is no punishment; and where there is no punishment there is no condemnation; and where there is no condemnation the mercies of the Holy One of Israel have claim upon them, because of the atonement**; for they are delivered by the power of him.*

> *For the **atonement satisfieth the demands of his justice** upon all those who have not the law given to them, that **they are delivered from** that awful monster, **death and hell, and the devil, and the lake of fire and brimstone**, which is endless torment; and **they are***

[290] Romans 5:13, 4:15.

restored to that God who gave them breath, which is the Holy One of Israel.[291]

This states that when they die they will not be subject to Satan and his buffeting and control. [See the underlined words]. It is difficult to describe their presence in the world of spirits. They would not be in darkness because they would not be subject to Satan.

It also states that they will be delivered from the *"lake of fire and brimstone."* Satan does not inflict this lake of fire and brimstone or fire. [Review the section "Everlasting Fire" in the essay "JUDGMENTS at MORTAL DEATH"]. Everlasting fire is created in the mind of man and is the torment of disappointment knowing they could have had a better eternal kingdom than what they earned. Since they had no knowledge of the truth in mortality they have nothing to compare that would create disappointment. Nor can their conscience be pricked to make that comparison.

The above quote also states that they will be delivered from "death". This death is not the death of the body which is suffered by all. It is spiritual death. In further explaining this Jacob stated in the above quote

> *they are restored to that God who gave them breath, which is the Holy One of Israel.*

Prior to this earth life we all knew that Jesus Christ would be the Savior of the world and would provide the atonement. Because of his status the Savior gave us all breath in the sense of being resurrected. The Savior will visit and minister to

---

[291] 2 Nephi 9:25–26; Moroni 8:22.

those in the terrestrial kingdom. Joseph and Sidney Rigdon saw a vision of those in the terrestrial kingdom,

> *Behold, these are they who died without law;*

And,

> *These are they **who receive of the presence of the Son**, but not of the fulness of the Father.*
>
> *Wherefore, they are bodies terrestrial.* [292]

Those without law have the opportunity to accept the gospel teachings. If they accept the teachings they are able to receive the full blessings of the celestial kingdom. If they do not accept the teachings they are assured of being in the terrestrial kingdom and to see and know the Savior.

The Savior said of those without law.

> *And then shall the heathen nations be redeemed, and they that knew no law shall have part in the first resurrection; and it shall be tolerable for them.*[293]

All of these will be resurrected prior to the final judgment and the resurrection of those in hell.

---

[292] D&C 76:72, 77-78.

[293] D&C 45:54.

----- JUDGMENTS -----

This book has already addressed some judgments and inferred judgments by describing their results. Some of these are

> ➤ Individual sins – the Savior takes upon him our individual sins when we repent and he gives us forgiveness. When he forgives us he does not remembers those sins.
>
> ➤ Temple marriage by his priesthood – This is required along with enduring to the end by repenting of all our sins. Then we are made clean and held guiltless before the Father. These inherit the highest degree in the celestial kingdom and can have their posterity (clearly their children) probably to the third or fourth generation with us in the celestial kingdom.
>
> ➤ Those without law – These ae guaranteed to be in the terrestrial kingdom but may be in the celestial kingdom.
>
> ➤ Little children – They do not suffer in hell. They will be in the celestial kingdom but in is unknown which degree.
>
> ➤ Those who know the of Jesus Christ and his gospel and die in their sins cannot repent in the world of spirits.

This collection of essays describes the judgments made by the Savior while mortals still live and at their death. Sons of perdition and their qualification are covered in this section.

CHRIST'S JUDGMENTS in MORTALITY

Most of us are probably knowledgeable about many judgments that humankind experiences in this mortal existence. The Savior actually tells us of the kinds of judgments that he gives in our mortal state. He spoke of using the descendants of Laman and Lemuel as a scourge to keep the Nephites in remembrance of the Savior.

> *And the Lord God said unto me: They* (the descendants of Laman and Lemuel) ***shall be a scourge unto thy seed**, to stir them up in remembrance of me; and inasmuch as they will not remember me, and hearken unto my words, they shall scourge them even unto destruction.* [294]

The Lord gave us some insight into some of the other judgments he takes during our mortality.

> *Hearken, O ye people, and open your hearts and give ear from afar; and listen, you that call yourselves the people of the Lord, and hear the word of the Lord and his will concerning you.*
>
> *Yea, verily, I say, hear the word of him whose anger is kindled against the wicked and rebellious;*
>
> ***Who willeth to take even them whom he will take, and preserveth in life them whom he will preserve;***
>
> ***Who buildeth up at his own will and pleasure; and destroyeth when he pleases, and is able to cast the soul down to hell.***
>
> *Behold, I, the Lord, utter my voice, and it shall be obeyed.* [295]

The following are judgments that he described.

1. He takes life as he wills
2. He preserves life as he wills

---

[294] 2 Nephi 5:25.

[295] D&C 63:1-5.

3. He builds as he pleases
4. He destroys as he pleases
5. He is able to cast the soul down to hell

He declares that his word "*will be obeyed*".

Taking and Preserving Life

When it comes to taking life and preserving life there are two excellent examples. One is dealing with Abraham and the other concerns the wives and children of husbands who were converts to Alma's teachings and who were chased out of Ammonihah.

The Priests of the god of Elkenah and Pharaoh did "violence" on Abraham and took him as a human sacrifice to these false gods. Undoubtedly this was to silence Abraham. As he was about to be sacrificed he called upon God to preserve his life. Jehovah responded by causing his bands to be loosened and the priests of the false gods to be killed. Abraham's life was preserved because of his righteousness.[296] At the time Abraham's life was preserved Jehovah told Abraham:

> *As it was with Noah so shall it be with thee; but through thy ministry my name shall be known in the earth forever, for I am thy God"*[297].

Abraham was the father of the Jewish people through his son Isaac and the father of the Arab people through his son Ishmael.

The lives of the righteous are not always preserved. In the Book of Mormon. The wives and children of Ammonihah converts were burned along with their records. Alma and

---

[296] Abraham 1:10-20.

[297] Abraham 1:19.

Amulek had preached to the people of Ammonihah.[298] Many men agreed with their message including Zeezrom. These men including Zeezrom were cast out of Ammonihah and men were sent to cast stones at them.[299] Then the wicked people of Ammonihah took the wives and children of the convert husbands who believed or had taught their families to believe Alma's and Amulek's message.[300] They cast them into a fire along with their records. Amulek wanted to use priesthood power to save the lives of the wives and children but Alma felt constrained. For Alma said,

> *The Spirit constraineth me that I must not stretch forth mine hand;* **for behold the Lord receiveth them up unto himself, in glory; and he doth suffer that they may do this thing,** *or that the* <u>people may do this thing unto them, according to the hardness of their hearts, that the judgments which he shall exercise upon them in his wrath may be just; and the blood of the innocent shall stand as a witness against them,</u> *yea, and cry mightily against them at the last day.*[301]

The lives of the righteous were taken but they were received unto God with glory. The leaders of the people of Ammonihah continued to mock and batter Alma and Amulek until Alma cried for release from these wicked men. In response to Alma's plea the walls crumbled and the leaders were killed.[302] Alma

---

[298] Alma Ch 9-14.

[299299] Alma 14:7.

[300] Alma 14:8.

[301] Alma 14:11.

[302] Alma 14:14-27.

and Amulek walked out of the prison. The Lamanite armies invaded Ammonihah killing all of the wicked inhabitants.[303]

The Lord allowed the martyrdom of the women and children that his judgments against the people of Ammonihah would be just. The lives of these innocent people would stand "*against them at the last day*" which is the final judgment that will occur. It is very likely that the people of Ammonihah became sons of perdition by this act of taking innocent lives. [See the section "Murder – Shedding Innocent Blood" in the essay "SONS OF PERDITION"]

When Samuel, the Lamanite, preached from the walls of Zarahemla he said this,

> *Yea, wo unto this great <u>city of Zarahemla</u>; for behold,* ***it is because of those who are righteous that it is saved;*** *yea, wo unto this great city, for I perceive, saith the Lord, that there are many, yea, even the more part of this great city, that will harden their hearts against me, saith the Lord.*
>
> *But blessed are they who will repent, for them will I spare. But behold,* ***if it were not for the righteous who are in this great city, behold, I would cause that fire should come down out of heaven and destroy it.*** [304]

This is an example of the Lord sparing the righteous even though he would like to send down fire from heaven to destroy the wicked intermingled among them. The Lord takes and preserves lives of individuals as he will.

---

[303] Alma 16:2-3.

[304] Helaman 13:12-13.

Building

The most obvious example of building by the Lord is to look at the Church today and the growth from its early days. Its influence is relative great when compared to the size of the world.

When the Church was first organized the headquarters were in Fayette, New York. Due to persecution the Lord commanded Joseph by revelation[305] in December 1830 to gather to Kirtland, Ohio. In January 1831 Joseph and Emma moved to Kirtland, Ohio. The first recorded revelation[306] received there was on 4 February 1831. It was in Kirtland that the Church had it greatest early growth. While the Church headquarters was there many revelations were received and the Church structure was organized.

The following list of events was taken from studies at Brigham Young University. [307]

Some 73 revelations were received in Kirtland and nearby areas

> ➤ Zion was identified as Independence, Missouri to be the gathering place for the Saints. Church leaders were called to reside and preside in Zion
> ➤ Temple built and Priesthood Keys restored by Elias, Moses and Elijah.
> ➤ Endowment partially given to a few
> ➤ Church Priesthood Quorums were established
>> • First Presidency

---

[305] D&C 37.

[306] D&C 38.

[307] Backman, Regional Studies in Latter-day Saint history, 90-99.

- Apostles
- 70 apostles[308] with 7 who presided
- Bishoprics in Kirtland and Zion
- Elders
- Priests
- Teachers
- Deacons

➢ Many were called to serve proselyting missions in many areas including Canada
➢ Revelations and organizations established to hold things "in common"
➢ In November 1831 a decision to publish the revelations in a book form and to organize the "Literary Firm" as the publishing arm of the Church to operate. In 1832 a Church printing office established in Zion by W. W. Phelps, a printer and editor by trade
  - Printing press purchased in Cincinnati and installed
  - Started printing the "Evening and Morning Star" Several revelations were published in the Star
  - Copyright for the book secured in February 1833
  - Book of Commandments was published but not bound (contained errors). In July 1833, the printing press was destroyed by mob and also destroyed most of the copies of the Book of Commandments

---

[308] Used here refers to Seventies.

- The Literary Firm moved to Kirtland and a new Church printing office established. The Book of Commandments was edited, published and presented to the various quorums and general membership of the Church for acceptance and accepted

It is amazing that the organizing, the teaching of principles and establishing so many fundamental values could have occurred in so short a time.

Saving Some

In a revelation to the Elders at Kirtland the Lord said,

> *I will not that my servant Frederick G. Williams should sell his farm, for I, the Lord, will to retain a strong hold in the land of Kirtland, for the space of five years, **in the which I will not overthrow the wicked, that thereby I may save some.**[309]*

With regard to the unrighteous in Kirtland the Lord had this to say:

> *Wherefore, I, the Lord, am not pleased with those among you who have sought after signs and wonders for faith, and not for the good of men unto my glory.*
>
> ***Nevertheless, I give commandments, and many have turned away from my commandments and have not kept them.***
>
> *There were among you adulterers and adulteresses; some of whom have turned away from you, and others remain with you that hereafter shall be revealed.*[310]

---

[309] D&C 64:20-21.

During this period there were some who apostatized and tried to do harm to Church leaders or interfere with the progress of the Church. The Lord allowed this by refraining from overthrowing the wicked in Kirtland while he protected the righteous as he saw fit. He allowed the saints and the wicked to live together.

The Savior tried to build Zion in Jackson County Missouri but was unsuccessful because the Saints were not obedient. The Saints driven out of Jackson County, Missouri, settled in neighboring counties. Of this the Lord said:

> *I, the Lord, have suffered the affliction to come upon them, wherewith they have been afflicted, in consequence of their transgressions;[311]*
>
> *Behold, I say unto you, there were jarrings, and contentions, and envyings, and strifes, and lustful and covetous desires among them; therefore by these things they polluted their inheritances.*
>
> *They were slow to hearken unto the voice of the Lord their God; therefore, the Lord their God is slow to hearken unto their prayers, to answer them in the day of their trouble[312]*

The Lord did not give up on these Saints for he said:

> *Verily I say unto you, notwithstanding their sins, my bowels are filled with compassion towards them.* **I will**

---

[310] D&C 63:12-14.

[311] D&C 101:2.

[312] D&C 101:6-7.

***not utterly cast them off; and in the day of wrath I
will remember mercy.***[313]

*Yet I will own them, and they shall be mine in that day
when I shall come to make up my jewels.*

*Therefore, they must needs be chastened and tried,
even as Abraham, who was commanded to offer up his
only son.*

*For all those who will not endure chastening, but deny
me, cannot be sanctified.*[314]

Even though these saints endured hardship they will be
"owned" by the Savior if they endure. The expulsion from
Jackson County was followed by the famous Missouri State
extermination order of 27 Oct 1838[315] in which all the Saints
were ordered driven from the state. These same principles
quoted above apply to the saints subjected to both expulsion
events.

The prophet Samuel quoted an angel[316] concerning the city of
Zarahemla when he said:

*Yea, wo unto this great city of Zarahemla; for behold,
**it is because of those who are righteous that it is
saved**; yea, wo unto this great city, for I perceive, saith
the Lord, that there are many, yea, even the more part
of this great city, that will harden their hearts against
me, saith the Lord.*

---

[313] D&C 101:9.

[314] D&C 101:3-5.

[315] Smith, History of the Church, 3:178.

[316] Helaman 13:6-8.

But blessed are they who will repent, for them will I spare. But behold, if it were not for the righteous who are in this great city, behold, I would cause that fire should come down out of heaven and destroy it.

But behold, it is for the righteous' sake that it is spared. [317]

The Lord is very concerned about his people and does look after them!

Destroying

Because the Missourians drove the Saints from Missouri without justification and with vicious intent they were under the condemnation of the Lord. Joseph prophesied of the retribution of the Lord against the nation.

> *And now I am prepared to say by the authority of Jesus Christ, that not many years shall pass away before the United States shall present such a scene of bloodshed as has not a parallel in the history of our nation; pestilence, hail, famine, and earthquake will sweep the wicked of this generation from off the face of the land,* [318]

Elder Brigham H. Roberts best describes the results of this condemnation at the Church Conference in 1907.

> *In the year 1864, Sterling Price, (the man who riveted the shackles upon the limbs of Joseph Smith, Hyrum Smith, Parley P. Pratt, and Sidney Rigdon, in Richmond prison, Ray county, Missouri), at the head of twelve thousand men, entered the state of Missouri in*

---

[317] Helaman 13:12-14.

[318] Smith, History of the Church, 1:316.

the southeast borders of it, and cut a zigzag swath of destruction through the state, for a distance of more than fourteen hundred miles. During that time he fought 43 battles and skirmishes; he destroyed more than ten millions of dollars in property, and chiefly among his own friends. His raid extended through the very counties formerly inhabited by the Saints, from thence he made his escape into the state of Kansas. In 1863, western Missouri having been a hot-bed of treason, rebellion, and guerilla warfare where southern sympathizers could recruit their horses and provisions, General Thomas Ewing, then in command at St. Louis, determined to break up these conditions, and hence issued his celebrated "Military Order No. 11," admitted to be one of the most drastic military orders ever issued in this or any other country, when you take into account the manner in which it was executed. It gave the people of named localities fifteen days to move from their homes, and designated the places to which they might go. The orders were most drastically executed. The scenes of suffering Passed through by the Latter-day Saints in 1833 were enacted on a larger scale. Houses were burned, the furniture was stacked in the front yards and burned before the eyes of the owners; old age was not respected; men and women were shot down in cold blood. Everywhere desolation reigned, and the roads were thronged with the people escaping from the cruel execution of this order.

It was from this incident that G. E. Bingham, the noted artist, painted from scenes enacted in Jackson county, Missouri, his celebrated painting, now in the Capitol at Washington, entitled "Civil War,' which he "dedicated to the lovers of civil liberty.' In that painting you may see the aged patriarch, the tender maiden, the black slave, the weeping matron, the startled children leaving the grand old mansion, of southern style, in flames, and everywhere the chimneys of neighboring houses standing as monuments of the abounding desolation.

This brings to my remembrance a circumstance connected with the Prophet Joseph Smith and General Doniphan. General Doniphan was the friend of Joseph Smith; a friend who, on one occasion, nobly stood out against the execution of a mob-militia court-martial order-and some of those who took Dart(part) in the court-martial, by the way, were ministers, or so-called ministers, of the Lord Jesus Christ. This court-martial condemned the Prophet Joseph to be shot in the public square of Far West, in the presence of his people.

On one occasion, when General Doniphan was in consultation with the Prophet, a Missourian came in to settle a bill with Doniphan, and offered in settlement of his bill some lands in Jackson county, and Doniphan told him he would think of it. Then the Prophet said to Doniphan: **'Doniphan, I advise you not to take that Jackson county land in payment of that debt; God's wrath hangs over Jackson county; God's people have been ruthlessly driven from it, and you will live to see the day when it will be visited by fire and sword; the Lord of Hosts will sweep it with the besom of destruction; the fields and farms and houses will be destroyed, and only the chimneys will be left to mark the desolation.'**

193

This was uttered in 1834. In 1863, L. M. Lawson, a man of standing in the commercial world, in the state of New York, a brother-in-law to General Doniphan, visited him. Those of you who are acquainted with Doniphan's history know that although he was a veteran soldier in the Mexican war, he took no part in the Civil War, only as a sorrowful spectator. With his brother-in-law, Mr. Lawson, he rode out into Jackson county, on the occasion of the visit above mentioned, and coming upon the crest of a hill, and seeing nothing but the chimneys of houses standing for miles around them, the monuments of once splendid homes, General Doniphan related the circumstance of the prophecy of Joseph Smith and said that he was much impressed by what the "Mormon" Prophet had told him.[319]

Missouri became desolate during the Civil War because of their actions against the Saints.

When Joshua led the children of Israel into the land promised to Abraham and his descendants. God commanded the area inhabitants destroyed by the Israelites. Everything was to be destroyed including the people and all animals, except the silver, gold and vessels of brass and iron, which were to be taken for the "*treasury for the Lord.*" The People were to keep nothing personal for themselves. Jericho was the first and is an example.

And ye, in any wise keep yourselves from the accursed thing, lest ye make yourselves accursed, when ye take of the accursed thing, and make the camp of Israel a curse, and trouble it.

---

[319] Roberts, Church Conference Report, October 1907, 124.

But all the silver, and gold, and vessels of brass and iron, are consecrated unto the Lord: they shall come into the treasury of the Lord.

So the people shouted when the priests blew with the trumpets: and it came to pass, when the people heard the sound of the trumpet, and the people shouted with a great shout, that the wall fell down flat, so that the people went up into the city, every man straight before him, and they took the city.

And they utterly destroyed all that was in the city, both man and woman, young and old, and ox, and sheep, and ass, with the edge of the sword. [320]

This is bothersome to some. Why would the Lord command the Israelites to kill all of the people and destroy everything?

Nephi had this to say to his rebellious brothers prior to their building their ship to come to the Promised Land. They complained about building a ship and going to some other land. Nephi reviewed the Israelites leaving Egypt by Moses as an example of what they were doing. He spoke of the Israelites conquering and destroying the inhabitants of the land promised to Abraham, Isaac and Jacob.

Behold, the Lord esteemeth all flesh in one; he that is righteous is favored of God. But behold, this people [the inhabitants whom Israel conquered] *had rejected every word of God, and they were ripe in iniquity; and the **fulness of the <u>wrath of God</u> was upon them**; and the Lord did curse the land against them, and bless it unto our fathers; **yea, he did curse it against them***

---

[320] Joshua 6:18-21.

unto their destruction, and he did bless it unto our fathers unto their obtaining power over it.[321]

What Nephi is saying here is that the wicked inhabitants of the land which was promised to Abraham Isaac and Jacob were so wicked that in the eyes of the Lord they needed to be destroyed. The Lord used the Israelites to destroy them. Why the Lord chose Israel to destroy them rather than some other means is not known. One plausible explanation is that the Lord desired to establish Israel as a strong righteous nation in the absence of wicked neighbors that would influence Israel.

Subsequent to Jericho, Joshua sent an army to destroy the people of Ai. However, Ai defeated that army. Joshua humbled himself and petitioned the Lord, who told him that at Jericho some had kept some of the contraband contrary to God's command. He commanded Joshua to find out who it was[322] and gave him a process to use. Joshua following a prescribed procedure and determined it was Achan who confessed

> *When I saw among the spoils a goodly Babylonish garment, and two hundred shekels of silver, and a wedge of gold of fifty shekels weight, **then I coveted them, and took them**; and, behold, they are hid in the earth in the midst of my tent, and the silver under it.*[323]

Achan did not follow the Lord's command and kept a garment, silver and gold and buried them in his tent. He had stolen from the Lord. All silver, gold and precious things were

---

[321] 1 Nephi 17:35.

[322] Joshua 7:5-11.

[323] Joshua 7:21.

to be put in the *"treasury of the Lord"*[324] Achan and his family was punished with the same punishment as the people of Jericho. Their family was stoned, their animals killed and all was burned. [325]

Casting Souls to Hell

When disobedient people die, such as Achan and his family, their spirits become subject to Satan because of their wickedness. Being subject to Satan is suffering in hell.

An example of this type of judgment where the Lord did the destroying is Sodom and Gomorrah. In Genesis we read

> *Abram dwelled in the land of Canaan, and Lot dwelled in the cities of the plain, and pitched his tent toward Sodom.*

> *But the men of Sodom becoming sinners, and exceedingly wicked before the Lord, the Lord was angry with them.*[326]

Fire rained down from heaven destroying this people. Of their wickedness Jude wrote,

> *Even as Sodom and Gomorrha, and the cities about them in like manner, giving themselves over to fornication, and going after strange flesh, are set forth for an example, suffering the vengeance of eternal fire.*[327]

Moreover, Peter wrote,

---

[324] Joshua 6:19.

[325] Joshua 7:24-26.

[326] Gen 13:10-11.

[327] Jude 1:7.

And turning the cities of Sodom and Gomorrah into ashes condemned [them] with an overthrow, making [them] an ensample unto those that after should live ungodly; [328]

The people of Sodom and Gomorrah and the surrounding area were condemned because they would not repent of their sins and they knew better than to commit those sins. They were thrust down to hell to suffer eternal fire and the buffetings and torment of Satan [Read the essay "JUDGMENTS at MORTAL DEATH"].

Common Judgments

Generally, the Lord's judgment of individuals occurs in two ways. If a person is righteous the Lord gives to them "tender mercies" and if they are not righteous the Lord "hedges up their way that they prosper not" [329].

Tender mercies are in fact "blessings." The term "tender mercies" is perhaps more descriptive. It emphasizes God's great mercy and the tender love that he extends to his righteous children and even to some who are not so righteous.

The first recorded use of the term "tender mercies" in the scriptures is in the Psalms of David. David used this term ten times and it appears that he may have coined that term being the first to use it in our current scriptures. If he did not coin the term he certainly emphasized it. For example, David wrote the following

The LORD [is] gracious, and full of compassion; slow to anger, and of great mercy.

---

[328] 2 Peter 2:6.

[329] Mosiah 7:29.

*The LORD [is] good to all: and his **tender mercies**
[are] over all his works.*[330]

These tender mercies sometimes come with great challenges
in difficult situations. The command to build the Kirtland
Temple[331] when the saints were desperately poor is one of
those tender mercies with a challenge. The purpose was to
have a temple where the Lord could dwell and provide temple
tender mercies to his people. The challenge was the building
of a structure that was worthy of the Lord's presence when so
many were so poor. After great sacrifice and dedication the
saints completed the temple. [332] Shortly after the dedication
Joseph Smith and Oliver Cowdery were in the temple and
knelt in prayer. The Savior, Moses, Elias and then Elijah
visited them. Each gave keys and authority for their
dispensations. Elijah gave the keys and authority relating to
temple ordinances including ordinances for the salvation of
the dead. The temple ordinances are tender mercies to all
righteous saints.

Nephi told of the "tender mercies" to Lehi in protecting him
from the people to whom Lehi preached.

> *In addition, when the Jews heard these things they
> were angry with him* [Lehi]; *yea, even as with the
> prophets of old, whom they had cast out, and stoned,
> and slain; and **they sought his life**, that they might
> take it away. But behold, **I, Nephi, will show unto you**
> that the <u>tender mercies</u> of the Lord are over all those*

---

[330] Ps 145:8-9.

[331] D&C 88:119; See S. 109.

[332] D&C S. 109.

*whom he hath chosen, **because of their faith, to make them mighty even unto the power of deliverance.***[333]

Nephi is referring to his father Lehi, whose life was threatened by the Jews. Nephi then recorded that his father had a dream or a vision in which the Lord commanded Lehi to take his family, leave his home and many of his earthly possessions and go into the "wilderness."[334] Lehi and his family followed that command. Ishmael and his family joined with them. It was a difficult journey for all. The wives bore children as they traveled. They were required to eat raw meat for food and the wives were able to nurse their children. That indeed was a tender mercy. There were many challenges including building the boat to carry them to their Promised Land but they did it.

Luke[335] and James[336] used the term "tender mercy" in their epistles. Moroni wrote of the Jaredites as they arrived at their Promised Land that they,

> *did humble themselves before the Lord, and did shed tears of joy before the Lord, because of the **multitude of his tender mercies** over them.*[337]

The word "tender mercies" may be the words of Moroni, in this instance, as he translated their record.

JUDGMENTS at MORTAL DEATH

---

[333] 1 Nephi 1:20.

[334] 1 Nephi 2:1-3.

[335] Luke 1:78.

[336] James 5:11.

[337] Ether 6:12.

One of the questions that many ask is "What really happens when we die?" Alma wanted to know the state of people between mortal death and our resurrection. He wrote this to his son, Corianton,

> *Now, concerning the state of the soul between death and the resurrection--Behold, it has been made known unto me by an angel, that **the <u>spirits of all men</u>, as soon as they are departed from this mortal body, yea, the spirits of all men, whether they be good or evil, <u>are taken home to that God who gave them life</u>.***
>
> *And then shall it come to pass, that the spirits of those who are righteous are received into a state of happiness, which is called paradise, a state of rest, a state of peace, where they shall rest from all their troubles and from all care, and sorrow.*
>
> *And then shall it come to pass, that the spirits of the wicked, yea, who are evil--for behold, they have no part nor portion of the Spirit of the Lord; for behold, they chose evil works rather than good; **therefore the spirit of the devil did enter into them, and take possession of their house--and these shall be cast out into outer darkness; there shall be weeping, and wailing, and gnashing of teeth, and this because of their own iniquity, being led captive by the will of the devil,***[338]

The bolded part of the first quoted verse states that when all mortals die their spirits "are taken home to that God who gave them life." If we were to interpret this literally it suggests that the wicked would go where the Savior's home is located.

---

[338] Alma 40:11-13.

However, the Savior's "home" is with the Father. Prior to his coming to mortality he was with the Father. After his resurrection he returned to his Father.[339] However, the third verse states the wicked have become subject to the devil. Because of their wickedness they cannot withstand the presence of the Father and because subject to Satan.

The expression that spirits "are taken home to that God who gave them life" should be interpreted as a judgment of God. The righteous are received into a state of happiness, peace and rest from all care and sorrow and the wicked are subject to Satan. This judgment will be final for some in the sense that their eternal status will have been determined at this judgment. As we shall see in the essay "JOSEPH F. SMITH REVELATION," others will have the opportunity to repent in the world of spirits.

World of Spirits
When we die our soul or spirit separates from our body. Where is the place for our spirits when we die? Joseph Smith explained the word "paradise" as the Savior told the thief on the cross "Today shalt thou be with me in paradise." [340]

> *I will say something about the spirits in prison. There has been much said by modern divines about the words of Jesus to the thief, saying, 'This day shalt thou be with me in paradise.' King James' translators make it out to say paradise. But what is paradise? It is a modern word it does not answer at all to the original word that Jesus made use of.* **There is nothing in the original word in Greek froze [from] which this was**

[339] John 20:17.

[340] Luke 23:43.

taken that signifies paradise; but it was-This day thou shalt be with me in the world of spirits " [341]

And continuing

> There has been much said about the word hell, and the sectarian world have preached much about it, describing it to be a burning lake of fire and brimstone. But what is hell? It is another modern term, and is taken from hades. ...
>
> **Hades, the Greek, or Shaole, the Hebrew: these two significations mean a world of spirits. Hades, Shaole, paradise, spirits in prison, are all one: it is a world of spirits.**
>
> **The righteous and the wicked all go to the same world of spirits until the resurrection.** [342]

This world of spirits has both righteous and wicked people including Satan who was cast out to the earth to tempt us. At a conference in Nauvoo Joseph Smith made some comments about James Adams during which he said,

> He had had revelations concerning his departure, and had gone to a more important work – of opening up a more effectual door for the dead. **The spirits of the just are exalted to a greater and more glorious work –** hence they are blessed in departing hence. <u>**Enveloped in flaming fire,**</u> **they are not far from us, and know and understand our thoughts, feelings and [e]motions, and are often pained therewith.** " [343]

---

[341] Smith, History of the Church, 5:425.

[342] Smith, History of the Church, 5:25.

The just are enveloped in flaming fire? This may be new to some, but Lehi and Nephi nevertheless saw this in their vision. After his marvelous vision Lehi told part of his vision to his family and expressed serious concern for Laman and Lemuel because they had not partaken of the precious fruit.

Afterwards the brothers were discussing Lehi's comments and Nephi explained many things to his brothers. During his comments to his brothers he said this

> *And I said unto them that it was an awful gulf, which separated the wicked from the tree of life, and also from the saints of God.*
>
> *And I said unto them that it was a representation of that awful hell, which the angel said unto me was prepared for the wicked.*
>
> *And I said unto them that our father also saw that the justice of God did also divide the wicked from the righteous; and the* **brightness thereof was like unto the brightness of a flaming fire, which ascendeth up unto God forever and ever, and hath no end.** [344]

Since this quote about flaming fire refers to our spirits, it appears that the spirits of the just have brightness that radiates from them. This may be the glory that is promised. When a person dies he is received either into paradise with a glory of brightness like a flaming fire, which is a state of happiness, peace and rest, or into prison. The unrepentant are in a state which we sometimes refer to as hell not meaning the world of spirits. This hell is suffering under Satan's control where there

---

[343] Ehat, Words of Joseph Smith, 253-254.

[344] 1 Nephi 15:28-30.

is weeping, wailing and gnashing of teeth because of their wickedness.

Weeping, and Wailing, and Gnashing of Teeth
Most of us understand and hope for happiness, peace and rest from mortal cares. Because of the importance of the title of this subsection as it relates to the eternal status of some we will focus on the meaning of this phrase.

It is important to review Satan's appearance to Moses following a visit that Moses had with God. Moses recorded

> *And again Moses said: I will not cease to call upon God; I have other things to inquire of him: for his glory has been upon me, wherefore I can judge between him and thee. Depart hence, Satan.*
>
> *And now, when Moses had said these words,* **Satan cried with a loud voice, and ranted upon the earth, and commanded, saying: I am the Only Begotten, worship me.**
>
> *And it came to pass that <u>Moses began to fear exceedingly; and as he began to fear, he saw the bitterness of hell.</u> Nevertheless, calling upon God, he received strength, and he commanded, saying: Depart from me, Satan, for this one God only will I worship, which is the God of glory.*
>
> *And now Satan began to tremble, and the earth shook; and Moses received strength, and called upon God, saying: In the name of the Only Begotten, depart hence, Satan.*
>
> *And it came to pass that* **Satan cried with a loud voice, with weeping, and wailing, and gnashing of teeth;**

and he departed hence, even from the presence of
Moses, that he be held him not. [345]

The important part of this quote is that Satan actually cried
with his voice and he was "weeping, wailing and gnashing of
teeth."

To repeat Alma's words to Corianton that describes the
suffering of the wicked.

> *... therefore the spirit of the devil did enter into them,*
> *and take possession of their house--and* ***these shall be***
> ***cast out into outer darkness; there shall be weeping,***
> ***and wailing, and gnashing of teeth****, and this because*
> *of their own iniquity, being led captive by the will of*
> *the devil.* [346]

From this verse, we learn that unrepentant spirits react as
Satan reacted. They will be "weeping, wailing and gnashing
their teeth." This quote also states that they are captive to the
will of Satan. Exactly what direct power Satan has over
wicked spirits is not exactly known, but he causes pain and
anguish to those under his control.

We can readily understand weeping and wailing but perhaps
"gnashing of teeth" needs some explanation. The definition of
gnash is

> *To grind your teeth together, especially in pain, anger*
> *or frustration.*

Probably spirits would express their anger and frustration
through their facial expressions perhaps by grimacing

---

[345] Moses 1:18-22.

[346] Alma 40:13.

combined with showing their teeth with their weeping and wailing.

President Joseph F. Smith saw in vision the Savior visiting the world of spirits. Of this he wrote

> *But unto the wicked he did not go, and among the ungodly and the unrepentant that had defiled them while in the flesh, his voice was not raised;*
>
> *Neither did the rebellious that rejected the testimonies and the warnings of the ancient prophets behold his presence, nor look upon his face.*
>
> ***Where these were, darkness reigned***, *but among the righteous there was peace.*[347]

There has been a separation between the wicked and the faithful whom the Savior visited. There is still darkness where the wicked reside with Satan. You will note from Alma's description to his son, Corianton, that the wicked reside in darkness in the world of spirits. This is confirmed by President Smith's revelation.

This separation was breached by the Savior's commission for the gospel to be preached to the dead.[348] [For more information about preaching the gospel in the world of spirits read the essay "JOSEPH F. SMITH REVELATION"].

Everlasting Fire
The Lord describes those who will inherit the telestial kingdom

---

[347] D&C 138:20-22.

[348] D&C 138:29-32.

These are they who are liars, and sorcerers, and adulterers, and whoremongers, and whosoever loves and makes a lie.

*These are they who suffer the **wrath of God** on earth.*

*These are they who suffer the **vengeance of eternal fire.*** [349]

These verses speak of the wicked. Notice the kinds of sins committed by these wicked which are adultery, fornication, liars, etc. These are "serious sins" that would send a soul to hell and eventually to the telestial kingdom. Of course all sin is serious but the term "serious sin" is used to identify this category of sins that qualify a person for the telestial kingdom. Those who commit these sins are the ones that will suffer the wrath of God by being in hell and under the control of Satan. The Lord describes them as suffering the "vengeance" of eternal fire. Vengeance means that this fire is very intense. What is this fire?

The term fire as used in the scriptures is referring to a principle taught by the Prophet Joseph Smith which is

*The great misery of departed spirits in the world of spirits, where they go after death, is to know that they come short of the glory that others enjoy and that they might have enjoyed themselves, and **they are their own accusers*** [350]

And also

---

[349] D&C 75:103-105.

[350] Smith, History of the Church, 5:425.

A man is his own tormentor and his own condemner. Hence the saying, They shall go into the lake that burns with fire and brimstone. **The torment of disappointment in the mind of man is as exquisite as a lake burning with fire and brimstone.** [351]

Joseph identifies that departed spirits will know in the world of spirits, prior to their resurrection, that they have fallen short of the glory they might have received. Their disappointment will be a torment that will be as intensive as a "lake burning with fire and brimstone." Whenever this quoted expression or other similar expressions are found in the scriptures it always refers to this great disappointment in the mind of a man. In addition to this disappointment, they will suffer the buffetings of Satan which also causes pain and despair.

It seems to this author that this great disappointment is because they will know that their life in mortality is contrary to the teachings of the Savior and will recognize that Jesus Christ is the Savior and Messiah. They will fear his judgment.

King Benjamin spoke of this fire to his people when he said

> *And if they be evil they are consigned to an **awful view of their own guilt and abominations, which doth cause them to shrink from the presence of the Lord into a state of misery and endless torment**...*
>
> ***And their torment is as a lake of fire and brimstone, whose flames are unquenchable, and whose smoke ascendeth up forever and ever.*** [352]

---

[351] Smith, History of the Church, 6:314.

[352] Mosiah 3:25, 27.

This statement by King Benjamin states that this fire will last "forever and ever." This fire will never cease. Nephi taught this principle of eternal fire.

> *And assuredly, as the Lord liveth, for the Lord God hath spoken it, and it is his eternal word, which cannot pass away, that they who are righteous shall be righteous still, and they who are filthy shall be filthy still; wherefore, **they who are filthy are the devil and his angels; and they shall go away into everlasting fire, prepared for them; and their torment is as a lake of fire and brimstone, whose flame ascendeth up forever and ever and has no end.***

> *O the greatness of the mercy of our God, the Holy One of Israel! For he delivereth his saints from that awful monster the devil, and death, and hell, and that lake of fire and brimstone, which is endless torment.* [353]

Even Samuel, the Lamanite, spoke of this fire from the walls of Zarahemla.

> *Yea, and it bringeth to pass the condition of repentance, that **whosoever repenteth the same is not hewn down and cast into the fire; but whosoever repenteth not is hewn down and cast into the fire;** and there cometh upon them again a spiritual death, yea, a second death, for they are cut off again as to things pertaining to righteousness.* [354]

These quotes mean that this torment of disappointment will not cease with their resurrection. A person will always know

---

[353] 2 Nephi 9:16, 19.

[354] Helaman 14:18.

throughout eternity that they could have had a better life in eternity had they lived differently. Joseph said

> *Those who have done wrong always have that wrong gnawing them.* [355]

Anyone who is not in the highest degree of the celestial kingdom will have this "gnawing" feeling. The Lord gave a brief statement to the Nephites which identified the heart of his atonement. He called this his "Gospel." [Read the essay "C"]. In it he said

> *And he **that endured not unto the end**, the same is he that is hewn down and **cast into the fire, from whence they can no more return**, because of the justice of the Father.*[356]

Those who do not "endure to the end" are those who receive the gospel and do not continue in it. They have been taught that Jesus is the Christ and have exercised faith in his atonement. They have repented of their sins, been baptized and received the gift of the Holy Ghost. They have been forgiven and the Savior has taken upon him their sins by forgiving them. They have been active in attending church and partaking of the sacrament. They could have been doing these activities for a short duration or a very long duration but then they change and no longer participate. There are a number of reasons why this activity could have stopped. Then they reach the time of their life when their bodies fail and they die. They were not faithful to the end of their mortal lives.

---

[355] Smith, History of the Church, 6:366.

[356] 3 Nephi 27:17.

The Savior says of them that they are "cast into the fire" and they cannot return. They cannot return to their life when they had fully accepted the gospel and actively lived it. They are foreclosed from inheriting the highest degree in celestial kingdom and returning to the presence of the Father. Throughout eternity, they will have this fire or gnawing feeling.

In describing those in the terrestrial kingdom, Joseph and Sidney recorded

> *These are they who are not valiant in the testimony of Jesus; wherefore, they obtain not the crown over the kingdom of our God.* [357]

The question that should be addressed is whether those who are "not valiant" will suffer in hell before being consigned to the terrestrial kingdom. If their lack of being valiant is because they have become liars, adulterers, thieves, etc, they will suffer in hell but they will not inherit the terrestrial kingdom, they will be consigned to the telestial kingdom. These will suffer the "vengeance" of this fire. [358]

Those who are not valiant are those who do not endure to the end of their lives. They include good people but slothful and not dedicated and consequently did not endure in faith to the end of their lives. It also includes those who have received temple ordinances but dropped out of activity. They will have this fire. They will always know that they could have had a better estate than what they will receive.

---

[357] D&C 76:79.

[358] D&C 75:105.

212

Those who are not valiant in their testimony who inherit the terrestrial kingdom will receive of the Savior's *"glory but not of his fulness"*[359] and will be personally visited by the Savior.[360] There must be some consolation in this as it pertains to the intensity of this fire that will be eternally felt.

Consider also the children of faithful parents who do not qualify for the highest degree of the celestial kingdom. The parents will have these children in the celestial kingdom with them. However, these children will be in a lower degree in the celestial kingdom. [Read the section "Marriage Covenant Children" in the essay "MARRIAGE COVENANT" on page153]. They will feel that fire to some extent. The love of family and continued association will provide consolation in lessening this fire; however, this fire will never be extinguished. As Joseph said

> *Those who have done wrong always have that wrong gnawing them.* [361]

Buffetings of Satan
The expression "buffetings of Satan" is found five (5) times in the Doctrine and Covenants. It does not appear in any other scriptures.

The term "buffetings" appears in modern dictionaries and is defined as a "shaking of an airplane." Those who have flown in turbulent weather know that some airplanes can be tossed about, sometimes violently. The passengers, if not using seat belts, can be thrown out of their seats.

---

[359] D&C 76:76.

[360] D&C 76:77.

[361] Smith, History of the Church, 6:366.

The root word "buffet" has several meanings. From several dictionaries the applicable common meaning is

1. A blow, especially by the fist

2. Something that affects like a blow

This root word is used in the New Testament to describe abuse to the Savior

> *Then did they spit in his face, **and buffeted him; and others smote him with the palms of their hands,***
>
> *Saying, Prophesy unto us, thou Christ, Who is he that smote thee?* [362]

Both of these quotes seem to make a difference between the tormentors slapping the Savior with the palm of their hands and hitting him with their fists. When they "buffeted him", they used their fists as the definition indicates.

The term "buffetings of Satan" is some sort of turbulence, agitation or happening that comes directly from Satan. It would be something powerful like a physical blow or a strong happening. This is something that Satan will inflict. The Savior referred to this "buffeting" but used different terms. He told Peter

> *And the Lord said, Simon, Simon, behold, **Satan hath desired to have you, that he may sift you as wheat:***
>
> *But I have prayed for thee, **that thy faith fail not**: and when thou art converted, strengthen thy brethren.* [363]

---

[362] Matthew 26:67-68.

[363] Luke 22:31-32.

This scripture references Peter's activities after the Savior's resurrection and not those prior to the Savior's death. (See the essay "PETER DENYING CHRIST" for justification of this statement).

The harvest of wheat was completed by putting the wheat and chaff into baskets and tossing the mixture into the air to separate the wheat chaff from the kernels. This method has been used for centuries. Although this action separates the chaff and the kernels this tossing activity puts the wheat kernels into constant motion, turbulence or agitation. This properly characterizes the "buffetings of Satan." When people suffer the buffetings of Satan in mortality their lives are in a constant turmoil.

The Savior prayed that Peter's "faith fail not." If Peter did not continue in faith he would not endure to the end. If Peter would have turned from the faith he would then suffer the "buffetings of Satan" or sifted as wheat. If a person exercises true faith they get rid of the chaff or sins through repentance.

The Savior gave the Nephites the same warning.

> *he turned again unto the multitude and said unto them:*
>
> *Behold, verily, verily, I say unto you, ye must watch and pray always lest ye enter into temptation; for **Satan desireth to have you, that he may sift you as wheat.*** [364]

These buffetings of Satan can begin in our mortal lives. The Prophet Joseph Smith wrote of a Brother Draper who is believed to be William Draper:

---

[364] 3 Nephi 18:17-18.

*In the afternoon we had an exhortation and communion service. Some two or three weeks since, Brother Draper insisted on leaving the meeting before communion, and could not be prevailed on to tarry a few moments, although we invited him to do so, as we did not wish to have the house thrown into confusion. He observed that he "would not," if we excluded him from the Church. Today he attempted to make a confession, but it was not satisfactory to me, and **I was constrained by the Spirit to deliver him over to the buffetings of Satan, until he should humble himself and repent of his sins, and make satisfactory confession before the Church.*** [365]

Joseph's purpose was to spur him to repentance and to rejoin in full activity. Paul did this same thing as he recorded in his letter to Timothy.

This charge I commit unto thee, son Timothy, according to the prophecies which went before on thee, that thou by them mightest war a good warfare;

Holding faith, and a good conscience; which some having put away concerning faith have made shipwreck:

__Of whom is Hymenæus and Alexander; whom I have delivered unto Satan, that they may learn not to blaspheme.__ [366]

William W. Phelps and John Whitmer were sustained as Presidents of the Church in Missouri and were later dismissed

---

[365] Smith, History of the Church, 2:326.

[366] 1 Timothy 1:18-20.

by a united vote of the Church. William W. Phelps and John Whitmer were claiming some $2000 of Church funds as their own funds. A court was held:

> *it was decided that William W. Phelps and John Whitmer be no longer members of the Church of Christ of Latter-day Saints, and **be given over to the buffetings of Satan, until they learn to blaspheme no more against the authorities of God, nor fleece the flock of Christ.***
>
> *The vote was then put to the congregation, and was carried unanimously.* [367]

William W. Phelps did repent, asking forgiveness of the Church members and those that he offended. After he rejoined the Church in 1840 he penned fifteen (15) poetic verses which were set to music and currently appear in the Church hymnbook. Perhaps the most notable is the hymn "Praise to the Man" giving honor and recognition to the Prophet Joseph Smith whom he had offended and of whom he had spoken evil.

John Whitmer did not repent of his transgressions and retained records of the history of the Church that he had while serving as clerk.[368] He assisted those who were commissioned by the authorities of Missouri to see that the Saints were removed from Missouri. On 5 April 1839, he and seven (7) others including the county judge met with Theodore Turley who had been working through the legal process to get those in Liberty jail released. This committee of eight was part of the group

---

[367] Smith, History of the Church, 3:8 (See pages 6-8).

[368] Smith, History of the Church, 6:66.

that was commissioned to see that the Saints were removed from the State of Missouri. John Whitmer had provided this committee a copy of the revelation[369] that stated that the apostles should dedicate the Far West temple site on 26 April 1839. This event was to take place just three weeks from the meeting time of this committee.

Brother Turley was told that if the apostles came they would be murdered to which he jumped up and said "In the name of God that revelation will be fulfilled." He was derided for his statement and they charged him to deny his position and join them. Brother Turley then asked John Whitmer what his position was. In response, John Whitmer did say he saw and handled the plates and described them but said he did not know whether the translation was correct. He contradicted his previous testimony that he had given when so active in the Church.[370] According to Joseph's quote above John Smith qualified himself to suffer the buffetings of Satan following his death.

The missionary group of apostles met just after midnight on 5 April 1839 and dedicated the Far West temple site thus fulfilling the revelation. They completed their business and then left for their missions as they had previously determined.

As mentioned earlier, there are five (5) occurrences of the expression "buffetings of Satan" in the Doctrine and Covenants. All of these references concern members of the Church who have broken covenants, transgressed or sinned Three of those references have a common expression. The offender,

---

[369] D&C S. 118.

[370] Smith, History of the Church, 3:307.

*...shall be delivered over to the **buffetings of Satan until the day of redemption**.*[371]

One other states that the transgressor

*...cannot escape the **buffetings of Satan until the day of redemption**.*[372]

These quotes show that there is an end to the buffetings of Satan. That end is the day of redemption. The day of redemption for William W. Phelps was the day he repented and returned to the Church. If there is no repentance the day of redemption occurs at the day of resurrection. When a person suffers the buffetings of Satan and dies, the buffetings of Satan continue because that person will be in hell with Satan. His redemption will occur when he is resurrected, forgiven and released from the realm of Satan. (See the section "Forgiveness and Glory" in the essay SALVATION OF MAN").

The Lord spoke of those who inherit the telestial kingdom.

These are they who are liars, and sorcerers, and adulterers, and whoremongers, and whosoever loves and makes a lie.

*These are **they who suffer the wrath of God on earth**.*

These are they who suffer the vengeance of eternal fire.

*These are **they who are cast down to hell and suffer the wrath of Almighty God, until the fulness of times**,*

---

[371] D&C 78:12; 82:21; 132:26.

[372] D&C 104:9.

when Christ shall have subdued all enemies under his feet, and shall have perfected his work; [373]

As we see from the second and fourth verses these are they who suffer the wrath of God on earth and are cast down to hell and suffer the wrath of God *"until the fulness of times"* when they are resurrected. In this context, the terms "wrath of God" and "buffetings of Satan" are equivalent terms and refers to being in hell.

The expression *"fullness of times"* is at the end of the millennium when those in hell shall be resurrected and the final judgments are made. They will be subjected to Satan and his follower's buffeting or torment until that time.

Eternal fire is not the same thing as the buffetings of Satan or the wrath of God.

The everlasting fire is personal and within each individual and stays with the individual throughout eternity. The buffetings of Satan stop when the person is released from Satan's control, resurrected and forgiven.

SONS OF PERDITION

There is a considerable misunderstanding about who are or can become sons of perdition. Many members have the impression there are only a few people who have become sons of perdition. In actuality there are more than a few people who have become sons of perdition. The question is "From the scriptures how can we recognize the qualification of those who have become or will become sons of perdition?"

Information about Satan and sons of perdition are revealed in the 76th section of the Doctrine and Covenants. We will begin

[373] D&C 76:103-106.

our discussion by quoting from this section. The Lord said this of the sons of perdition:

> *31 Thus saith the Lord concerning **all those who know my power, and have been made partakers thereof, and suffered themselves through the power of the devil to be overcome, and to deny the truth and defy my power**—*
>
> *32 They are they who are the **sons of perdition**, of whom I say that it had been better for them never to have been born;*
>
> *33 For **they are vessels of wrath, doomed to suffer the wrath of God, with the devil and his angels in eternity;***
>
> *34 **Concerning whom I have said there is no forgiveness in this world nor in the world to come**—*
>
> *35 **Having denied the Holy Spirit after having received it**, and having denied the Only Begotten Son of the Father, having crucified him unto themselves and put him to an open shame.*
>
> *36 These are they **who shall go away into the lake of fire and brimstone, with the devil and his angels**—*
>
> *37 **And the only ones on whom the second death shall have any power;***
>
> *38 **Yea, verily, the only ones who shall not be redeemed in the due time of the Lord**, after the sufferings of his wrath.*
>
> *39 For all the rest shall be brought forth by the resurrection of the dead, through the triumph and the glory of the Lamb, who was slain, who was in the bosom of the Father before the worlds were made.*[374]

And continuing

> *43 Who* [the Savior] *glorifies the Father, and **saves all the works of his hands, except those sons of perdition** who deny the Son after the Father has revealed him. 44 Wherefore, **he saves all except them**—they shall go away into everlasting punishment, which is endless punishment, which is eternal punishment, to reign with the devil and his angels in eternity, where their worm dieth not, and the fire is not quenched, which is their torment—*

The verse numbers have been left on this quote for ease of discussing the concepts quoted. One of the first things that we should recognize is the punishment of the sons of perdition.

In verse 33, the Lord states directly that they will suffer God's punishment, which is being with Satan and his hosts throughout eternity. There will be no telestial, terrestrial or any other salvation for the sons of perdition. This is reconfirmed a few verses later.

One statement clearly identifies a person whose conduct qualifies him or her as a son of perdition. Verse 34 contains that statement. It is the sons of perdition have *"no forgiveness in this world nor in the world to come."* Any time that this expression occurs in the scriptures, it identifies a son of perdition event, which if a person does that event, they become a son of perdition.

This expression relates to verse 38 wherein the Lord states that sons of perdition are *"the only ones who shall not be redeemed in the due time of the Lord."* This expression means that when they are resurrected they will not qualify for any of the

---

[374] D&C 76:31-40.

kingdoms, i.e. celestial, terrestrial or telestial. The Lord further states (verse 37) that there is a "second death" that will be suffered and the sons of perdition are the only ones that will suffer this second death which means that they are the only ones who shall not be redeemed from hell. [See verse 38].

We neither know nor understand the extent of punishment or the location of the torment that the sons of perdition will suffer when they are returned to dwell with Satan. The Savior said

> *And the end thereof, neither the place thereof, nor their torment, no man knows;*
>
> *Neither was it revealed, neither is, neither will be revealed unto man, except to them who are made partakers thereof;*
>
> *Nevertheless, I, the Lord, show it by vision unto many, but straightway shut it up again;*
>
> *Wherefore, the end, the width, the height, the depth, and the misery thereof, they understand not, neither any man except those who are ordained unto this condemnation.*[375]

At the end of the millennium there will be a resurrection of all that are in hell including the sons of perdition. Many will be consigned to the telestial kingdom but sons of perdition will be placed back with Satan and his host, to be with them throughout eternity. At this resurrection time there will be a forgiveness given to all except the sons of perdition. Joseph Smith stated

---

[375] D&C 76:45–48.

All sins shall be forgiven, except the sin against the Holy Ghost; for Jesus will save all except the sons of perdition. [376]

Those who do not receive forgiveness in mortality will receive it when they are resurrected except for the sons of perdition. The Savior expressly stated in verse 34 that for the sons of perdition *"there is no forgiveness in this world nor in the world to come"*. Those who commit the sin that qualifies them to be a son of perdition have no forgiveness. The sin that qualifies them for this status is often referred to as the "unpardonable" sin. There is no pardon or forgiveness ever given to them. Therefore when one reads the expression "unpardonable sin" in the scriptures it is referring to the sin that makes a person a son of perdition.

In verse 31, we are told that sons of perdition will "deny the truth and defy my power." Joseph Smith describes this denying the truth and defying God when he said this

> *When a man begins to be an enemy to this work, he hunts me, he seeks to kill me, and never ceases to thirst for my blood. He* **gets the spirit of the devil-the same spirit that they had who crucified the Lord of Life-the same spirit that sins against the Holy Ghost.**
>
> **You cannot save such persons; you cannot bring them to repentance; they make open war, like the devil, and awful is the consequence.** [377]

This quote from Joseph Smith identifies another characteristic associated with those who are sons of perdition. That

---

[376] Smith, History of the Church, 6:314.

[377] Smith, History of the Church, 6:315.

characteristic is that they thirst for the blood of the righteous. This is the extreme attitude. After the martyrdom of Joseph and Hyrum Smith on July 27, 1844, three members of the Quorum of the Twelve, W. W. Phelps, Willard Richards and John Taylor wrote a communication dated July 1, 1844, to members of the Church. They counseled the members to not seek retribution for these deaths. They were to be peaceable and calm letting the authorities do their duty. They continued by saying if the authorities did not do their job in prosecuting the murderers it should be left to God. Near the end they penned

> *and blessed are they that hold out faithful to the end,* **while apostates, consenting to the shedding of innocent blood, have no forgiveness in this world nor in the world to come.** [378]

By this statement they are saying that apostates having the attitude of wanting to kill Church leaders or "consenting" thereto would be sons of perdition. They need not actually participate in the martyrdom of Joseph and Hyrum to become sons of perdition. They will be returned to Satan following their resurrection.

Murder – Shedding Innocent Blood

Innocent blood is the taking of life without justification. Certainly, the Nephites were not guilty of shedding innocent blood when they fought and killed Lamanites in battle. They were defending themselves, their families and their liberties. The blood they spilt was not innocent.

The Lord revealed to Joseph Smith the following:

---

[378] Smith, History of the Church, 7:152.

*And now, behold, I speak unto the church. Thou shalt not kill; and **he that kills shall not have forgiveness in this world, nor in the world to come.***

And again, I say, thou shalt not kill; but he that killeth shall die. [379]

A person who is a member of this church and takes the life of an innocent person becomes a son of perdition by virtue of his act of killing. The Savior said of those who kill, they *"shall not have forgiveness in this world, nor in the world to come."* These are the exact words that the Savior said of the sons of perdition as quoted in the previous section. The death identified in this last verse is the second death suffered by the sons of perdition when they receive no salvation.

Joseph Smith said,

> *The **unpardonable sin** is to shed innocent blood, or **be accessory thereto.*** [380]

One does not have to commit the murder themselves. They can be an accessory and become a son of perdition. Alma chastised his son Corianton during which he stated this

> *whosoever murdereth against the light and knowledge of God, it is not easy for him to obtain forgiveness; yea, I say unto you, my son, that it is not easy for him to obtain a forgiveness.* [381]

Probably the most famous example of shedding innocent blood is Judas Iscariot. Judas did not actually commit the

---

[379] D&C 42:18-19.

[380] Smith, History of the Church, 5:392.

[381] Alma 39:6.

murder but took action to arrest the Savior from which the Savior was tried, condemned and crucified. When Judas understood the effect of what he had done he realized he was an accessory to the Savior's slaying and had committed the unpardonable sin. He had become a son of perdition for he is quoted as saying,

> *I have sinned in that I have betrayed the innocent blood* [382]

Cain is perhaps the second most famous. Cain killed his brother, Abel. He was taught by angels and had conversed directly with the Lord. In fact, it was the Lord who condemned Cain[383]. Certainly, he qualified as knowing the Lord and he still committed the murder of Abel for gain. Cain was the first to commit murder. He is known as "perdition"[384] and he loved Satan more than God.[385] Consequently, those who know God and then follow Satan become Cain's sons or are "sons of perdition."

Laman and Lemuel became sons of perdition. An angel appeared to them and chastised them for striking their younger brothers, Sam and Nephi, with a rod. The angel told them that Nephi would rule over them. The angel commanded them to return to Jerusalem and Laban would be put into their hands.[386]

When Nephi made tools to build a ship which was to take the group to their promised land, the brothers rebelled. Nephi

---

[382] Matthew 27:4.

[383] Genesis 4:9-11

[384] Moses 5:24.

[385] Moses 5:28-33.

[386] 1 Nephi 3:29-30.

recounted the travels and activities of the Israelites under the leadership of Moses. Then he had this to say about his brothers:

> *Wherefore, the Lord commanded my father that he should depart into the wilderness; and the Jews also sought to take away his life; yea, and **ye also have sought to take away his** [Lehi's] **life; <u>wherefore, ye are murderers in your hearts</u>** and ye are like unto them.*
>
> *Ye are swift to do iniquity but slow to remember the Lord your God. **Ye have seen an angel, and he spake unto you; yea, ye have heard his voice from time to time**; and he hath spoken unto you in a still small voice, but ye were past feeling, that ye could not feel his words; **wherefore, he has spoken unto you like unto the voice of thunder, which did cause the earth to shake as if it were to divide asunder.**[387]*

The brothers were humbled and helped build the ship. After they arrived at the Promised Land they tried to kill Nephi.[388] After Nephi and his group separated themselves from Laman and Lemuel, his brothers waged war against them. Nephi, using the sword of Laban, defended his group but was not killed.[389] After all the events of seeing an angel, hearing God's voice they rebelled and were *"murderers in your hearts."* Laman and Lemuel waged war and were responsible for the shedding of innocent blood, even after an angel had appeared to them and they heard the voice of God. It is not known

[387] 1 Nephi 17:44-45.

[388] 2 Nephi 5:1-3.

[389] Jacob 1:10.

whether they directly had killed any of Nephi's followers but they were, as Joseph Smith stated, accessories to or instigators of these killings.

Laman and Lemuel became sons of perdition because they caused innocent blood to be shed and were murderers in their hearts ignoring having seen an angel hearing the voice of God.

David's Murder of Uriah

The Lord had this to say about those who receive the new and everlasting covenant and shed innocent blood:

> *The <u>blasphemy against the Holy Ghost</u>, **which shall not be forgiven in the world nor out of the world, is in that ye commit murder wherein ye shed innocent blood**, and assent unto my death, **after ye have received my new and everlasting covenant**, saith the Lord God; and he that abideth not this law can in nowise enter into my glory, but shall be damned, saith the Lord.*[390]

David who slew Goliath became a son of perdition. Bathsheba and David committed adultery and Bathsheba became with child. David personally interviewed Uriah, her husband, and during that conversation tried to get Uriah to go home so that the adultery could be concealed. However, Uriah did not go home.[391] Since Uriah did not go home, Bathsheba was destined to be stoned for having committed adultery. To avoid this, David sent a note to Joab, his commander, saying,

> *Set ye Uriah in the forefront of the hottest battle, and retire ye from him, that he may be smitten, and die.*[392]

---

[390] D&C 132:27.

[391] 2 Samuel 11:2-18.

Uriah died in battle. When he died David had shed innocent blood by his command to Joab.

When David became king, he had many wives and concubines that were given to him by temple marriage. The Lord said,

> *David's wives and concubines were given unto him of me, by the hand of Nathan, my servant, and others of the **prophets who had the keys of this power**; and in none of these things did he sin against me save in the case of Uriah and his wife; and, **therefore he hath fallen from his exaltation**[393]*

Notice that the prophets who performed the marriages "had keys of this power". These keys were keys of the priesthood. So David was married in the new and everlasting covenant.[394] To refresh our memory the Savior's words were

> *The <u>blasphemy against the Holy Ghost</u>, **which shall not be forgiven in the world nor out of the world, is in that ye commit murder wherein ye shed innocent blood**, and assent unto my death, **after ye have received my new and everlasting covenant.** [395]*

David entered the new and everlasting covenant. Anyone who receives the marriage covenant and sheds innocent blood whether directly or by assistance will have committed "blasphemy against the Holy Ghost" and becomes a son of perdition. David became a son of perdition by commanding Uriah's death.

---

[392] 2 Samuel 11:15 [6-17].

[393] D&C 132:39.

[394] D&C 131:2 (1-3).

[395] D&C 132:27.

The Lord had this to say about the sons of perdition:

*Thus saith the Lord concerning all those who know my power, and have been made partakers thereof, and suffered themselves through the power of the devil to be overcome, **and to deny the truth and defy my power**—*[396]

David never did deny Christ nor defy his power but he did commit blasphemy against the Holy Ghost by the murder of Uriah. He lost his exaltation. His wives were given to another.[397] According to the revelation on the sons of perdition he was not to have forgiveness in this world nor in the world to come. Not having this forgiveness means that he would be returned to the torment of Satan after his resurrection and he would have no hope of changing that eternally.

David knew of his situation and knew he would suffer in hell throughout eternity. Nevertheless, David tried to repent by sincerely petitioning the Lord for forgiveness. He spent a long time in this repentance process. The Lord did not grant him forgiveness in this world and he is suffering the torment of Satan in hell. However, David received a promise that his soul would not be left in hell. David received this message with gladness for he recorded,

Therefore my heart is glad, and my glory rejoiceth: my flesh also shall rest in hope.

For thou wilt not leave my soul in hell.[398]

---

[396] D&C 76:31.

[397] D&C 132:38-39.

[398] Psalms 16:9–10.

Since his soul would not be left in hell he would receive forgiveness at his resurrection. This is the only case that the author knows where a person has become a son of perdition where forgiveness will be given "in the world to come." It is because of David's sincere repentance, not denying Christ nor defying Christ but giving Christ his love and devotion over a period of years that the Lord finally granted that his soul would not be left in hell. Joseph Smith confirmed this in a sermon on 10 March 1844. According to Franklin D. Richards he said,

> *because that he* [David] *had not spoken against the spirit and because that he had not done this he obtained promise that God would not leave his soul in hell.*[399]

Holy Ghost – Denying Christ

This section gives more information on those sons of perdition who qualify under this scripture:

> **Having denied the Holy Spirit after having received it, and having denied the Only Begotten Son** *of the Father, having crucified him unto themselves and put him to an open shame.*[400]

Joseph Smith had this to say:

> *All sins shall be forgiven, except the sin against the Holy Ghost; for Jesus will save all except the sons of perdition. What must a man do to commit the unpardonable sin? He must receive the Holy Ghost, have the heavens opened unto him, and know God, and*

---

[399] Ehat, Words of Joseph Smith, 335.

[400] D&C 76:31-35; See also Alma 39:5-6.

then sin against him. After a man has sinned against the Holy Ghost, there is no repentance for him. He has got to say that the sun does not shine while he sees it; he has got to deny Jesus Christ when the heavens have been opened unto him, and to deny the plan of salvation with his eyes open to the truth of it; and from that time he begins to be an enemy. [401]

Some members of the Church have read this quote and have claim that this is the only way to become a son of perdition because Joseph Smith said it. This view is totally misplaced as we have shown that there are others ways to become a son of perdition. However, this quote describes this category well. Note that Joseph stated that these sons of perdition fight against God as Satan does now.

Jacob, the younger brother of Nephi, experienced an encounter with one Sherem who was preaching that there was no Christ and that Jacob was teaching false doctrines.[402] Jacob confounded Sherem following which Sherem asked for a sign. Jacob declined to give a sign but said that if it were the will of God that a sign would be given. Sherem was overcome and nourished for several days. Sherem then asked that the people to be brought together so that he could speak to them.

And he spake plainly unto them, that he had been deceived by the power of the devil. And he spake of hell, and of eternity, and of eternal punishment.

*And he said: **I fear lest I have committed the <u>unpardonable sin</u>**, for I have lied unto God; for I*

---

[401] Smith, History of the Church, 6:314.

[402] Jacob 7:6-7.

*denied the Christ, and said that I believed the
scriptures; and they truly testify of him. And because I
have thus lied unto God I greatly fear lest my case
shall be awful; but I confess unto God.*

*And it came to pass that when he had said these words
he could say no more, and he gave up the ghost.* [403]

Another example is Nehor. Nehor set up a separate church and
contended against the church of God. He taught that all would
be saved and would have eternal life. He taught that the priests
and teachers should be "popular" and supported by the people.[404]
He contended against Gideon who was instrumental in
planning and getting King Limhi's people away from
Lamanite bondage. When Nehor could not best Gideon he
drew his sword and killed Gideon.

He was bound and brought before Alma, who was in his first
year as chief judge of the land, to be judged according to the
crimes that he committed. Nehor had practiced "priestcraft"
and tried to enforce it with the sword. Nehor had shed the
innocent blood of righteous Gideon. He was condemned to die
for his crimes and just before his death, he acknowledged
*"that what he had taught to the people was contrary to the
word of God."* [405] Nehor knew what the truth was and denied
that knowledge by teaching against it. In so doing he became a
son of perdition prior to killing Gideon. By killing Gideon, he
shed innocent blood, which also qualified him to becoming a
son of perdition.

---

[403] Jacob 7:18-20.

[404] Alma 1:3-4.

[405] Alma 1:7-15.

234

There is one more story from the Book of Mormon. Korihor was a person who went from land to land within the Nephite territory preaching against the church, telling people that there was no God. He taught that the Nephites were in bondage to the performances and ordinances laid down by ancient priests. He also said that looking forward to a "remission of your sins" was the result of a "frenzied mind" and that "this derangement of your minds" [406]was because of traditions. He said that they believed in things that were not so.

Eventually he was confronted by Alma which resulted in Korihor pressing for a sign. Finally, Alma gave him a sign and Korihor was struck dumb. Following this curse Korihor wrote

> *I know that I am dumb, for I cannot speak; and I know that nothing save it were the power of God could bring this upon me; yea, and* **I always knew that there was a God.**

> *But behold, the devil hath deceived me; for he appeared unto me in the form of an angel, and said unto me: Go and reclaim this people, for they have all gone astray after an unknown God. And he said unto me: There is no God; yea, and he taught me that which I should say. And I have taught his words; and I taught them because they were pleasing unto the carnal mind; and I taught them, even until I had much success, insomuch that I verily believed that they were true; and for this cause I withstood the truth, even until I have brought this great curse upon me.* [407]

---

[406] Alma 30:12-16.

[407] Alma 30:52–53.

All three of these men knew that there was a God and knew that Christ was the Savior but denied him by preaching against the truth and denying the Savior.

Knowing God's Power

The Lord chastised the people in the cities of Chorazin, Bethsaida and Capernaum by saying,

> *Then began he to upbraid the cities **wherein most of his mighty works were done, because they repented not:***
>
> *Woe unto thee, Chorazin! woe unto thee, Bethsaida! for if the mighty works, which were done in you, had been done in Tyre and Sidon, they would have repented long ago in sackcloth and ashes.*
>
> *But I say unto you, **It shall be more tolerable for Tyre and Sidon at the day of judgment, than for you.***
>
> *And thou, **Capernaum, which art exalted unto heaven, shalt be brought down to hell**: for if the mighty works, which have been done in thee, had been done in Sodom, it would have remained until this day.*
>
> *But I say unto you, That **it shall be <u>more tolerable for the land of Sodom in the day of judgment, than for thee.</u>*** [408]

When the Lord named these cities he was speaking of the populace living within those cities. We should recognize that some individuals within these groups were good people. The Savior called Peter, James and John to follow him. They were in Capernaum at the time. There probably were some people

---

[408] Matthew 11:20–25.

in the cities that were healed and otherwise blessed that may have accepted Christ as their Savior and repented. However, these were few in comparison to the group as a whole.

In these quoted verses the Lord is comparing two groups of people. On the one hand, there are the wicked cities of Tyre, Sidon, and Sodom. Sodom and several other cities in that area including Gomorrha were destroyed by fire from heaven.[409] They were destroyed to make an example of them because of their wickedness.[410] The people of those cities were in hell at the time of the Savior. They are in hell at the present time awaiting their resurrection and the final judgment following which they will generally be consigned to the telestial kingdom. Their fate at the time of the Savior was already known.

On the other hand the cities of Chorazin, Bethsaida and Capernaum, in which *"most of his mighty works were done"*, were still living at the time the Savior made his statement. By the Savior's statement the people is those cities had not repented and were still wicked in spite of seeing these mighty miracles. They should have known that he was the son of God by these miracles.

First, the Lord said that it would be "more tolerable" for Tyre and Sidon than for Chorazin and Bethsaida at the "day of judgment." Another word which means the same as tolerable is acceptable. Therefore, the Lord means that it is more acceptable for Tyre and Sidon, two wicked cities, than for Chorazin and Bethsaida in the "day of judgment." Why was it more acceptable? If the miracles which were performed in

---

[409] Genesis 19:23-28.

[410] 2 Peter 2:6; Jude 1:7.

Chorazin and Bethsaida, were performed in Tyre and Sidon, the people in those cities would have repented. The same comparison was made between Capernaum and Sodom. If the miracles which were performed in Capernaum were performed in Sodom the people of Sodom would have repented. However, the people in Chorazin, Bethsaida and Capernaum did not repent and therefore, were condemned to a greater condemnation than Bethsaida, Tyre and Sidon.

To which judgment day was the Savior referring? It is the final judgment at the end of the Millennium. This was the only judgment left for the people of Tyre, Sidon and Sodom at the time the Savior made his statement.

By saying that it will be" more acceptable" for Tyre, Sidon and Sodom at the final judgment than for Chorazin, Bethsaida and Capernaum, the Savior is saying they will NOT have the same judgments. The people in the cities of Tyre, Sidon and Sodom will be consigned to the telestial kingdom. If the people in Chorazin, Bethsaida and Capernaum were consigned to the telestial kingdom, there would be no difference in their final judgment and the Savior's statement would be meaningless.

The only judgment that would be different and less tolerable (or more severe) for those in the cities of Chorazin, Bethsaida and Capernaum is being consigned to be with Satan through all eternity and thus they would be sons of perdition having no forgiveness in the world to come.

We ask the question, "What is the gospel standard that would make the people of Chorazin, Bethsaida and Capernaum be sons of perdition?" The pertinent scripture is:

*Thus saith the Lord concerning all **those who know my power, and have been made partakers thereof, and suffered themselves through the power of the devil to be overcome, and to deny the truth and defy my power***

They are they who are the sons of perdition, of whom I say that it had been better for them never to have been born.[411]

How does one know of God's power and be made partakers thereof? They know and made partakers of his power by the miracles performed. Well did Nicodemus state the principle of how the people should respond to the Savior performing "mighty miracles" when he addressed the Savior:

*Rabbi, we know that thou art a teacher come from God: **for no man can do these miracles that thou doest, except God be with him.*** [412]

Remember what the Savior said about Chorazin and Bethsaida.

*Woe unto thee, **Chorazin!** woe unto thee, **Bethsaida!** for if the mighty works, which were done in you, had been done in Tyre and Sidon, they would have repented long ago in sackcloth and ashes.*[413]

He stated that had the miracles been done in Tyre and Sidon they would have repented. Why? Because they would have recognized, like Nicodemus, that the miracles testify that the

---

[411] D&C 76:31-32.

[412] John 3:2.

[413] Matthew 11:21

Savior came from God and God was with him. Having mighty miracles performed among them is the same as knowing God's power because they witnessed these miracles. Jacob, Nephi's brother, quoted an angel as saying that the Savior:

> *should come among the Jews, among those who are the more wicked part of the world; and they shall crucify him—for thus it behooveth our God, and there is none other nation on earth that would crucify their God.*
>
> **For should the mighty miracles be wrought among other nations _they would repent, and know that he be their God_**.[414]

The Savior spoke of John the Baptist and his testimony or light concerning the Savior and said,

> *But I have greater witness than that of John: **for the works which the Father hath given me to finish, the same works that I do, _bear witness of me_,** that the Father hath sent me.* [415]

All of these works performed in Chorazin and Bethsaida show that the inhabitants in these two cities were more wicked that those in Tyre and Sidon. The inhabitants of Capernaum were the same. Having seen God's miracles or power classify the inhabitants as knowing God's power and turning from it makes them sons of perdition.

Others within Israel fall into this same category but not the soldiers who were cruel to the Savior. When the Savior was on

---

[414] 2 Nephi 10:3-4.

[415] John 5:36.

the cross he asked the Father to forgive the soldiers. Luke wrote,

> Then said Jesus, Father, **forgive them**; for they know not what they do [meaning the soldiers who maltreated and crucified him]. And they parted his raiment, and cast lots.[416]

Joseph Smith identified the soldiers in his translation of the New Testament as being those who should be forgiven.

The Savior was totally silent with regard to the Jewish leaders and others who demanded his death. The Jewish leaders knew of Christ's miracles. They saw many healed and many other miracles were reported to them. The same thing can be said of these as was written regarding the people of Chorazin, Bethsaida and Capernaum.

The Jewish leadership should have known, as Nicodemus did, that he was the Messiah. Instead, they were seeking to kill him. They had previously decided to arrange killing him because his miracles and actions interrupted their income and authority.[417] Not only did they want to kill the Savior but also, they wanted to kill Lazarus whom Christ raised from the dead.[418]

However, the Jewish leadership feared the people and did not know how they would react.[419] Therefore, with the help of Judas Iscariot, the Jewish leaders arrested the Savior at night and began their judgments out of the sight and knowledge of the people. The Jewish leaders and those who cried for the

---

[416] Luke 23:34 with footnote; see JST Luke 23:35.

[417] Matthew 26:3-4.

[418] John 12:10.

[419] Mark 11:18; Mark 12:12; Luke 20:19; Luke 22:2.

241

crucifixion of Christ became sons of perdition by their key role in the shedding of the innocent blood of Christ.

Joseph Smith said

> *When a man begins to be an enemy to this work, he hunts me, he seeks to kill me, and never ceases to thirst for my blood.* **He gets the spirit of the devil-the same spirit that they had who crucified the Lord of Life-the <u>same spirit that sins against the Holy Ghost.</u>**
>
> **You cannot save such persons; you cannot bring them to repentance; they make open war, like the devil, and awful is the consequence.** [420]

We can see from these scriptures of the extreme wickedness of the people of Chorazin, Bethsaida and Capernaum and the Jewish leadership. This wickedness had extreme consequences for the nation. Quoting the prophet Zenos, Nephi wrote,

> *And as for those who are at Jerusalem, saith the prophet, they shall be scourged by all people, because* **they crucify the God of Israel, and turn their hearts aside<u>, rejecting signs and wonders,</u> and the power and glory of the God of Israel.**
>
> *And because they turn their hearts aside, saith the prophet, and have despised the Holy One of Israel, they shall wander in the flesh, and perish, and become a hiss and a byword, and be hated among all nations.*
>
> *Nevertheless, when that day cometh, saith the prophet, that they no more turn aside their hearts against the Holy One of Israel, then will he remember the covenants which he made to their fathers.* [421]

---

[420] Smith, History of the Church, 6:315.

We need to be careful and not ascribe the request of the Savior to forgive the soldiers for his crucifixion as requesting the forgiveness of those who are sons of perdition and caused his death. As did the Savior, we should remain silent as their acts condemned them as sons of perdition.

---

421 1 Nephi 19:13-16.

----- OTHER RELATED TOPICS -----

These essays do not fit into other categories. They address topics that generally have questions concerning them. For example, in the Law of Moses a section was added the relates to Elijah taking the temple sealing keys from the earth. That raises the question of what priesthood remained and the effect on those in Israel, including Lehi and Nephi.

One of the great questions is "Why did Peter deny knowing the Savior three times?

The third essay attempts to give a better picture of events on the night of the Savior's arrest, trial and maltreatments leading to his crucifixion the next day.

LAW OF MOSES

Moses was called to be a prophet to Israel out of the burning bush.[422] Prior to this Moses received the Melchizedek Priesthood from his father-in-law, Jethro.[423] The children of Israel were led out of Egypt and traveled through the Sinai Peninsula until they arrived at Mount Sinai. By this time, Moses had held the Melchizedek Priesthood for many years. He ordained others to that priesthood as he led the children of Israel out of Egypt and taught them. At Mount Sinai, the Lord gave a number of commandments to Moses who in turn taught them to the Israelites. It is easy to think that Moses only went up to the Mount one time especially after seeing the movie "The Ten Commandments." However, Moses went up a number of times to receive commandments, and returned to

---

[422] Exodus 3:1-15.

[423] D&C 84:6.

teach them to the Israelites. He received their commitment to live those teachings. These visits include:

> Moses went up to converse with the Lord where the Lord commanded that the people wash their clothes and prepare themselves for the Lord to appear on Mount Sinai before all the people. The people were not to encroach upon the Mount lest they see God and die. On the third day, the Lord appeared among smoke and fire. Moses went up again to talk with the Lord.[424]

> God gave to Moses the Ten Commandments while on the Mount and upon returning the people said "Speak thou with us, and we will hear: but let not God speak with us, lest we die." Whereupon Moses said " Fear not: for **God is come to prove you**, and that his fear may be before your faces, that ye sin not." [425]

> The Lord reveals his laws pertaining to servants, marriage, the death penalty for various offenses, the giving of an eye for an eye and a tooth for a tooth, and the damage done by oxen. [426]

> The Lord reveals his laws pertaining to stealing, destructions by fire, care of the property of others, borrowing, lascivious acts, sacrifices to false gods, afflicting widows, usury, reviling God, and the firstborn of men and of animals—The men of Israel are commanded to be holy." [427]

---

[424] Exodus Ch. 19.

[425] Exodus Ch. 20.

[426] Exodus 21, Heading.

➢ The Lord reveals his laws pertaining to integrity and godly conduct—The land is to rest during a sabbatical year—The children of Israel are to keep three annual feasts—An angel, bearing the Lord's name, will guide them—Sickness will be removed—The nations of Canaan will be driven out gradually." [428]

These headnote quotes demonstrate that Moses went up many times to talk with the Lord. The Lord revealed himself to all Israel in the midst of smoke and fire which caused them to be fearful. Moses received instructions with regard to the individual conduct of the Israelites. Finally, Moses instructed the people on an important covenant.

*And he took the **book of the covenant, and read in the audience of the people**: and they said, All that the LORD hath said will we do, and be obedient.*[429]

This author believes that this "covenant" related to the everlasting covenant or marriage covenant. This covenant detailed the qualifications to receive the marriage covenant which Israel accepted and promised obedience. This was not receiving the covenant but was receiving principles relating thereto.

Following this Moses, Aaron, Nadab, Abihu and seventy of the elders of Israel went up to Mount Sinai and all saw the God of Israel.[430] All of these men who beheld God with Moses

---

[427] Exodus 22, Heading.

[428] Exodus 23, Heading.

[429] Exodus 24:7.

[430] Exodus 24:9-10.

held the Melchizedek Priesthood. They could not have seen the God of Israel if they did not hold that priesthood. Joseph Smith's vision of the Father and the Son was different in that there was no one on the earth that held the Melchizedek Priesthood. Joseph was called of God to restore this priesthood with its keys and blessings. In Israel, the Melchizedek Priesthood was active and held by many among the Israelites.

Moses went back to the mount to receive further instructions from the Lord. These instructions described the Tabernacle of the Congregation. The purpose of this tabernacle was:

> *And let them make me a sanctuary; that I may dwell among them.*[431]

This was a command to build a sanctuary in which the priesthood keys would be exercised which would include the initiatory, endowment and the marriage covenant. Moses was on the mount for forty days and nights. While there the people demonstrated that as a people they could not live the laws given by Moses from the Book of Covenant for they built a golden calf, worshiped it and engaged in riotous activities.[432] In the revelation on priesthood to Joseph Smith the Lord said

> *Therefore, in the ordinances thereof* [Melchizedek Priesthood], *the power of godliness is manifest.*
>
> *And without the ordinances thereof, and the authority of the priesthood, the power of godliness is not manifest unto men in the flesh;*
>
> *For without this no man can see the face of God, even the Father, and live. Now this* **Moses plainly taught to**

---

431 Exodus 25:8-9.

432 Exodus 32.

the children of Israel in the wilderness, and sought diligently to sanctify his people that they might behold the face of God;

*But **they hardened their hearts** and could not endure his presence;*

*Therefore, **he took Moses out of their midst, and the Holy Priesthood also.**[433]*

The teachings of Moses were to sanctify the people to receive the marriage covenant that they might return to the presence of God and behold his face which required them to be married in the marriage covenant. Because of the worship of the golden calf and the riotous activities the Lord "*took Moses out of their midst, and the Holy Priesthood also.*"[434]

The Holy or Melchizedek Priesthood was taken from "their midst" means that the general population of men in Israel were not eligible to be ordained to that priesthood. Consequently, they could not receive the full temple ordinances that are now available to us. The Lord also took Moses "out of their midst". Moses was directly involved in the administration of the people. That stopped. Moses was still the prophet but his relationship to the people changed.

In place of withdrawing Moses and the Melchizedek Priesthood and associated ordinances from the general population a large number of performances and ordinances were instituted and became known as the Law of Moses. Moses continued in the overall leadership of Israel. Moses was instructed to call Aaron and his sons to be priests to administer

---

[433] D&C 84:20-25.

[434] D&C 84:25.

these new performances and ordinances. It is important to note that Nadab and Abihu were sons of Aaron.[435] Moses, Aaron, Nadab and Abihu were all Levites or of the tribe of Levi.[436]

*AND take thou unto thee **Aaron thy brother, and his sons with him,** from among the children of Israel, **that he may minister unto me in the priest's office.***[437]

Bring the tribe of Levi near, and present them <u>before Aaron the priest</u>, that they may minister unto him.

*And **they shall keep his charge.***[438]

Aaron had charge of the Levites in the administration of their priest duties and he ministered *"in the priest's office."* Possibly Aaron and definitely those that followed would be called the "high priest" which is not to be confused with the office of high priest in the Melchizedek Priesthood. Although Aaron held the Melchizedek Priesthood he functioned as a Priest and administrator over all the activities and duties of the Levitical or Aaronic Priesthood. Thus, he was the "high" priest. When we read of the High Priest or Chief Priest in the New Testament that priest was functioning in a similar capacity as Aaron.

Some of these performances and ordinances were performed in the Tabernacle of the Congregation. The men of the Levite tribe were called as a group and given authority to administer the ordinances in the Tabernacle of the Congregation and to care for the instruments therein.[439] Zacharias was attending to

---

[435] Exodus 6:23.

[436] 1 Chronicles 23:14.

[437] Exodus 28:1.

[438] Numbers 3:6-7.

some of these duties in the temple when he was informed by an angel that his wife would give birth to a son.[440] The authority or priesthood was called both the Aaronic Priesthood because Aaron was the first priest and administrator and sometimes called the Levitical Priesthood because the tribe of Levi was called as a group of priests to minister in the Law of Moses. It is the same priesthood.

The Melchizedek Priesthood continued to preside in Israel. Aaron still reported to Moses. Joshua was ordained by Moses to lead Israel following Moses' administration.[441] Joshua directed many activities including the destruction of the walls of Jericho and the settlement of Israel in that Promised Land.

The keys within that Priesthood to perform the sacred ordinance of temple marriage were held and administered by some prophets. They performed these sacred ordinances for some people in Israel until Elijah was taken from the earth. King David was married to his wives by the prophet Nathan and others who had the temple sealing keys.[442] [Read the section "Murder – Shedding Innocent Blood" in the essay "SONS OF PERDITION" for information concerning David].These ordinances pertaining to the marriage covenant were conducted concurrently with those duties of the Aaronic Priesthood in the tabernacle or temple.

Elijah and the Temple Keys

---

[439] Numbers 3:5-9.

[440] Luke 1:5-14.

[441] Deuteronomy 34:8-9.

[442] D&C 132:39.

Elijah lived during the reign of King Ahab of the Northern kingdom of Israel which was about the Ninth century prior to the birth of the Savior. Almost all of us know of his restoration of the priesthood keys to Joseph Smith and Oliver Cowdery in 1836. In a treatise on the Priesthood Joseph Smith wrote,

> **Elijah was the last Prophet that held the keys of the Priesthood**, *and who will, before the last dispensation, restore the authority and deliver the keys of the Priesthood, in order that all the ordinances may be attended to in righteousness. ...'And I will send Elijah the Prophet before the great and terrible day of the Lord,' etc., etc.* **Why send Elijah?** **Because he holds the keys of the authority to administer in all the ordinances of the Priesthood;** *and without the authority is given, the ordinances could not be administered in righteousness.*[443]

Since Elijah was the last prophet to hold these keys, then obviously, they were not passed on to anyone following him. Elisha followed Elijah as a prophet in Israel. Elijah did not confer the priesthood keys upon Elisha. When Elijah was taken up by a chariot of fire, his protégé, Elisha, saw him go and by a previous promise, Elisha received a double portion of the spirit of Elijah[444] and he did many miracles. However, that double portion did not include the priesthood sealing keys which Elijah took with him. Elisha held the Melchizedek Priesthood but not the temple sealing keys. His priesthood is manifest by the miracles he performed and because he received a double portion of the spirit of Elijah. The sealing

---

[443] Smith, History of the Church, 4:211.

[444] 2 Kings 1-14.

keys would have been given by the laying on of hands and not by seeing Elijah go into the heavens by chariot.

The taking of the keys of the priesthood was a very significant event in Israel. It affected the priesthood administration process and eliminated the ability for anyone living to receive the marriage covenant sealed by the priesthood keys. Joseph Smith in the marriage covenant revelation revealed that only one person on the earth holds those keys at any one time.

> *All covenants, contracts, bonds, obligations, oaths, vows, performances, connections, associations, or expectations, that are not made and entered into and sealed by the Holy Spirit of promise, **of him who is anointed**, both as well for time and for all eternity, and that too most holy, by revelation and commandment through the medium of **mine anointed, whom I have appointed on the earth to hold this power** (and I have appointed unto my servant Joseph to hold this power in the last days, **and there is never but one on the earth at a time on whom this power and the keys of this priesthood are conferred**), are of no efficacy, virtue, or force in and after the resurrection from the dead; for all contracts that are not made unto this end have an end when men are dead.* [445]"

The important point of this quote is that only one person holds these keys of the priesthood at any one point in time on the earth. The President of the Church of Jesus Christ of Latter-day Saints currently holds the active keys in the priesthood. We commonly know that the members of the Quorum of the Twelve and the members of the First Presidency have all been

---

[445] D&C132:7.

ordained with those keys but only the President is authorized to exercise those keys. In Elijah's time there was no such arrangement. Joseph Smith wrote that Elijah was the last prophet to hold those keys. There were others who held the Melchizedek Priesthood including Elisha but only Elijah held the sealing keys.

We should not be confused with Elijah's taking the sealing keys from the earth, with the special powers given to the prophet Nephi by the Lord just prior to the birth of the Savior. Nephi was extremely dedicated and righteous and was given a special power to call the people to repentance. This power was not the keys that Elijah held. The keys Elijah held are only conferred by the laying on of hands. Nephi's power was not given by the laying on of hands as did Elijah to Joseph Smith and Oliver Cowdery. It was declared by the Lord to expand Nephi's existing priesthood powers but not giving him priesthood keys. The following is the declaration of the Lord to Nephi:

> *Behold, thou art Nephi, and I am God. Behold, **I declare it unto thee** in the presence of mine angels, **that ye shall have power over this people, and shall smite the earth with famine, and with pestilence, and destruction, according to the wickedness of this people.***

> *Behold, I give unto you power, that whatsoever ye shall seal on earth shall be sealed in heaven; and whatsoever ye shall loose on earth shall be loosed in heaven; and thus shall ye have **power among this people.***

> ***And thus, if ye shall say unto this temple it shall be rent in twain, it shall be done.***

253

And if ye shall say unto this mountain, Be thou cast down and become smooth, it shall be done.

And behold, if ye shall say that God shall smite this people, it shall come to pass.

And now behold, I command you, that ye shall go and declare unto this people, that thus saith the Lord God, who is the Almighty: Except ye repent ye shall be smitten, even unto destruction. [446]

Some read the underlined portion of this quote without understanding the bolded portion of this quote. This power was given to Nephi because he would use it to provide judgments upon the wicked that they might repent. This power was limited to calling this people to repentance. There was no laying on of hands to provide the marriage sealing power to Nephi. This power was given to him verbally. He would not ask that which is contrary to the will of the Lord.[447] The Lord would recognize his requests accordingly. This power was not the sealing priesthood keys held by Elijah which requires the laying on of hands.

What Priesthood Authority Remained?
After Elijah, what priesthood would have remained? We have to go to modern revelation to get the answer to this question. The Lord had this to say about the office of high priest:

High priests after the order of the Melchizedek Priesthood **have a right to officiate in their own standing,** <u>**under the direction of the presidency**</u>, *in*

---

446 Helaman 10:6-12.

447 Helaman 10:5.

administering spiritual things, and also in the office of an elder, priest (of the Levitical order), teacher, deacon, and member. [448]

High priests can "officiate in their own standing" but under the "direction of the presidency." When Elijah was in mortality he had the priesthood keys which make him the "president" of those who held the Melchizedek Priesthood. Having left mortality with those keys, there was no president. Those holding the Melchizedek Priesthood after he left would be high priests because they are the only ones who could "officiate in their own standing."

It should be noted that a stake president functioning as a high priest in his own ministry can ordain others as high priests, elders, priests, teachers and deacons. However, he cannot ordain bishops in the same manner. The President of the Church has to approve someone to be ordained a bishop[449]. Note that the office of bishop is not listed in the offices above in the quoted scripture. This will be important to note as we discuss the Nephites and their priesthood.

Elisha held the office of high priest. After Elijah, all the prophets would have been ordained high priests. Lehi being a prophet was a high priest. Lehi was not a Levite but held the Melchizedek Priesthood. He did not hold the temple sealing keys because those temple keys were not had in Israel at that time. Consequently, since Elijah was taken up to heaven in a chariot none of the prophets in Israel held these keys until Elijah restored them to living prophets. If Elijah had performed the marriage covenant for others during his

---

448 D&C 107:10.

449 D&C 68:18-19 [14-20).

mortality that ordinance would be effective for them. However, following his departure there was no one who could perform that ordinance.

We should recognize that the Melchizedek Priesthood has the "power, that whatsoever ye shall seal on earth shall be sealed in heaven; and whatsoever ye shall loose on earth shall be loosed in heaven." When a person is ordained an elder by another elder or high priest it is recognized and sealed in heaven. In the Church the only way for a person to lose that priesthood is to be excommunicated.

Alma was a priest of King Noah and all were unrighteous until Abinadi called them to repentance. Only Alma repented and gathered people at the waters of Mormon and baptized them which baptism was recognized in heaven. It is not clear whether Alma at this time held the office of priest in the Aaronic Priesthood or held the Melchizedek Priesthood. He was later given the power to create churches among the Nephites and to ordain others with the priesthood. [450] He could have received the office of high priest at that time.

Sealings Keys Taken by Elijah

Since the sealing keys were taken away by Elijah all the prophets following Elijah were not married by the marriage covenant. This means that Isaiah, Daniel, Jeremiah, Ezekiel, Lehi, Nephi, Jacob, Alma, King Benjamin and many other prophets of the Old Testament and of the Book of Mormon were not married in the new and everlasting covenant or marriage covenant during their mortality. They held the office of high priest in the Melchizedek Priesthood and could qualify for the new and everlasting covenant (marriage covenant) but

---

[450] Mosiah 25:19.

no one on the earth had the priesthood keys to perform the ordinance. At first reaction one might say this could never be! These prophets exercised great leadership and received many visions and made prophesies some of which apply to our day. They did marvelous things in the name of God.

From the quote above a high priest administers in spiritual things and can accomplish all that is described that the later prophets have done. How could they be deprived of the marriage covenant? We revere these prophets greatly and admire their deeds and faithfulness.

Why the Lord took Elijah with his keys from Israel is not clear but it undoubtedly relates to the wickedness of the Israelites. It would appear that they would be denied this most holy ordinance but that is not the case. They just did not receive it in their mortality. Regardless of the reason that the Lord took the sealing keys from the earth, that is what the Lord did.

The faithful Israelites will not be denied the marriage covenant blessing. These prophets and others like them lived faithfully to the full extent of the gospel law that was available to them and have fulfilled all that they were able to do. They have earned the right to the marriage covenant. However, that ordinance must be performed on their behalf. As we know in our dispensation that we research our ancestors and perform these ordinances on their behalf. The Lord will see that these ordinances will be completed for these dedicated and righteous men and women.

As one thinks on these things they need to answer this question: "Does it really matter in eternity whether they receive the marriage covenant ordinance in mortality or by proxy?"

We should not be disturbed that these righteous prophets were not married by the sealing keys of the Melchizedek Priesthood during their mortality. Other good and holy men have lived on this earth to fulfill righteous and holy missions. Not all of them were members of the Savior's church during their mortality. One group of such men and women were born to make the United States free and independent with a constitution of guaranteed freedoms.

Wilford Woodruff had this to say about these men and women shortly after experiencing a visit from them while he was the President of the St. George Temple. He described that visit at a conference shortly following their visit to him.

> *I will here say, before closing, that two weeks before I left St. George, the spirits of the dead gathered around me, wanting to know why we did not redeem them. Said they, '**You have had the use of the Endowment House for a number of years, and yet nothing has ever been done for us. We laid the foundation of the government you now enjoy, and we never apostatized from it, but we remained true to it and were faithful to God.**' These were the <u>signers of the Declaration of Independence, and they waited on me for two days and two nights</u>. I thought it very singular, that notwithstanding so much work had been done, and yet nothing had been done for them. The thought never entered my heart, from the fact, I suppose, that heretofore our minds were reaching after our more immediate friends and relatives. I straightway went into the baptismal font and called upon brother McCallister to baptize me for the signers of the Declaration of Independence, and fifty other eminent men, making one hundred in all, including John*

258

Wesley, Columbus, and others; I then baptized him for every President of the United States, except three; and when their cause is just, somebody will do the work for them. [451]

Brian H. Stuy compiled additional information from the journal of Wilford Woodruff and the St. George temple records relating to this event which was published in the Collected Discourses, volume 3 in the appendix of that book. At the beginning paragraph in the appendix, he wrote,

No vision received by Wilford Woodruff is more well known than the appearance of the Signers of the Declaration of Independence. This vision, received "two weeks before leaving St. George," prompted Wilford Woodruff to compile a list of prominent men and women of the seventeenth and eighteenth centuries. On 21 August 1877, Wilford Woodruff, assisted by John Daniel Thompson McAllister (St. George Stake President), David H. Cannon (son of President George Q. Cannon) and **Lucy Bigelow Young (plural wife of President Brigham Young), performed the baptismal work for the one hundred seventy-one names on his list.** He <u>then called on the Saints of St. George</u> **to perform the endowment and sealing work, which was accomplished by February 1878.**

He continued quoting Wilford Woodruff as writing the following

When Br. McAllister had Baptized me for the 100 Names I baptized him for 21, including Gen.

[451] Young, Journal of Discourses, 19:223.

Washington & his forefathers and all the[Preside[n]ts of the United States that were not in my list. Except [Buchannan [,] Van Buren & Grant.

Of the sisters, he wrote

Sister Lucy Bigelow Young went forth into the font and was Baptized for Martha Washington and her family and seventy (70) of the Eminent women of the world [baptisms were performed by John Daniel Thompson McAllister, with confirmations by William Fawcett] [452]

President Wilford Woodruff again talked of this event in the fourth day of the April 1898 Church Conference in the second afternoon session during which he said

*Brother Cannon has been laying before you something with regard to the nation in which we live and what has been said concerning it. I am going to bear my testimony to this assembly, if I never do it again in my life, that **those men who laid the foundation of this American government and signed the Declaration of Independence were the best spirits the God of heaven could find on the face of the earth. They were choice spirits, not wicked men. General Washington and all the men that labored for the purpose were inspired of the Lord.***

Another thing I am going to say here, because I have a right to say it. Every one of those men that signed the Declaration of Independence, with General Washington, called upon me, as an Apostle of the Lord Jesus Christ, in the Temple at St. George, two

---

[452] Stuy, Collected Discourses, 3: Appendix.

consecutive nights, and demanded at my hands that I should go forth and attend to the ordinances of the House of God for them. Men are here, I believe, that know of this, Brothers J. D. T. McAllister, David H. Cannon and James G. Bleak. Brother McAllister baptized me for all those men, and then I told these brethren that it was their duty to go into the Temple and labor until they had got endowments for all of them. They did it. Would those spirits have called upon me, as an Elder in Israel, to perform that work if they had not been noble spirits before God? They would not.

Several general authorities have quoted and emphasized this bolded quote of President Woodruff showing how noble and great these people were. Ezra Taft Benson talked of this work in the November 1987 Church Conference in his talk entitled "Our Divine Constitution." He emphasized that these people were great men and women some of the best that God could find.

He further explained that

President George Washington was ordained a high priest at that time. You will also be interested to know that, according to Wilford Woodruff's journal, John Wesley, Benjamin Franklin, and Christopher Columbus were also ordained high priests at that time. [453]

These above quotes were cited to show great men, the signers of the constitution and the other men and women fulfilled the charge that God gave to them even though they were not

[453] Benson, Teachings of Ezra Taft Benson, 604.

members of his Church. Yet these people had earned the right to have their temple work and sealings completed. They demanded it of Wilford Woodruff because they had served God in what they did.

There is another group of such holy men, not specifically identified, whom the Lord is reserving to himself. The Lord said

> *Wherefore, I will that all men shall repent, for all are under sin,* **except those which I have reserved unto myself, holy men that ye know not of.** [454]

Who these men are and what they have accomplished or will accomplish is not known. We can be assured that they will have served God in their accomplishments and will be rewarded accordingly with all the eternal blessings that we have.

There is one other point that should be made at this time. Joseph Smith saw a vision of Alvin, his older brother, in the celestial kingdom with his parents and he marveled because Alvin died prior to the restoration of the priesthood and the ordinance of baptism. Alvin was faithful and counseled Joseph to get the plates and do as God directs before he died. Alvin was not married prior to his death. Alvin cannot inherit the highest degree in the celestial kingdom without a companion and the marriage covenant being performed for them. Alvin will not be denied this blessing. At the appropriate time, revelation will be given to the appropriate person to have the marriage covenant performed on behalf of Alvin and his companion and he will have this blessing throughout eternity.

---

[454] D&C 49:8.

Law of Moses - Nephites

Probably the first issue that should be addressed is how the priesthood functioned during the Nephite period. Lehi was not a Levite and therefore could not have held the Levitical Priesthood by direct lineage. As already established, the prophets in Israel held the Melchizedek Priesthood with the office of high priest and Lehi being a prophet held that priesthood and office. Nephi received the same from his father.

Jacob held the Melchizedek Priesthood. In addressing the people as recorded by Nephi he states,

> *Behold, my beloved brethren, I, Jacob, **having been called of God, and ordained after the manner of his holy order** ... "* [455]

The term "holy order" refers to the Melchizedek Priesthood. Joseph Smith in answering a question by the brethren on a scripture, used the same language referring to men being ordained to the office of high priest.

> *We are to understand that those who are sealed (in their foreheads) are high priests, ordained unto the holy order of God, to administer the everlasting gospel* [456]

In addition, Jacob and Joseph were ordained as Priests and Teachers to function in the requirements of the Law of Moses. They were ordained by Nephi because he held the office of high priest, which he received from his father.

---

[455] 2 Nephi 6:2.

[456] D&C 77:11.

For I, Jacob, and my brother Joseph had been consecrated priests and teachers of this people, by the hand of Nephi. [457]

Nephite Organization

Lehi's migration group consisted of his family, Ishmael's family and a single individual, Zoram, who had been the servant of Laban. There was no church established in the group. They were led by a prophet, Lehi, who was commanded to leave Jerusalem. Being Israelites they were still subject to the Law of Moses. They acted as a group like the patriarchal order. As Lehi knew he was about to leave mortality he gathered the group together[458] and left his blessings and admonitions upon them similar to what Adam did.[459] This was a patriarchal order.

We have used modern scripture to show that prophets following Elijah held the office of high priest. Lehi and subsequently, Nephi, were high priests. Nephi "anointed" the person who followed him as king who was called second Nephi.

*Now Nephi began to be old, and he saw that he must soon die; wherefore, he **anointed a man to be a king and a ruler over his people now, according to the reigns of the kings.***

... the people were desirous to retain in remembrance his name. And whoso should reign in his stead were

---

[457] Jacob 1:18.

[458] 2 Nephi 1:1-4:12.

[459] D&C 107:53-57.

called by the people, second Nephi, third Nephi, and so forth, according to the reigns of the kings [460]

[461] Kings reigned as governors and as spiritual leaders until King Mosiah's time.

When he was getting old King Benjamin,[462] father of Mosiah, gathered the people together at the temple that he might address them. There were so many that he caused a tower to be built. Even then not all could hear his message so he caused his message to be written and circulated among the people.[463] We therefore have an accurate record in the Book of Mormon of his message. The people made an oath to follow the commandments of God. Then Mormon records

> *And again, it came to pass that when king Benjamin had made an end of all these things, and had* **consecrated his son Mosiah to be a ruler and a king over his people, and had given him all the charges concerning the kingdom,** *and also* **had appointed priests to teach the people, that thereby they might hear and know the commandments of God, and to stir them up in remembrance of the oath which they had made,** *he dismissed the multitude, and they returned, every one, according to their families, to their own houses.* [464]

---

[460] Jacob 1:9, 11.

[461] Jacob 1:11.

[462] See Mosiah Ch. 1 to 6

[463] Mosiah 2:1-8.

[464] Mosiah 6:3.

As we have stated earlier the Levitical Priesthood was not had in the Promised Land. King Benjamin would have ordained Mosiah with the Melchizedek Priesthood office of high priest if he did not already hold it. We see how King Benjamin exercised his priesthood to call priests to teach the people. During King Mosiah's reign he gave power and authority to Alma to organize and preside over the Church.

> *And it came to pass that king Mosiah granted unto Alma that he might establish churches throughout all the land of Zarahemla;* **and gave him power to ordain priests and teachers over every church.** [465]

We can see from these quotes that King Benjamin and then King Mosiah exercised their Melchizedek priesthood.

Alma was authorized to set up churches over all the land. This was the first time that organized churches are mentioned in The Book of Mormon. The reason this had to occur was that the population had grown too large to collect the people to the temple to preach to them in the manner of the patriarchal approach. They had to set up churches in each Nephite land and appoint priests and teachers in each land to administer to the spiritual needs of the people.

> *And now, Alma was their* **high priest, he being the founder of their church.**
>
> **And it came to pass that none received authority to preach or to teach except it were by him from God.** *Therefore he consecrated all their priests and all their teachers; and none were consecrated except they were just men.* [466]

---

[465] Mosiah 25:19.

This mention of Alma being a high priest is referring to the office of high priest in the Melchizedek Priesthood and not to the same office as Aaron held. Aaron's office was a managing priest in the Levitical Priesthood. The authority or priesthood was given to Alma by King Mosiah who received it from his father, King Benjamin, who received it from the kings, who received it from Nephi. Alma the younger received his priesthood from his father.

> *And it came to pass that Alma was appointed to be the first chief judge, he **being also the high priest, his father having conferred the office upon him, and having given him the charge concerning all the affairs of the church.*** [467]

Alma, son of Alma, actually gave a discourse on the office of high priest.[468] This church organization continued until the Savior appeared to the Nephites after his resurrection.

As we have seen a high priest can minister in his own right concerning spiritual things. There were no bishops in this organization. The office of bishop has to be approved and set apart under the authority of the president of the high priesthood.[469] Following Elijah there was no one with keys that had authority to call and set apart a person as a bishop. In fact, in the Book of Mormon the office of "bishop" is not even written. There were other offices mentioned as Jarom wrote

---

[466] Mosiah 23:16;17.

[467] Mosiah 29:42, Alma 4:4.

[468] Alma Ch. 13.

[469] D&C 107:16-17.

*Wherefore, the **prophets, and the priests, and the teachers**, did labor diligently, exhorting with all long-suffering the people to diligence; **teaching the law of Moses, and the intent for which it was given; persuading them to look forward unto the Messiah**, and believe in him to come as though he already was. And after this manner did they teach them.*[470]

The "prophets" mentioned in the scripture were probably men who held the Melchizedek Priesthood, perhaps Elders or High Priests.

Spirituality – Law of Moses

When the Savior appeared to the Nephites, he commanded that they needed to approach him with a "broken heart and a contrite spirit."[471] This was not a new commandment. This teaching was had with Lehi and Nephi as part of the Law of Moses which, if properly followed, points to Christ. Lehi taught this same principle as a principle of the Law of Moses when he left his blessing to his children and followers. In his blessing to Jacob he said,

Wherefore, redemption cometh in and through the Holy Messiah; for he is full of grace and truth.

*Behold, he offereth himself a sacrifice for sin, to answer the ends of the law, **unto all those who have a broken heart and a contrite spirit; and unto none else** can the ends of the law* [of Moses] *be answered.*[472]

---

[470] Jarom 1:11.

[471] 3 Nephi 9:20, 12:19.

[472] 2 Nephi 2:6-7.

Nephi recognized this principle of the broken heart and contrite spirit when he prayed for his forgiveness for the anger he felt toward his brothers, Laman and Lemuel. [Read the essay "Nephi's Anger" in the essay "ANGER – SAVIOR'S PERFECTION] Nephi prayed,

> *O Lord, wilt thou redeem my soul? Wilt thou deliver me out of the hands of mine enemies? Wilt thou make me that I may shake at the appearance of sin?*
>
> *May the gates of hell be shut continually before me,* **because that my heart is broken and my spirit is contrite!** *O Lord, wilt thou not shut the gates of thy righteousness before me, that I may walk in the path of the low valley, that I may be strict in the plain road!* [473]

The way that this attitude was achieved was explained by Nephi when he wrote

> *And, notwithstanding we believe in Christ, we keep the law of Moses, and look forward with steadfastness unto Christ, until the law shall be fulfilled.*
>
> *For, for this end was the law given; ...* **and we are made alive in Christ because of our faith; yet we keep the law** [of Moses] **because of the commandments.**
>
> *And we talk of Christ, we rejoice in Christ, we preach of Christ, we prophesy of Christ, and we write according to our prophecies, that our children may know to what source they may look for a remission of their sins.* [474]

---

[473] 2 Nephi 4:31-32.

[474] 2 Nephi 25:24-26.

By focusing on the Savior to whom the Law of Moses pointed and writing his atonement in their hearts, it would lead the Nephites to have a broken heart and a contrite spirit. Following the procedures or mechanics of offering the sacrifices does not provide the atonement although necessary to follow the Law of Moses. When performing these sacrifices, the message or intent thereof had to be internalized within their souls in order for them to have a broken heart and a contrite spirit.

Fulfillment of the Law

The Savior came to fulfill the Law of Moses. One of the early events that started this process was the Sermon on the Mount[475] the principles of which the Savior also taught to the Nephites.[476] This sermon is found in the Gospel of Matthew. The head note at the beginning of the sermon (chapter 5) had this expression.

Its teachings replace and transcend some aspects of the Law of Moses—.

Throughout his ministry the Savior taught many parables and principles to his disciples and to the multitudes. He taught compassion, forgiveness, love for one another and the requirements to return to the presence of God.

The Savior could not fulfill all the requirements of the Law of Moses until he was crucified and resurrected. The Law of Moses was given specifically to point to these atonement events. One of the more challenging events during the Savior's ministry was when the Scribes and Pharisees brought an adulteress before him for judgment.

---

[475] Matthew Ch 5-7.

[476] 3 Nephi Ch. 12-14.

They say unto him, Master, this woman was taken in adultery, in the very act.

Now Moses in the law commanded us, that such should be stoned: but what sayest thou?

This they said, tempting him, that they might have (cause) to accuse him. But Jesus stooped down, and with his finger wrote on the ground, as though he heard them not. [477]

These Scribes and Pharisees understood the Savior's teachings that were contrary to the Law of Moses. This is indicated by their words because they quoted the law and asked *"What sayest thou?"* This seems to be a more difficult situation. The Savior was restoring the correct teachings and fulfilling the Law of Moses but it was not completed. How could he tell them that forgiveness was the proper way to handle this situation? He could not tell these leaders that he was the Messiah and would complete the fulfillment with his death and resurrection. Forgiveness was the proper course but they would never accept that explanation because of the Law of Moses.

Yet he had already taught forgiveness of others which the Scribes and Pharisees obviously understood as being contrary to the Law of Moses in this case of adultery. They used the situation to find cause against the Savior. The Savior paused and began writing in the sand. It seems like the Savior needed a minute or two to think through his answer. He then stood up and responded.

He that is without sin among you, let him first cast a stone at her. [478]

---

[477] John 8:4–11.

By this statement he did not discount the Law of Moses, but taught that if they were to be judges they must be clean of sin themselves. Not one person including the Scribes and Pharisees remained because each was condemned of their sins by their own conscience. When they were alone the Savior said,

> *Woman, where are those thine accusers? Hath no man condemned thee?*

> *She said, No man, Lord. And Jesus said unto her, Neither do I condemn thee: go, and sin no more.* [479]

After the Savior was resurrected he appeared to the Nephites and told them,

> *I came unto my own, and my own received me not. And the scriptures concerning my coming are fulfilled.*

> *And as many as have received me, to them have I given to become the sons of God; and even so will I to as many as shall believe on my name, for behold, by me redemption cometh, and **in me is the law of Moses fulfilled.***[480]

The Law of Moses was instituted because

> ***they hardened their hearts and could not endure his*** [God's] ***presence*** ...

> *Therefore, he took Moses out of their midst, and the Holy Priesthood also.*[481]

---

[478] John 8:7.

[479] John 8:10-11.

[480] 3 Nephi 9:16-17.

[481] D&C 84:23-24.

The expression that the "Holy Priesthood" was taken "out of their midst" means that the general male members could not be ordained to hold the Melchizedek Priesthood nor be married (temple marriage) in the Tabernacle of the Congregation. Only a few select worthy men could receive the Melchizedek Priesthood and then could receive temple marriage such as the prophets and David.

The Savior not only fulfilled the Law of Moses by his crucifixion and resurrection but he restored all that was taken away at the time the Law of Moses was instituted. In addition, the sealing keys were restored to Peter, James and John on the Mount of Transfiguration. If men were worthy they could receive the Melchizedek Priesthood and the full temple sealing ordinances were available to them.

Joseph Smith did not talk of the sealing keys being restored to the House of Israel at the time of Peter, James and John. His focus was restoring these teachings and principles to our dispensation. However, the prophets of our day have taught that these principles were restored to Peter, James and John, but temples were not available to them so that these ordinances were performed in other special places. Joseph Fielding Smith wrote

> *The first complete endowments in this dispensation were given in Nauvoo, May 4, 1842. These of course could not be given in the Temple, and were given elsewhere. In the time of poverty and when necessity requires the giving of blessings which belong to the House of the Lord, and there is no such house, they may be given in the wilderness, on a mountain or some other spot, **consecrated to that purpose**. The Savior had to give an endowment to Peter, James and John,*

273

on the Mount of Transfiguration. The Saints of that dispensation had to be baptized for the dead and give other ordinances for the dead in the wilderness, for the temple in Jerusalem was closed to them and had been desecrated, therefore the wilderness, mountain tops and rivers, had to be utilized for the temple work for their dead in that dispensation. [482]

In our dispensation the Lord commanded that temples were to be built. In the Kirtland temple sealing keys were restored by Elijah to Joseph Smith and Oliver Cowdery on 3 April 1836.[483] The appearance of Moses and Elijah on the Mount of Transfiguration[484] accomplished the same purpose as when they appeared to Joseph Smith and Oliver Cowdery. They restored the keys they possessed to Peter, James and John and then the Savior gave the endowment to Peter, James and John who then gave the endowment to others of that dispensation.

Initially it appears that some or all of the temple ordinances were performed at the temple in Jerusalem. Remember that the Lord cleansed the temple just prior to his crucifixion and resurrection and he taught them that the Law of Moses was fulfilled in him. They would not be going to the temple to perform any ordinances pertaining to the Law of Moses because it was fulfilled.

*And they, **continuing daily with one accord in the temple**, and breaking bread from house to house, did eat their meat with gladness and singleness of heart,*

---

[482] Smith, Church History and Modern Revelation, 4:138.

[483] D&C 110:13-16.

[484] Matthew 17:1-9; Mark 9:2-9; Luke 9:28-36.

Praising God, and having favour with all the people. And the Lord added to the church daily such as should be saved.[485]

As tribulations increased this use of the temple would have been terminated by the High Priests as Joseph Fielding Smith stated and other places were used.

Temple Work - Nephites

As we have already seen the temple sealing keys were not had among the Nephites from their migration until the time of the Savior's appearance to them. The Savior's teachings as recorded in the Book of Mormon are silent with regard to temple teaching, authority and ordinances. These people did have this authority with the attendant ordinances and blessings. Since there is no direct record we have to look at language clues and other gospel principles to show they had these things. Not everything that the Savior taught the Nephites was recorded. The prophet Mormon was commanded to leave many things out of his record.

*And now there cannot be written in **this book even a hundredth part of the things which Jesus did truly teach unto the people;***

*But behold **the plates of Nephi do contain the more part of the things which he taught the people.***

*And **these things have I written, which are a lesser part of the things which he taught the people;** and I have written them to the intent that they may be brought again unto this people, from the Gentiles, according to the words which Jesus hath spoken.*

---

[485] Acts 2:46-47.

And when they shall have received this, which is expedient that they should have first, to try their faith, and if it shall so be that they shall believe these things then shall the greater things be made manifest unto them.

And if it so be that they will not believe these things, then shall the greater things be withheld from them, unto their condemnation.

Behold, I was about to write them, all which were engraven upon the plates of Nephi, but the Lord forbade it, saying: I will try the faith of my people.

Therefore I, Mormon, do write the things which have been commanded me of the Lord. And now I, Mormon, make an end of my sayings, and proceed to write the things which have been commanded me. [486]

We will now look at some of the evidences that will show that the Nephites received the temple sealing authority and the accompanying ordinances. Moroni recorded a valuable insight into the Savior's giving his disciples priesthood authority.

*The words of Christ, which he spake unto his <u>disciples, the twelve whom he had chosen,</u> **as he laid his hands upon them—***

*And he called them by name, saying: Ye shall call on the Father in my name, in mighty prayer; and after ye have done this **ye shall have power that to him upon whom ye shall lay your hands, ye shall give the Holy Ghost; and in my name shall ye give it, for thus do mine apostles.***

---

[486] 3 Nephi 26:6-12.

Now Christ spake these words unto them at the time of his first appearing; and the multitude heard it not, but the disciples heard it; and on as many as they laid their hands, fell the Holy Ghost.[487]

This scripture records the resurrected Savior as laying his hands upon his disciples' heads and giving them authority. That authority was the right to give the gift of the Holy Ghost. Since we have an example of the Lord giving authority by the laying on of his hands and we know that he ordained the apostles in Jerusalem, then it is very reasonable to believe that he gave additional authority to his Nephite disciples in this same manner. Nephi confirmed this fact in his vision of the Savior's visit to Nephi's descendants when he wrote,

*And I also saw and bear record that the Holy Ghost fell upon twelve others; and **they were ordained of God, and chosen**.*

*And the angel spake unto me, saying: Behold the **twelve disciples of the Lamb, who are chosen to minister unto thy seed**.*[488]

These twelve ministers were called to minister unto the Nephites the same as the twelve apostles were called to minister unto those at Jerusalem and areas abroad in the near east. The Savior had fulfilled the Law of Moses and had told the Nephites that it was fulfilled. He taught the principles and laws which were the higher principles as contained in the Sermon on the Mount.[489] They were converted as a people and

---

[487] Moroni 2:1-3.

[488] 1 Nephi 12:7-8.

[489] 3 Nephi 12-14.

had all things in common among them as did the Saints in Jerusalem.[490]

These people were a righteous people for 200 years before they began to fall away.[491] These people were as righteous as were the faithful saints in this dispensation and as righteous as the faithful saints at Jerusalem.

Mormon recorded this during this righteous period of the Nephites:

> *And **they were married, and given in marriage**, and were blessed according to the **multitude of the promises** which the Lord had made unto them.*[492]

It should be noted that the Lord gave the Nephites a "multitude of promises" and especially a promise relating to marriage. What promise would the Lord give to the Nephites relating to marriage? The marriage promise given by the Lord to any people is that of the marriage covenant.

When the Savior fulfilled the Law of Moses he restored all of the things that were taken away when the Law of Moses was instituted. Remember that the Melchizedek Priesthood with its associated ordinances was withdrawn from the people and the administration was under the Aaronic Priesthood for the ordinances and commandments given.

In Jerusalem Peter, James and John were apostles and received the sealing keys or the keys of the Church presidency from Elijah. These same keys were given to Joseph Smith and

---

490 4 Nephi 1:2-3.

491 4 Nephi 1:22.

492 4 Nephi 1:11.

278

Oliver Cowdery at the beginning of our dispensation. These same keys would have been given to his Nephite disciples when the Savior visited them.

In all probability the Savior ordained his disciples with these keys. We have no record of how they received these keys but they truly had them. Mormon could not have written what he did about marriage and the multitude of promises including the marriage covenant given by the Lord if they did not have those keys.

Since the sealing keys were not had by Lehi or Nephi or any of the other prophets of the Book of Mormon prior to the visit of the Savior none of those prophets or people were married by the marriage covenant in mortality. They had been faithful to the gospel teachings that were available to them. They had earned the right to the "everlasting covenant" or "marriage covenant." However, the ordinance still needed to be conducted on their behalf as it will be done for all of our ancestors. After the Savior's ministry to the Nephites, these ordinances were performed.

PETER DENYING CHRIST

Why Peter denied the Savior during the night of the Savior's condemnation and maltreatment has been baffling to many people. Peter knew that the Savior was the Messiah and yet he denied knowing the Messiah three times. The Savior had this exchange with his Apostles and Peter

He saith unto them, But whom say ye that I am?

And Simon Peter answered and said, Thou art the Christ, the Son of the living God.

And Jesus answered and said unto him, Blessed art thou, Simon Bar-jona: for flesh and blood hath not

revealed it unto thee, but my Father which is in
heaven. [493]

The Savior clearly confirmed to Peter that the Father had revealed this truth to him. A little later as the Savior, Peter, James and John were returning from the Mount of Transfiguration, where they had seen Moses and Elijah, a special witness was given to them.

While he yet spake, behold, a bright cloud overshadowed them: and behold a voice out of the cloud, which said, This is my beloved Son, in whom I am well pleased; hear ye him.

And when the disciples heard it, they fell on their face, and were sore afraid. [494]

A careful review of the scriptures reveals that even though Peter and the other apostles had witness of his divinity they did not know what the mission of the Messiah really was and therefore their witness and understanding was incomplete.

In order to understand Peter's denial we need to go to the Scriptures and show what his real understanding was about Jesus Christ being the Messiah.

Messiah Understanding
It is common knowledge that the nation of Israel wanted to shed the Roman rule from their nation. The best scriptural example showing the common attitude is when the Savior appeared to Cleopas and a companion as they traveled from Jerusalem to the village of Emmaus. The Savior was unknown

---

[493] Matthew 16:15-17.

[494] Matthew 17:5-6; Mark 9:5-7; Luke 9:33-35.

to them. A conversation followed and Cleopas described part of the situation

> *Concerning Jesus of Nazareth, which was a prophet mighty in deed and word before God and all the people:*
>
> *And how the chief priests and our rulers delivered him to be condemned to death, and have crucified him.*
>
> ***But we trusted that it had been he which should have redeemed Israel"***[495]

What Cleopas was saying was that since Jesus of Nazareth was crucified and died he couldn't redeem Israel from the Romans. The expression "we trusted" was speaking of the followers of Jesus of Nazareth who believed he was the Messiah. But he had died and now he couldn't redeem Israel from the Romans. They were still under Roman rule.

The experience of Peter, James and John accompanied the Savior to the Mount of Transfiguration gives further clues as to the mindset of the apostles. When all was done and on their way down the mount the Savior told Peter, James and John

> *he charged them that they should tell no man what things they had seen, **till the Son of man were risen from the dead**.*
>
> *And they kept that saying with themselves, **questioning one with another what the rising from the dead should mean**.*[496]

---

[495] Luke 24:19-21.

[496] Mark 9:9-10.

They did not know anything about the resurrection. Understanding the resurrection was not a part of the Jewish culture at that time. Although we understand it his apostles did not understand it prior to the Savior's actual resurrection. The concept of the Savior dying and then being resurrected is fundamental to knowing the mission of the Messiah. There was no common knowledge of these concepts in Israel at the time.

Following Peter's first stated testimony that Jesus was the Son of God the scriptures record

> *From that time forth began Jesus to shew unto his disciples, how that he must go unto Jerusalem, and suffer many things of the elders and chief priests and scribes, and be killed, and be raised again the third day.*
>
> *Then **Peter took him, and began to rebuke him, saying, Be it far from thee, Lord: this shall not be unto thee**.*
>
> *But he turned, and said unto Peter, **Get thee behind me, Satan: thou art an offence unto me: for thou savourest not the things that be of God, but those that be of men.***[497]*

Here we have the Savior begin to teach his apostles and followers what would shortly come to pass and Peter rebuked the Savior. He clearly understood that he Savior was talking of his death. Peter said "this shall not be unto thee." He was the Messiah and he was going to deliver Israel from the Romans. He should not die.

---

[497] Matthew 16:21–23.

The Savior rebuked Peter for his comment actually calling Peter "Satan"

> *Get thee behind me, Satan: thou art an offence unto me: for thou savourest not the things that be of God"*[498]

This rebuke did not change Peter's mind. At the Last Supper, the Savior said this to Peter

> *I have prayed for thee, that thy faith fail not: and **when thou art converted, strengthen thy brethren.***
>
> *And he said unto him, **Lord, I am ready to go with thee, both into prison, and to death.***
>
> *And he said, **I tell thee, Peter, the cock shall not crow this day, before that thou shalt thrice deny that thou knowest me.*** [499]

This exchange is very important to understand. The Savior was trying to teach Peter to be prepared to strengthen his brethren. This suggests that Peter needed to be ready to take the lead with his brethren. Peter's mindset was that he was going to follow the Savior. He was

> *ready to go with thee, both into prison, and to death."*

This is a significant statement by Peter when in a matter of a very short time the Savior would be arrested. Peter was ready to defend the Savior and to die defending him if necessary. This strongly indicates that Peter would be quick to use his sword in the Savior's defense in support of his belief that the Savior would throw off the Roman rule.

---

[498] Matthew 16:23.

[499] Luke 22:32-34.

The Savior responded with his prophesy of Peter denying him three (3) times. When the Savior told Peter that he was not yet converted, the Savior knew that Peter did not understand that the Savior's mission was to die and provide the resurrection for all of humankind. The Savior had already told his disciples of his impending events that he must suffer and Peter did not understand. He did not understand but he was ready to fight.

For that matter, none of the other apostles understood his resurrection. Peter was not alone in his lack of understanding. Mark records this about the apostles' reaction when they were told of his resurrection.

> *And they, when they had heard that he was alive, and had been seen of her, believed not.*
>
> *After that he appeared in another form unto two of them, as they walked, and went into the country.*
>
> *And they went and told it unto the residue: neither believed they them.*
>
> *Afterward **he appeared unto the eleven as they sat at meat, and upbraided them with their unbelief and hardness of heart**, because they believed not them which had seen him after he was risen.* [500]

When Peter and John ran to the sepulcher the Savior was not there.

> *Then went in also that other disciple (John), which came first to the sepulchre, and he saw, and believed.*
>
> *For as yet they knew not the scripture, that he must rise again from the dead.* [501]

---

[500] Mark 16:11-14.

Peter Defending the Savior

Following the Savior's Garden event, the group came to arrest the Savior. The following was recorded by Matthew

> *And, behold, one of them* [Peter] *which were with Jesus stretched out his hand, and drew his sword, and struck a servant of the high priest's, and smote off his ear.*
>
> *Then said Jesus unto him,* **Put up again thy sword into his place: for all they that take the sword shall perish with the sword.**
>
> *Thinkest thou that I cannot now pray to my Father, and he shall presently give me more than twelve legions of angels?*
>
> *But how then shall the scriptures be fulfilled, that thus it must be?* [502]

All four gospels give a similar story that one disciple took a sword and cut off the ear of the servant of the High Priest. John identifies that disciple as Peter.

At the beginning of the arrest Peter now executed his mindset and his personal commitment of protecting the Savior. He reacted immediately taking his sword and swung it at the head of the high priest's servant. Striking at the head is the kind of blow that would kill or do serious injury. But Peter only cut off the ear whereupon the Savior healed the servant's ear and chastised Peter for using his sword telling him that those who use the sword will die by the sword.

---

[501] John 20:8-9.

[502] Matthew 26:51-55.

The Savior chose to tell Peter that he could have more than twelve (12) legions of angels because it described far more angels than the Romans had soldiers. He chose the term legions because it mentally links angels against the soldiers. Using the term "twelve legions of angels" emphasizes that the Savior did not need to rely upon Peter for his safety. The message was that he had the power to crush the Romans without Peter's help.

This was a severe chastisement to Peter. This was his Messiah whom he knew was the Messiah by revelation and by the voice of the Father. He had seen heavenly messengers with the Savior. He was helpless to protect the Savior. This exchange had to have caused Peter to be extremely unsettled concerning what to do. He had been so firm and hot in his commitment of defending the Savior and then chastised so strongly.

The Savior's mission had to be fulfilled. But Peter did not understand what that mission was. Following this exchange the Savior willingly placed himself into the hands of this arresting group. The arresting group showed great fear of the Savior when they came to arrest him.

> *Jesus therefore, knowing all things that should come upon him, went forth, and said unto them, Whom seek ye?*
>
> *They answered him, Jesus of Nazareth. Jesus saith unto them, I am he. And Judas also, which betrayed him, stood with them.*
>
> *As soon then as he had said unto them, I am he, **they went backward, and fell to the ground.***
>
> *Then asked he them again, Whom seek ye? And they said, Jesus of Nazareth.*

*Jesus answered, I have told you that I am he: if
therefore ye seek me, **let these go their way:*** [503]

Peter watched the arresting group react to their fear of the
Savior. This group knew of his miracles and feared him
because they did not know whether the Savior would use
miracles to do harm to them. Peter witnessed this fear. He also
understood the Savior's comment to "let these go their way."
He was in this deep quandary but he got the message that he
<u>must not be</u> with the Savior. The other disciples fled. Peter
was still concerned about the Savior and followed at a distance
trying to be discreet. By being discreet he felt he could remain
unknown and avoid being associated with the Savior and yet
observe what would happen.

It should be noted that the Savior was arrested after dinner and
relatively early in the night. [Read the essay
"DETERMINING PASSOVER EVENTS" for the justification
that it was fairly early in the evening].

We cannot place the time of the first two denials with
exactness but they probably happened during the Savior's
maltreatment. Matthew records Peter's first denial as follows,

> ¶ *Now Peter sat without in the palace: and a damsel
> came unto him, saying, Thou also wast with Jesus of
> Galilee.*

> *But he denied before them all, saying, I know not what
> thou sayest.*

The damsel challenged Peter directly. Here Peter did not
exactly deny that he was with Jesus. His response was to pled
ignorance by saying "*I know not.*"

---

[503] John 18: 4-8.

And when he was gone out into the porch, another maid saw him, and said unto them that were there, This fellow was also with Jesus of Nazareth.

And again he denied with an oath, I do not know the man.

Here the maid accused Peter of being with Jesus as a disciple to the others, who were present. He had tried to minimize the first challenge but now the charge was stronger, being made in his presence to the crowd present. Yet he knew he could not be identified as a disciple of Jesus. So his response was stronger by saying *"I do not know the man."*

And after a while came unto him they that stood by, and said to Peter, Surely thou also art one of them; for thy speech bewrayeth thee.

Then began he to curse and to swear, saying, I know not the man. And immediately the cock crew. [504]

Now the crowd was accusing him of being a disciple. Peter responded more strongly by cursing and denying the charge.

Peter witnessed many events throughout the night beginning with the arrest in early evening. In addition, he milled among the other spectators hearing their verbal exchanges. The Savior was condemned to die. He witnessed or heard of the Savior being buffeted with fists, slapping him with their open hands, plucking out his beard[505], spiting upon him and mocking him. They mocked him by covering his head, striking him on the head and then telling him to prophesy who struck him. This

---

[504] Matthew 26:69-74

[505] Isaiah 50:6 (This is not recorded in the New Testament but was prophesied in Isaiah. This act was done to shame the Savior).

continued for some time. Peter witnessed that the fear of the arresting group changed to vicious maltreatment. He knew he should not be caught up in this situation.

His faith was not fully developed at this time because he did not understand the true mission of the Savior. He previously showed that lack of faith when he feared while walking on the water.[506] As he began to sink into the water, the Savior took him by the hand and said "*O thou of little faith, wherefore didst thou doubt?*" He was severely chastised by the Savior and the events of the night caused him some fear. He witnessed the fear of the arresting party and the resulting attitude of brazen and harsh maltreatment. Then the cock crowed and Jesus turned to look at Peter.[507]

His love for the Savior was very great. He had a revelation that Jesus was the Son of God and heard the Father's voice confirming that Jesus was the beloved Son of the Father. This was the man who would not let the Savior wash his feet because he thought the Savior should not humble himself to do this lowly activity. Upon learning that he without this could have no part of the Savior, he wanted hands and head washed.[508] His desire and love was strong. But he had let the Savior down. He had denied knowing the Savior three times. This was a devastating realization for Peter and he wept bitterly because he had failed the Savior. This reaction shows Peter's great and driving love for the Savior and his commitment to save him from death.

---

[506] Matthew 14:28-31; JST Matthew 14:24-25

[507] Matthew 26:75; Luke 22:61-62.

[508] John 13:4-14.

Being Converted

On the morning of the resurrection the women went to the tomb to complete the preparation of the body for final burial and were told by the angel that the Savior had risen. They reported this to the apostles who ran to the site. Luke records this

> *Then arose Peter, and ran unto the sepulchre; and stooping down, he beheld the linen clothes laid by themselves, and departed, **wondering in himself at that which was come to pass.*** [509]

Previously Peter did not understand about the resurrection and the need for the Savior to die. He was beginning to get the picture as he began his "wondering." When Mary Magdalene reported to the apostles that she had seen the Savior, they doubted her.[510] Their doubt was removed when Cleopas returned to Jerusalem to report to the apostles they had seen the Savior and that he lived.

According to Luke the Savior then appeared to the attending apostles and Cleopas and his companion.[511] They were able to see and feel the scars from the nails. The risen Savior taught them and their understanding developed. They walked together to Bethany and then the Savior left them. Peter was converted. Peter and the others finally understood the resurrection and the message and they rejoiced in it. The Savior had been resurrected and had provided the atonement for humankind. Peter went forth with boldness, understanding

---

[509] Luke 24:12.

[510] Mark 16:9-10.

[511] Luke 24:33-36.

and conviction to lead Christ's church because he finally understood the true mission of the Messiah and was converted.

When the Savior told Peter "when thou art converted, strengthen thy brethren"[512] He was really saying "When you understand my mission, strengthen thy brethren." The term "converted" as used by the Savior requires that one come to the correct knowledge and understanding of the Savior's mission. Peter knew Jesus was the Messiah by revelation and the Father's words but did not understand what the mission of the Messiah really was.

DETERMINING PASSOVER EVENTS

The Savior ate the Passover dinner with his apostles and probably other disciples. We know the Passover day is observed in the spring time and begins in early evening because the Jewish day starts at dusk and ends the following evening at dusk. The significance of the Passover celebration is in recognition of Jehovah cursing the Egyptians by taking the life of their firstborn children while he preserved the firstborn of the Israelites, as recorded by Moses. This was done to cause the Pharaoh to release the Israelites from the Egyptian bondage.

> *Then Moses called for all the elders of Israel, and said unto them, Draw out and take you a lamb according to your families, and kill the passover.*

> *And ye shall take a bunch of hyssop, and dip [it] in the blood that [is] in the bason, and strike the lintel and the two side posts with the blood that [is] in the bason;*

---

[512] Luke 22:32.

and none of you shall go out at the door of his house until the morning.

For the LORD will pass through to smite the Egyptians; and when he seeth the blood upon the lintel, and on the two side posts, the LORD will pass over the door, and will not suffer the destroyer to come in unto your houses to smite [you].

And ye shall observe this thing for an ordinance to thee and to thy sons for ever.

And it shall come to pass, when ye be come to the land which the LORD will give you, according as he hath promised, that ye shall keep this service.

And it shall come to pass, when your children shall say unto you, What mean ye by this service?

That ye shall say, It [is] the sacrifice of the LORD'S passover, who passed over the houses of the children of Israel in Egypt, when he smote the Egyptians, and delivered our houses. And the people bowed the head and worshipped.[513]

The lamb's blood being spread upon the door posts and crossbeam was the requirement that would preserve the firstborn of the Israelites. The significance of this celebration was to remember the preservation of the Israelites. Unbeknown to the Israelites, because of the things he would suffer, this Passover day would be the preservation of not only Israel but of the whole world. It had great significance to the Savior.

---

[513] Exodus 12:21-27.

This essay is to estimate the time of the sunset, dusk, dawn and sunrise of the Passover day at the end of the Savior's earthly ministry. Understanding these things will help us to understand more fully what and how long the Savior suffered through that night and the following day.

We assume because of the consistency of the planetary system that the sun rise and sun set times on the day of Christ's Passover is the same or within minutes for the same calendar day for 2016.

From the internet, the beginning dates for Passover for a number of past years was identified. They varied from late March to late April. The date of April 10 was chosen as that is the date that Passover will start in 2017 and seemed to be near the middle of the dates. Assuming this to be the equivalent date for the Savior's Passover, we can now determine the time for dawn and dusk for that date. Obviously, this is not the correct date, however, it is within minutes of the actual time for the Savior's Passover.

We located a table at "timeanddate.com" that shows Jerusalem's times for April dates. It can be found at http://www.timeanddate.com/sun/israel/jerusalem?month=4& year=2016 .[514] The times in this table are daylight savings times. Since there was no such thing at the time of the Savior the times are adjusted to reflect the actual time. That table contains the following information:

DATE	TIME	EVENT/COMMENT
April 9	6 pm	Party arrival

---

[514] Last visited July 11, 2016

April 9	Dusk 6:29 pm	Passover start
	Candles lit	

April 9	6:40 pm	Dinner started

April 9	7:20 pm	Judas leaves

Conversation, Peter prophesy,

Intercessory Prayer

April 9	8:15 pm	Move to Gethsemane

Christ's Garden suffering

April 9	9:pm	Judas party arrives – Savior

arrested

April 9	9:45 pm	Meeting with Annas, then

Caiaphas, trial and maltreatment

April 10	Dawn 5 am	Cock Crowed, Peter's response

These estimates are offered because the author believes the Savior suffered the maltreatments for a considerable time through the night which added to his fatigue and eventual suffering from the entire affair.

The three gospels although using slightly different language state that when it was time they sat down to eat. It is likely that they arrived prior to the lighting of the candles. A likely time for the starting of the meal would be very soon following dusk. The meal would have lasted perhaps two (2) hours. The actual eating perhaps forty-five (45) minutes to an hour with some conversation following. It could have been shorter.

The Savior identified Judas Iscariot as his betrayer early during the meal. Matthew records the Savior as verbally identifying Judas following the dipping.

Then Judas, which betrayed him, answered and said, Master, is it I? He said unto him, Thou hast said.[515]

The latest that Judas left was probably at the end of the meal. He left to meet with those wishing the Savior's death to identify the Savior to the arresting party.

The chief priests, scribes and elders met with Caiaphas to consult how they could arrest Jesus out of the view of the people. They feared an arrest viewed by these people.[516] Judas had met earlier with this group with an offer to deliver the Savior for arrest out of the public view. They agreed on 30 pieces of silver.[517] Judas knew the place where the Savior and apostles often went after their meals, which was a Garden across "the brook Cedron"[518].

This arrest being preplanned would not take a large amount of time to implement. It took perhaps an hour and a half or perhaps a little less from the time that Judas Iscariot left the meal to gather the arresting party and return to the Garden. So somewhere about 2 hours from the start of the meal, Judas would be at the Garden.

The next crucial question is <u>"How long did the Savior suffer in the Garden?</u> The two events that were accomplished by the Savior in the Garden were

1. Atoning for the individual sins of humankind and
2. Eliminating all blood from his body so that he could return to the presence of the Father. (See the

---

[515] Matthew 26:25.

[516] Matthew 26:3-5.

[517] Matthew 26:14-16.

[518] John 18:1-2.

essay "BLOOD/RESURRECTION – SAVIOR"
for full information).

The Savior needed to suffer long enough to eliminate all of the blood from his system. He shed <u>from every pore</u> **large drops of blood** that lasted perhaps thirty (30) or so minutes. As soon as all of his blood was eliminated he would be released from Satan's torment relieving his pain. There would be no purpose to suffer longer as both purposes had been fulfilled by the time all the blood from his body was shed.

The arresting party came as soon as the Savior had completed his ordeal. The arrest probably took place about 9 pm. The trial before Caiaphas probably started about 10 pm. The point of this discussion is to show that before the cock crowed Peter would have witnessed the trial, death sentence and maltreatment that the Savior suffered. The maltreatments would have concluded about the time that the cock crowed.

John records

> *Peter then denied again: and immediately the cock crew.*
> *Then led they Jesus from Caiaphas unto the hall of judgment: and **it was early;*** [519]

The meeting with Pilate was probably started about 6:00 am. It was a short time following the cock crowing that they left to travel to the hall of judgment.

---

[519] John 18:27–28.

----- ATONEMENT PERSPECTIVES -----

This book was developed to explain some of the questions about the Savior's atonement and related scriptural events and issues. It is not a complete book covering every question, issue or related topic. It is hoped that it will give the reader a better understanding of what and how our Savior accomplished his mission. In accomplishing his mission, he always followed and accepted the will of the Father.

However, to qualify for eternal life one does not have to understand everything about the atonement of the Savior and every topic discussed in this book. It requires simple faith in him and his teachings and commandments and living a life like the Savior and enduring to the end of their life.

But we must consider what Joseph Smith said

> *And if a person gains more knowledge and intelligence in this life through his diligence and obedience than another, he will have so much the advantage in the world to come.* [520]

If you have read this book and if you do not agree with parts of it, you are trying to gain more knowledge and intelligence in this life. I wish you well in this endeavor.

---

[520] D&C 130:19.

BIBLIOGRAPHY

Backman, Milton V., Jr., Ed, *Regional Studies in Latter-day Saint church history: Ohio*; [Provo, Utah], Dept. of Church History and Doctrine, Brigham Young University; 1990.

Benson, Ezra Taft. *The Teachings of Ezra Taft Benson.* Salt Lake City, UT: Bookcraft, Inc., 1988.

Bible History Online. *Bible History Online.* http://www.bible-history.com.

Church of Jesus Christ of Latter-Day Saints. *"The Family: A Proclamation to the World."* http://www.lds.org/topics/family-proclamation?lang=eng.

Church of Jesus Christ of Latter-day Saints, Seventy-Eighth Semi-Annual Conference Report, Salt Lake City, Utah, Oct 1907; http://www.scriptures.byu.edu/gc-historical/1907-O.pdf.

Church of Jesus Christ of Latter-day Saints, Ninety Ninth Annual Conference Report, Salt Lake City, Utah, April 1929; http://www.scriptures.byu.edu/gc-historical/1929-A.pdf.

Dictionary.com, LLC. *Dictionary.com.* http://www.dictionary.com.

Ehat, Andrew F., and Lyndon W. Cook, comps. *The Words of Joseph Smith: The Contemporary Accounts of the Nauvoo Discourses of the Prophet Joseph Smith.* Provo, Utah: Religious Studies Center, Brigham Young University, 1980.

The Free Dictionary,
http://www.newworldencyclopedia.org/entry/Info:Main_Page

Journal of Discourses. 26 vols. Liverpool: F.D. Richards, 1855-86. [Brigham Young verbally authorized George D. Watt, who was skilled in stenography, to take his notes to England and publish them. Both felt that these publications could not be published in the United States because of the anti-Mormon sentiment. Each volume was entitled "Journal of Discourses" with the year of publication which contained the previous year's records. The first nineteen volumes were listed, "by President Brigham Young," signifying his verbal authorization for publication. The last seven volumes were listed, "by President John Taylor." David W. Evans and George W. Gibbs later assisted and continued in this work of publishing]

McConkie, Bruce R. *The Mortal Messiah.* 4 vols. Salt Lake City, UT: Deseret Book Co., 1979.

Merriam-Webster, Inc – An online dictionary:
http://www.merriam-webster.com

New World Encyclopedia, A Free Online Encyclopedia,
http://www.newworldencyclopedia.org/entry/New_World_Encyclopedia:About

Smith, Joseph. *History of the Church of Jesus Christ of Latter-Day Saints.* Intro and notes by B. H. Roberts. 7 vols. Salt Lake City, UT: Deseret Book Co., 1948.

Smith, Joseph Fielding. *Church History and Modern Revelation.* 4 vols. Salt Lake City, UT, Deseret Book Co., 1946. [These books were authorized as the

Melchizedek Priesthood course of study for the years 1947-1950, and were approved by the Quorum of the Twelve Apostles.]

Stuy, Brian H., ed., *Collected Discourses*, 5 Vol., Woodland Hills, B. H. S. Publishing, 1987.

Talmage, James E. *Jesus the Christ*. Salt Lake City, UT: Deseret Book Co., 1983.

Whiston, William, A.M., Trans. *Complete Works of Flavius Josephus*, Grand Rapids, Michigan, Kregel Publications. Josephus Writings are also available online at http://www.sacred-texts.com/jud/josephus/index.htm.

Wikimedia Foundation, Inc. *Wikipedia: The Free Encyclopedia*. http://www.wikipedia.org.

Zias, Joe, *Crucifixion in Antiquity*, Century One Foundation. http://www.centuryone.org/crucifixion2.html. Article no longer available at site, but is archived by Internet Archive Wayback Machine at http://web.archive.org/web/20110615201341/http://wwwcentu ryone.org/crucifixion2.html.

46463514R00174